FLY FISHING
BRITISH COLUMBIA

Edited By Karl Bruhn

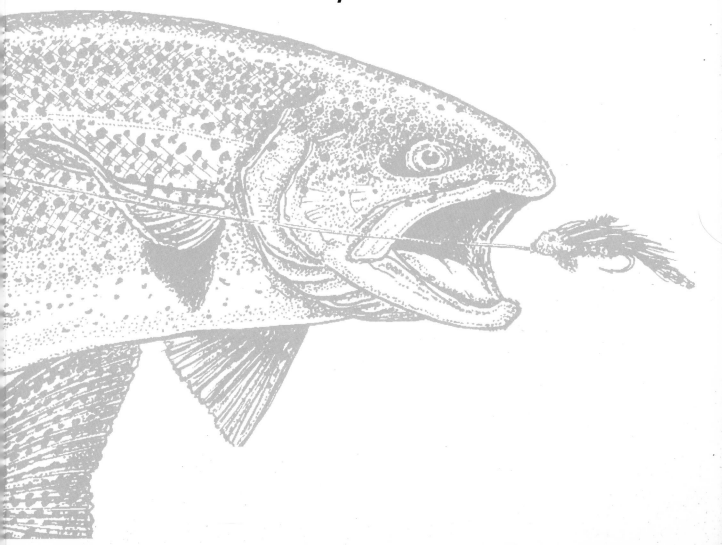

Copyright © 1999 Interactive Broadcasting Corporation

Canadian Cataloguing in Publication Data

Main entry under title:

Fly Fishing British Columbia

ISBN 1-895811-67-8

1. Fly Fishing—British Columbia. I. Bruhn, Karl.
SH572.B8F59 1999   799.1'24'09711   C99-910258-3

First edition 1999

Heritage House wishes to acknowledge the support of Heritage Canada through the Book Publishing Industry Development Program, the British Columbia Arts Council, and the permission of Douglas & McIntyre, Vancouver, B.C. to reprint the Roderick Haig-Brown quote on the opposite page.

Cover design: Debra Bevaart
Book design and layout: Dave Sharrock
Editors: Karl Bruhn, Mel-Lynda Andersen & Audrey McClellan

This book is published in association with Interactive Broadcasting Corporation. The bcadventure.com imprint recognizes the co-publishing program of Heritage House and Interactive Broadcasting to introduce new books supporting recreational adventure in British Columbia.

Heritage House Publishing Company Ltd.
Unit #8 - 17921 55th Ave., Surrey, BC V3S 6C4

www.bcadventure.com

Printed in Canada

FLY FISHING
BRITISH COLUMBIA

Fisherman's Summer

"Whether it be the stream of youth or the adopted stream of later years, a fisherman's home river (or it may be a home lake or some favorite bay in salt water) is of ultimate importance to him. It is a known, familiar place, full of memories and associations.

"Everything that happens on the home stream builds and increases and enriches knowledge until it becomes intimacy. Yet since weather is weather, water is water and fish are fish, knowledge is never complete. Instead, the standard changes and one seeks still greater intimacy."

Roderick Haig-Brown

Acknowledgements

As the producers and co-publishers of this book, we were astounded by the outpouring of creative energy and dedication from so many talented individuals as the ideas and visual images for this book took shape. A very special thanks are due to the Fly Fishing British Columbia team: Karl Bruhn, the team leader, whose love and knowledge of the outdoors combined with dedication and tireless effort quite simply made this whole book possible; Dave Sharrock for his ability to magically pull rabbits out of his hat to give this book its special look; Mel-Lynda Andersen, whose incredible energy was the catalyst to keep the team motivated and on track; Debra Bevaart for her outstanding angling art featured throughout the book; Ian Forbes for his many fine fly pattern drawings; Ken Kirkby for his wonderful Journal drawings; Ian Roberts for his beautiful fly pattern photography; Philip Rowley for his painstaking work on pattern selection; Peter Morrison for his knowledge and watchful eye; and Kevin Longard for his expertise and resourceful dedication.

Thanks to Ehor Boyanowsky, Peter Caverhill, Brian Chan, Rob Dolighan, Don Holmes, Doug Porter, Adam Lewis, Art Lingren, Peter MacPherson, Bob Melrose, Ron Nelson, Ron Newman, Ryan Pohl, Dave Stewart and Barry Thornton for unreservedly sharing so many fishing "secrets".

Thank you to all the fly tiers who contributed their special fly patterns and to the expert fly fishers whose pro tips will make us all better fishermen.

Special thanks to Rodger Touchie, Audrey McClellan and Darlene Nickull at Heritage House Publishing Company, our co-publisher, for their expertise, encouragement and support; to all the members of the Interactive Broadcasting Corporation team who have brought to this project and accompanying web site (www.flyfishingbc.com) the same level of dedication and excellence they display daily on the BC Adventure Network.

To all the book stores, fly shops, resorts and lodges, thank you for making *Fly Fishing British Columbia* available to your customers.

And finally, this book is dedicated to fly fishers everywhere who get that "special feeling" when they wet a line in the magical waters of this great province!

— *Jim Matheson & Dave Prentice*
Interactive Broadcasting Corporation

www.bcadventure.com

Foreword

This book is a collaborative effort on the part of the fly fishing community of British Columbia. Blending the voices of 15 main contributors, all acknowledged experts with almost 500 years of B.C. fly fishing experience among them, the book distils their knowledge as well as the wisdom, lore, art and science of the many fine anglers who blazed the trails we continue to explore today.

No single writer could have produced this multi-faceted work, nor could the contributors have achieved the level of detail revealed in these pages without the collected knowledge left by those who went before. In this respect the book is a celebration of British Columbia's angling heritage and so becomes a bridge between the past and the present.

None of this was clear at the outset. When Jim and Dave from Interactive Broadcasting Corporation contacted me about becoming involved in the writing of a definitive work on fly fishing in B.C., I was immediately intrigued. As the creator of B.C.'s premier tourism and outdoor recreation web site (www.bcadventure.com), IBC is a favorite in the province's angling community and recognized for outstanding quality. The proposed book seemed a natural extension of those efforts, and in the fall of 1998 I joined the team as editor and creative director. From there the project quickly took on a life of its own and with it came a lucky star that defies rational explanation. Each time it became apparent that remarkable talent and skill was required, it somehow became readily available.

Artist Debra Bevaart happened along just when it became clear we needed an artist capable of depicting the aquatic environment in exquisite detail. Renowned Canadian artist Ken Kirkby was captivated by the concept and consequently made available a vast selection of his many fine angling works. Photographer Ian Roberts not only had the exacting standards required to do justice to the book's color section, he is also a fly fisher and writer.

One after another they all appeared when they were needed and each one of them fell under the spell of a project that was clearly larger than any one of its many elements and perhaps even greater than the sum of all those varied parts. It has been a happy and fortuitous coming together of many individual voices, talents and skills. As editor, I like to think every reader will be as captivated as were those who worked on the project and that its underlying message of deep-seated respect, appreciation and conservation will be communicated to all who open these pages and cast a fly to the waters of British Columbia. ⚓

Fly Fishing British Columbia

Editor & Creative Director
Karl Bruhn

Art Director
Dave Sharrock

Artists
Debra Bevaart
Fly Pattern Drawings — Ian Forbes
Journal Paintings — Ken Kirkby

Copy Editor
Mel-Lynda Andersen

Thompson Okanagan
Brian Chan, Art Lingren & Dave Stewart

Cariboo Chilcotin Coast
Doug Porter, Karl Bruhn, Art Lingren, Barry M. Thornton, Ian Forbes, Don Holmes,
Ron Newman, Brian Chan, Bob Melrose, Rob Dolighan & Phil Rowley

The North
Art Lingren, Karl Bruhn, Peter Morrison, Adam Lewis, Bob Melrose, Ian Forbes, Ron Nelson & Doug Porter

The Rockies
Ron Nelson & Ian Forbes

Vancouver Island
Ian Forbes, Barry M. Thornton, Ian Roberts, Peter Morrison & Karl Bruhn

Vancouver Coast Mountains
Kevin Longard, Ian Roberts, Ehor Boyanowsky, Karl Bruhn, Peter Caverhill, Peter MacPherson & Ryan Pohl

Selected Menu
Phil Rowley

Fly Patterns
Shawn Bennett, Glenn Butler, Brian Chan, Dave Connolly, David Cooper, Kelly Davison, Colonel Esmond Drury, Bus Ellis,
Hermann Fischer, Bill Flintoft, Glenn Gerbrandt, Syd Glasso, Tyson Gogel, Peter Hobot, Dave Hofman, Shim Hogan, Gordon
Honey, Mike Labach, Duncan Laird, Harold Lohr, Kevin Longard, Peter MacPherson, Mike Maxwell, Bruce McLeod, Peter
Morrison, Bill Nation, Brian Niska, John O'Brien, Dave Paille, Larry Pemberton, Ryan Pohl, Bob Popovic, Doug Porter, Ian
Roberts, Phil Rowley, Ruddick's Fly Shop, Ken Ruddick, Dale Rutherford, Eric Schulz, Jack Shaw, Ron Tarnawski, Barry
Thornton, David Wallden, Rod Zavaduk

Color Photography of Fly Patterns
Ian Roberts

Photo Images
Karl Bruhn, Gordon Honey, Peter Morrison, Joe Raschendorfer, Dave Prentice, Mike Blenkar, Warren Goodman,
Naomi Yamamoto, Roderick Haig Brown — UBC Special Collections

Producers
Jim Matheson & Dave Prentice; Interactive Broadcasting Corporation

Contents

Chapter

1

Thompson Okanagan

The Thompson is British Columbia's trout fishing mecca. Rod-in-hand travel to the rolling, lake-dotted plateau framed by the Fraser River in the west and the Okanagan system in the east is like undertaking a pilgrimage. Anglers have been venturing here since the 1800s, lured by tales of a special breed of trout. The Kamloops trout and the waters it calls home produce the best small lake angling in the world. Hallowed names such as Stump, Lundbom, Peterhope, Tunkwa, Roche and Pass are celebrated by anglers the world over, but hidden in each fold of the region's softly rounded hills lie a score of more secret lakes, any one of which might rival the historically famous names.

Virtually all these waters share one important trait: they are nutrient rich in precisely the ways required to foster healthy, well-conditioned trout. As if by design, the region's lakes were created thousands of years ago as a result of glacial activity. Receding glaciers left a multitude of relatively shallow basins, many of which were landlocked or had only intermittent inlet and outlet creek systems. Underlying soils rich in basic elements such as calcium, magnesium and phosphorus remain the invisible ingredients that contribute to the creation of these famous trout lakes.

Until the late 1800s, most of the lake fishing opportunities were confined to waters connected to major river systems such as the Thompson, Adams and Nicola. Early written accounts of fishing in the Kamloops area document spectacular catches of large trout from these rivers. The potential of lake fishing was not really discovered until the early 1900s, which saw the start of major fish stockings and the development of fisheries management programs. The lakes were perfect in every way for trout, but the trout themselves were missing. Wild stocks of rainbow trout from Shuswap Lake were released into such lakes as Paul and

Pinantan and from there many more fertile waters received fish.

These initial stockings produced incredibly large trout and word quickly spread through the international fishing community. Grand fishing lodges catering to the wealthy soon began to appear on the shores of the most prolific trout lakes, signalling the start of the fishing resort industry. Over the years, ever more lakes were stocked and management policies fine tuned to produce today's network of well-groomed lakes.

Several key ingredients go into making a good trout lake. The right chemical composition of the water is of prime importance, but each lake must also have a balance of deep versus shallow water. Abundant shallow areas, where energy from the sun allows photosynthesis to grow lush aquatic plants, are essential. The vegetation creates important habitat for the insects and crustaceans that trout feed on. Deep-water areas provide habitat for the trout during the heat of

summer, affording cooler, more oxygenated water than in the shallows.

The third key ingredient is climate. Long summers mean a prolonged growing season for trout and trout food. This is important since all of the region's small angling lakes are frozen for up to five months each year. Not only is the summer long, it is dry as well, and this too plays a major role. Unlike their coastal counterparts, Interior lakes have minimal or no flushing action. Coupled with high rates of evaporation, this means essential nutrients not only remain in the lake, but are concentrated.

For all that, not all Thompson lakes are created equal. Difference in elevation, local climate and surrounding forest type all play a role

Callibaetis Mayfly Dry

Hook: Mustad 9671, #12–14
Tail: 4 strands moose mane
Body: Syn. dubbing mixture of tan, gry. & olv.
Hackle/Wing: Drk. griz. dun
Thorax: Drk. gry. dubbing pulled under & wound in front of hackle

Callibaetis Emerger

Hook: Mustad 9671, #12–14
Tail: Speckled wood duck clump
Body: Syn. dubbing mixture of tan & gry. wool
Thorax: Syn. dubbing mixture of brn. wool w/bits of olv. Flashabou dubbing mixed in, or brnz. peacock
Wing/Hackle: Drk. griz. hackle wound parachute style around closed-cell foam cylinder

in determining water quality. These variables significantly influence the water chemistry of specific lakes and thus dictate the diversity and abundance of both aquatic invertebrate and plant communities. These, in turn, determine angling quality. Low-elevation lakes of the grassland/Douglas fir zone are typically extremely and the pH levels are low enough that lily pads are the predominant emergent plants. The shorter open-water growing season of high-elevation lakes is often reflected in fish size. Variations on these typical scenarios abound for any number of reasons, so while low-lying lakes traditionally provide the best angling, larger fish and nutrient rich waters may well be found at both mid- and high elevations.

Phil Rowley: Learning to adopt a bottom-to-top philosophy, as opposed to concentrating solely on the surface, stretches any hatch, especially Callibaetis. In preparation for their surface swim, mature mayfly nymphs rise and fall from bottom. A #12 or #14 *Callibaetis Nymph* fished near the bottom off a floating line and long leader will do well, particularly patterns with a glimmer of Flashabou to mimic the sheen of air and gases trapped in the nymphal shuck. A slow hand-twist retrieve, coupled with pauses, duplicates the dart-and-stop action of the nymphs. When surface-bulging trout are seen, switch to the emerger. Trout gorge on the hanging nymphs, showing only their backs or tails as they feed. The parachute hackle of the *Callibaetis Emerger* pattern suspends it perfectly as it bobs amongst the naturals. Finally, when duns litter the surface like hundreds of small sailboats and trout literally boil on the surface, switch to the *Callibaetis Dun/Spinner*. Target the feeding path of a specific fish and let the pattern sit, allowing the ambient current to do the rest. When the fly drifts off the shoal over deep water, be prepared: trout love to vault upward from the security of deeper water.

productive. Examples include Lundbom, Peterhope, Stump, Campbell and Six Mile Lake. Aquatic vegetation thrives in nutrient rich waters, chiefly bulrush, cattails and Chara. The surrounding soils, forest types and subsequent runoff supply high concentrations of the base elements important for sustaining aquatic invertebrate life. As a result of higher levels of dissolved solids, pH levels remain high, further improving habitat conditions. These lakes also have a very long, warm growing season. A precise combination of all these ingredients creates ideal trout habitat. Summer blue-green algal blooms, although unsightly, are a by-product of these extremely productive lakes.

Mid-elevation lakes are often situated in lodgepole pine forests, where soils are less productive and runoff water is lower in pH. Typically, lakes in this zone will be lower in productivity and the water may appear darker or tannic stained. Lakes in the higher-elevation Englemann spruce/sub-alpine fir zone will have less diversity of aquatic invertebrate and plant life. The water is typically tannic or tea-stained

The majority of the well-known lakes are stocked with rainbow trout on a regular basis. Carefully designed stocking rates, in combination with lake-specific regulations, produce a variety of angling opportunities. Visiting anglers will find a mix of challenges, although the majority of waters are managed for family recreation. The province's fish culture program has developed a number of special rainbow stocks with a view to providing quality fishing. These include all-female and triploid (sterile) female stocks, which grow fast and live longer, especially in highly productive landlocked waters. Quality lakes can be identified by reading the provincial government's sport-fishing regulations synopsis. Most often quality waters are those with reduced limits and/or catch and release regulations, in combination with single barbless hook restrictions and bait bans.

Lakes with self-sustaining, wild stocks of rainbow trout do exist and are carefully nurtured. The majority of these are found north of Kamloops, particularly in Bonaparte Provincial Park, which contains about 70 small wild-stock wilderness lakes. There is no road access to these waters, a popular feature for anglers seeking hike-in fishing experiences. Several wilderness resorts within the park cater both to anglers and those who come merely to enjoy the solitude. Abundant populations of small- to medium-sized trout are the hallmarks of these lakes, but a scattering of waters holding larger fish are found throughout the park. Slightly further north lie the secluded wild-stock lakes of the Caverhill and Thuya Lake chains. Wilderness Emar Lake Provincial Park, west of the town of Little Fort, is home to a series of small lakes connected by a trail system. Ideally explored by canoe, the portages between these pristine lakes are short, allowing maximum fishing time.

Stocked brook trout are available in a number of lakes, and these char grow large and incredibly plump in the food-rich lakes of the region. Brook trout provide a different fishing experience that is just now becoming evident to stillwater fly fishers. Highly selective and notoriously moody, they are a real challenge to catch on the fly. Their preference for deeper water through much of the year makes them that much more difficult to catch. Well-known brook trout waters include Edith, Horseshoe and Red near Kamloops, as well as Edna and Second lakes near Merritt.

Prolific populations of aquatic invertebrates are responsible for the rapid growth rates and trophy sizes attained by rainbow and brook trout in the Thompson-Okanagan, but the single most important food item is the fresh-water shrimp. Found in the region's many calcium-rich lakes, Gammarus and Hyalella shrimp are the food sources which give Kamloops trout their famous deep orange flesh color. Available throughout the year, Gammarus shrimp are largely responsible for the superb condition of the region's trout.

Abundant populations of chironomids or midges are found in every lake. These insects emerge in large numbers during the spring months and continue to hatch in smaller numbers throughout the open-water period. Callibaetis mayflies, damselflies and dragonflies hatch in late spring and mid-summer months. Trout know when these various emergences occur and switch their diet accordingly.

The most exciting dry fly fishing of the year occurs when the travelling sedge or caddis hatches peak. It is hard to imagine a more frenzied feeding spree than that of big trout slashing and chasing

down these moth-like insects as they attempt to fly off the water.

By late summer the majority of insect hatches are complete, and trout and char turn to the elusive leeches that frequent all waters. In the fall months fish return to a staple diet of shrimp and any immature insects that might be available. The ability to identify the various food sources and know their preferred habitats and life cycles is critical to successfully fishing these rich and complex stillwaters.

The wild rainbow trout found in such river systems as the Thompson, Adams, Clearwater and Mahood round out the region's angling challenges. These rivers were the lifeblood, which over time established fish populations in many connected lake systems. The Thompson River is a brawling piece of water which does not give fish up easily. Only those anglers willing to learn the river on an intimate level will have repeated success. The Adams, Mahood and Clearwater are large freestone rivers that support beautifully conditioned rainbows reared on caddisflies, stoneflies and mayflies. These rivers offer a blend of scenic beauty and pristine conditions that is hard to find elsewhere.

Okanagan

Fly fishing the Okanagan region provides its own unique mix of varied and diverse challenges. Besides the big lakes – Mabel, Okanagan and Skaha – there are alpine tarns, semi-desert ponds, high plateau lakes and several trout-filled rivers. Species include lake trout, kokanee, Kamloops trout, high-mountain cutthroat trout, brown trout in the Kettle River, introduced brook trout, bull trout and warm-water species such as bass, perch and bluegills.

Lakes holding Kamloops trout tend to be nestled in groups surrounded by the pine and fir forests typically found in the rain shadow of the Coast mountain range. The Okanagan Valley, from

Callibaetis Nymph
Hook: Mustad 9671, #12–14
Tail: Speckled wood duck or gry. partridge clump
Body: Syn. dubbing mixture of tan wool
Rib: Copper wire
Thorax: Syn. dubbing mixture of brn. wool w/bits of olv. flashabou dubbing mixed in
Legs: Speckled wood duck clump spread to hook's sides
Head: Brnz. peacock

Stillwater Caddis

(Contributed by Ruddick's Fly Shop)

Hook: Mustad 9671, #12
Body: Sparse olv. dubbing
Hackle: 3 wraps of brn. hackle trimmed on bottom
Under-Wing: 10 strands of deerhair
Over-Wing: Grouse body feather smoothed w/glue

Vernon to Osoyoos, has hot summers, low precipitation and fairly mild winters. East of the Okanagan Valley, the land rises through a series of mountain ranges to the Monashee wilderness, the dividing line between the Okanagan and the Rockies (Kootenays).

Mountains in Cathedral Park rise to over 8,500 feet. Wonderful fly fishing can be found in a group of trout-filled lakes in the park. Big rainbows swim in the clear waters of Ladyslipper Lake, and westslope cutthroat trout abound in Quiniscoe Lake, Pyramid Lake and Lake of the Woods. A private lodge on Quiniscoe Lake provides accommodation and transportation to this spectacular area throughout the summer season. The Ashnola River drains the Cathedrals and from mid-summer to late fall provides excellent fishing for small rainbows. An all-season gravel road parallels the entire length of the river.

The Similkameen, of which the Ashnola is a tributary, drains the southwestern corner of the Okanagan. Although not noted as a prime trout stream, it does have fair fishing away from roadside access. The Kettle River and its tributary, the Granby, are fine trout streams in spring and late summer. Although the trout are not particularly big, they come willingly to the fly. Both rivers also contain whitefish and a very few brown trout. The upper Kettle Valley is home to numerous trout lakes nestled in pine and fir forests.

Southeast of Vernon on a 4,500-foot-high plateau, a group of small lakes provides fair fishing in spring and early summer, then again in the fall. During the heat of summer, lakes such as Oyama, Streak, King Edward, Aberdeen, Haddo, Swalwell and Dee become too warm for daytime fishing, but there is often an evening rise.

Gardom Lake near Enderby holds plump brook trout, and the fishing can be quite good in the spring and fall. Low-elevation lakes are best avoided during the Okanagan's notoriously hot summer season, but a number of high-elevation lakes provide ready alternatives. North of Falkland, Bolean, Arthur and Spa lakes are situated at almost 5,000 feet and stay cool enough to produce consistent action for medium-sized trout all summer long. Pinaus, Little Pinaus and Square lakes are a group of small, fertile lakes found south of Falkland.

Pacific salmon migrate all the way to the cold, clear water of Mabel Lake, in the Shuswap watershed. Mabel offers the best large-lake fishing in the Okanagan. Lake trout, bull trout, kokanee, and rainbow trout all inhabit this beautiful lake. Trolling is the most popular method of fishing, but the big rainbows will come to the surface in the evening and can then be taken on the fly.

Many of the most fertile lakes are located north of Princeton. This hilly grassland and aspen-fir-pine forested area has numerous pockets of lakes, most of which are of the small size favored by fly fishers. The more popular of these lakes, such as the Thalia group, are stocked each season. Others are managed as quality waters with fewer, but larger, trout. Eastmere and Westmere are examples of lakes left for those willing to pack in a canoe or float tube. ✺

A Brief History

The Kamloops trout's reputation as a strong, hard-fighting fish began in the late 1800s and early 1900s when rainbow trout fry from tributaries of Shuswap Lake were released into a number of small lakes in the Kamloops area. These were extremely productive lakes which were barren of fish life. Soon after, news of anglers catching 15- to 20-pound rainbows in lakes like Knouff, Peterhope and Badger spread like wildfire through the fishing community.

Lakes that supported wild populations of rainbow trout were also being discovered. Lac Le Jeune, or Fish Lake as it was known in the late 1800s, boasted incredible catches of trout: One record documents a three-day catch by two anglers totalling 1,500 trout, all caught on flies.

Much of the history focusses on Paul Lake and the incredible opportunities available during the 1920s and 30s. Originally barren of fish, Paul Lake was stocked in 1908 by the then-provincial game commission. Within a few short years fishing was so good a road was pushed in to the lake, a resort was built and the game commission established a fish hatchery to seed more lakes in the Thompson-Okanagan area. The lake's phenomenal fishing caught the attention of an angling guide by the name of Bill Nation who had been working out of the Little River at Shuswap Lake.

Bill Nation was born in England and had guided in New Zealand and fished extensively throughout the southern Interior of B.C. He moved his guiding service to Echo Lodge on Paul Lake and soon developed an international client base. An observant naturalist/angler, Nation understood the importance of aquatic invertebrates as trout food and believed that barometric pressure influenced the feeding activity of fish. He created many trout patterns that imitated specific trout food sources, including *Nation's Black*, likely the first chironomid pupa

imitation ever dressed. Other flies he designed included *Nation's Fancy*, tied to imitate a Gammarus shrimp; *Nation's Green Sedge*, a caddis pupa imitation; and *Nation's Grey* and *Green Nymphs*, developed to represent the large darner dragonfly nymphs found in Interior lakes. These patterns, plus many more attributed to Bill Nation, definitely laid the foundation for imitative stillwater fly tying as we know it today. Soon other innovative fly fishers and tiers followed in Nation's footsteps. Tommy Brayshaw, John Dexheimer, Heber Smith, Barney Rushton and Jack Shaw all played important roles in further developing the sport as it is practised on the lakes of the southern Interior by those who seek the renowned Kamloops trout. ⤙

Bill Nation with his first fish of the season, April 1939.

Nation's Fancy
(By Bill Nation)
Hook: Limerick or round bend, #8
Thread: Blk. silk
Tail: Gold. pheas. tippet feather strands (orng. & blk.)
Body Rear 1/2: Silv. tinsel
Body Front 1/2: Blk. floss
Under-Wing: Several strands gold. pheas. tippet
Over-Wing: Speckled gry. mallard flank feather
Hackle: Beard-style speckled guinea

Educated Trout

Watching for fish cruising the shoal areas of lakes is a hallmark of experienced, observant stillwater anglers – for good reason. Most of the productive lakes of the southern Interior are marked by extraordinarily clear water and white marl-covered shoals. These marl-shoal lakes are rich in calcium, a basic element for ensuring abundant shrimp and other invertebrate populations. Such lakes can grow very large trout and, not surprisingly, the shoals are where the fish do the majority of their feeding.

Fish of similar size or age class typically travel together. Large numbers of trout in the 12- to 14-inch class will group together, while fish in the 16- to 20-inch size range will travel in smaller groups. Occasional pods of a select few large fish, normally weighing more than five pounds and which likely have been caught at least once during their lifetimes, are the ones anglers refer to as 'educated' trout. Catch and release does make fish more tentative, and only the most cautious fish will attain the largest sizes. Trophy-sized fish will have heard a lot of boats and motors, seen a lot of flies or lures, and been harassed numerous times by loons or ospreys. Catching these "experienced" trout requires special tactics and no end of patience. Targetting such fish is not a numbers game.

Big fish do have to feed on the shoal just like every other trout in the lake, but they are far and away more cautious. Their tendency is to feed along the deeper edges of the shoal or to come onto the shoal for only very short periods before slipping silently back into deeper water.

Since sound travels five times faster in water than in the air, it is vital anglers be as quiet as possible, particularly when probing the shoals. Sound is amplified underwater as well, so even hitting the gunnel of the boat with an oar will send big fish scurrying for cover,

Ian Forbes: The *Floating Scud* was designed to be fished very slowly over marl or weedbeds in super clear water. In hard-fished lakes trout are wary of any sort of retrieve and this pattern can be fished dead drift until a trout approaches. Trout seldom waste energy chasing active scuds but will quickly pick up stationary ones. Best bet is to give the scud a subtle twitch to get the trout's attention, then let the fly rest. The silvery packing foam is left natural to imitate scuds over marl beds. Dye can be added to the thin glue to match the color of the naturals.

which normally means deep water. Take the time to lay outdoor carpeting in the bottom of the boat and have equipment organized to reduce the amount of movement while fishing. False casts should be kept to a minimum as the line, both in the air and splashing the water, will be heard or seen by fish. If cruising fish are seen, chances are they can see the angler as well, so keeping a low profile – sitting rather than standing – makes good sense, as does wearing polarized sunglasses to help cut surface glare.

Having every detail of tackle prepared for the big moment is vital, considering how few such opportunities come by in any given season. Use good-quality leader and tippet materials as they are very fine in diameter for their strength. Double check leader knots each time prior to fishing and take special care when tying flies on. Plain clinch knots will eventually slip and the improved version only takes an extra five seconds to tie. Good practice also requires tippets be checked after each fish and replaced after three or four fish have been caught. Nicked or frayed tippets are among the prime causes of lost fish.

If big fish can be seen cruising on and off the shoal, all attention and effort should be focussed on the deeper edges. If at all possible estimate how close the fish are to the lake bottom. In most cases big fish will feed closer to the bottom to avoid predators. A floating line and long leader will allow effective coverage of deeper water on the shoal's edges. The key to successful long-leader nymphing is waiting long enough for the fly to reach the bottom before initiating any retrieve. To reduce the time it takes for the fly to get down to the right depth, add some soft putty lead to the last tippet knot before the fly. Split shot crimped onto the leader works, but it can weaken the monofilament – a big factor when playing large, heavy fish. Shrimp, chironomid larvae and pupae, mayflies, and damselflies can all be effectively fished with the long-leader nymphing technique.

The best time of the year to hook a quality fish is during the very late fall period, normally long after most anglers have stored their rods for the season. Fish feed aggressively in anticipation of winter, and the majority of feeding is in shallow water, often tight to cattail and bulrush patches. Big fish travel together, so if only smaller fish are being caught, move to another shoal. Late fall fishing often means short periods of feeding activity. Be prepared to spend the entire day on the water and really concentrate on finding moving fish; they are the ones most likely to be actively feeding. Effective fall shallow-water patterns include bead-headed maroon leeches, shrimp and juvenile damselfly nymphs.

Catching big trout means fishing in water that has the productive capacity to grow large fish. Select productive waters by the type of fishing regulations in place: quality managed lakes will have bait bans, single barbless hook restrictions, winter angling closures, and very limited harvest or zero bag limits. Stocking rates on these lakes are closely monitored to ensure the majority of the fish will reach trophy sizes before natural mortality occurs.

Floating Scud

Hook: Mustad 9671, #12–14
Body: Rough dubbing of olv./gry. fur or syn. mixture w/bits of olv. Flashabou mixed in
Rib: 2 strands of Krystal Flash twisted together or 4-lb.-test mono.
Shell Back: Thin strip of packing foam protected w/pliable glue (thinned Goop or Soft Body glue); add dye to glue to change color

Ron Newman: Large trout will often sweep a marl or mud bottom with their tail, causing food material to rise in the water column. They then return to prey on what has been stirred up. To catch these trophy fish, let your fly sink into the mud and use a slow retrieve. Your fly disturbing the bottom material lets the trout know where to use the 'tail-sweep' technique. Often you will feel a bump and then the strike a few seconds later. Be patient on the bumps and wait for the strike; the bump is usually the fish's tail hitting your fly or leader. Occasionally you will foul-hook a fish with this technique and legally it must be released.

Thompson Steelhead

Majestic but difficult aptly describes both the Thompson River and its unique run of summer steelhead.

Flowing though a steep-walled desert valley, the river is dauntingly large by the standards of coastal steelhead streams, even when at low flows of about 10,000 cubic feet per second. Boats may be used for transportation, but all fishing must be done from shore. Aluminum cleats or good wading boots with hobnails and a wading staff are a must, given the river's slippery rocks. Even so, only small portions of the river's huge pools can be covered with the fly. The setting is majestic indeed, but the size of the river and the tough wading make it very difficult to fish.

Thompson River summer-run steelhead are renowned for their strength and stamina. Averaging between 12 and 15 pounds in weight, these legendary fish will readily take a fly – provided the angler can find them. The river is huge and the run, which has averaged about 2,000 fish annually between 1985 and 1995, will be scattered over many miles of river and in pools often beyond the reach of even the longest casts.

For all that, the river does yield fish to the fly,

notably in the runs in and around Spences Bridge, which are well-known favorites among fly fishers. The season usually starts in early October and extends through to the December 31 closure. In the early season, water temperatures hover in the mid- to high 50s, but as late fall approaches, water temperatures drop; temperatures in the mid-40s are typical of mid-November. In the early season, the fish will rise more readily to take a fly fished near or skated across the surface. The floating-line technique will work in shallower water even with water temperatures in the low 40s, but the deeply sunk fly technique is the staple method of fishing most anadromous fish, Thompson steelhead included.

To be successful on such big pieces of water as the Y Pool, Hotel Run, Murray Creek Run or the Graveyard, anglers must be able to gauge the river's velocity and select a sinktip of the correct length and density to sink the fly as close to bottom as possible without hanging up. Double-handed rod users usually loop their tips to the ends of floating lines and carry a variety of tips in various densities and lengths, typically ranging from five to 15 feet. Single-handed rod users more often rely on manufactured lines in different densities with tips ranging from 10 to 20 feet.

With runs as wide as 500 feet across, the temptation on the Thompson is to cast more line than can be comfortably or capably handled. Given

Bomber

Hook: TMC 7999, Partridge Wilson, Bartleet, Alec Jackson

Tail: Light tan elk hair clump

Body: Nat. or dyed deer-hair; spun, packed & trimmed

Wing/Hackle: Light tan elk hair flared towards front & sides

the careful line manipulation required, it makes sense to concentrate on water within comfortable wading and casting range and forget about what might be happening further out. Fishing a sunk line is a difficult skill to master – any number of factors will affect the drift of the fly – and unless it is properly presented, the fish will not take the offering. Slow and deep are the two basic criteria, but meeting them requires a series of fine judgements involving current speed and the angle of the cast required in relation to the water being fished.

Sinktips backed by floating lines, either manufactured or attached by loops, allow far more control when fishing the deep-sunk fly than was afforded with the old full-sinking lines. Casts can be more directly out from the angler, thus allowing the fly to fish at optimum depth during the more productive part of the drift. With a deeply sunk line, most steelhead will be caught from about a 45-degree angle upstream of the flow to almost directly below the angler. Once the line is cast, the floating portion is readily mended, sometimes a number of times as the fly fishes across. Properly done so as not to interrupt the smooth passage of the fly through the water, mending decreases the belly of the line to the current and allows the fly to fish slower across the lie. Practice is definitely required to get it right.

Although the big-fish, big-fly axiom is often a fallacy when steelhead fishing, it does bear consideration when selecting a fly to fish the deep reaches of the Thompson. Big flies such as the *General Practitioner*, *Woolly Bugger* and *Popsicle*-type flies on #2 hooks and larger do attract big Thompson River steelhead, particularly when water temperatures drop into the 40s. Dark-toned patterns with lively movement seem to work better than bright, compact, lifeless flies.

Success will increase by methodically working a piece of water from the top to the bottom of the run. The two-step method comes into its own here: cast, fish the cast, take two steps downstream, cast again and repeat. Going through the water a second time can be worthwhile, particularly if fish are showing or being caught by others. 🐟

Chironomids & Mayflies

May is the prime angling month. Low and mid-elevation lakes will have completed spring turnover and the water will be clear, well oxygenated and at ideal temperatures. Comfortable on the shoals, the fish will be avidly feeding on such items as shrimp and early mayfly emergences, but it is the chironomids in all their infinite variety which will be the mainstays.

Typically, several different species of chironomids hatch at the same time or at different times during the same day. Trout key exclusively to one particular pupal color and size, spurning the thousands of other slightly different pupae emerging at the same time. To determine the color and size preference of the day, or hour, anglers must constantly scan for pupae as they rise to the surface. Samples captured with an aquarium net will reveal the actual color and size of hatching pupae. Matching imitations can then be tested, but if the fish fail to respond, or stop responding, the sequence must be repeated – chances are another emergence will have commenced and the fish, ever finicky, will have switched preferences.

Chironomid emergences are often heavier or more prolonged in one area of a shoal or bay than the rest of the lake, so anglers should be prepared to shift anchor and explore.

The majority of chironomid pupal fishing occurs in water less than 20 feet deep. Trout take rising pupae at any depth between the lake bottom and surface, but often prefer to feed close to the bottom, taking the pupae just as they begin their upward ascent. Floating fly lines with leaders at least two feet longer than the depth anchored in are ideal in this situation. For example, if the hatch is coming off in 16 feet of water and the leader is 18 feet long, the extra two feet of length allows for the angle the leader takes as the retrieve is initiated.

Critical to the formula is allowing sufficient time for the fly to reach bottom before beginning any retrieve. If unsuccessful, reduce the wait time before starting the next set of casts so that the fly fishes higher in the water column.

Callibaetis mayflies also emerge in May and observant anglers will see the signs: discarded nymphal cases or newly emerged duns sitting on the water. Trout taking duns will show classic swirling or head-and-tail rise forms. More often than not, the trout will be feeding most aggressively on the nymphs during their surface swim, making slow/intermediate sinking lines and mayfly nymphs an effective combination. In shallow water, floating lines and long leaders are best. Overcast days with calm or light winds make ideal mayfly emergence weather. Typically, several short emergences occur sporadically over the course of a day, underlining once again the need to be ever vigilant.

Bead Head Chironomid

Hook: Mustad 9671 or similar, #14
Under-Body: Red myl. tinsel
Over-Body: Olv. Super Floss
Thorax: Peacock sword
Head: Clear glass bead
Gills: Small tuft wht. floss or syn. wool

Callibaetis Nymph

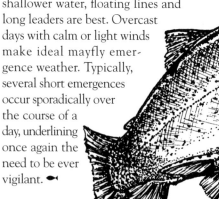

Fishing Calendar

Damsel & Caddisflies

June is the month of transition. The intensity of the chironomid hatches dwindles, mayfly emergences peak, and damselfly and caddisfly hatches come into their own. Trout will still have chironomids on their minds, but after a month-long diet of little else, any strong mayfly emergence will be greeted with enthusiasm, while newly hatching damsel and caddisflies will trigger an all-out spree.

It is not uncommon to have damselflies and caddisflies hatching simultaneously in the same lake. Normally the caddis begin hatching first and peak as the damselfly nymph migration begins in earnest.

Caddisflies (sedges) offer some of the most exciting dry fly fishing of the season. Newly emerged adults scampering across the surface film in an attempt to get airborne not only draw large, normally wary trout to the surface, they also trigger truly aggressive responses. Telltale bucket-sized swirls or boils on the surface are a sure sign of caddis-feeding trout as they inhale one adult after another.

For all the surface drama, as much or more feeding occurs unseen as the pupae swim from the bottom of the shoal to the surface of the lake to hatch. Swimming pupae are a safe, easy meal; ever-alert avian predators make the surface a dangerous place for trout. Expect to encounter caddis hatches both during daylight hours and at night. Obvious signs of an emergence are adults skating across the surface of a lake, but look too for cast pupal casings floating in the surface film. Nighthawks and Bonaparte gulls also key to caddis hatches, so their activity can be a tip-off. The several caddis species found in Interior lakes range in size from three-eighths of an inch to over one inch in body length. Most pupae have a prominent bright green rib through the abdomen, which fly tiers should incorporate in their imitations.

Mature damselfly nymphs swim from vegetation-covered shoals to cattail or bulrush patches to emerge into the adult form. Anglers will see the nymphs swimming within three feet of the surface of the lake. The nymphs crawl out of the water onto shoreside plant stems where the adult form emerges from the nymphal case. The slow-swimming nymphs are easy targets and trout will follow them into mere inches of water, feeding all the way.

Damselfly emergences typically occur between mid-morning and late afternoon. Floating fly lines and 12- to 16-foot-long leaders are a good combination for imitating the emergence swim. Damselfly nymphs range in color from various shades of green to a very dark brown. Imitations must match the naturals as closely as possible, especially as the hatch progresses and the trout become increasingly selective. Adult patterns can be important; strong winds will push adult damsels into the surface film, providing inviting morsels for cruising trout.

Big attractor flies like bead-headed leeches, *Woolly Buggers* or matuka-style patterns are used for the noise and commotion they create. Trout use their excellent eyesight and pressure-sensitive lateral line to zero in on these pulsating flies. Try casting parallel to the outside edge of weed patches, as the fish will be cruising in and out of the vegetation in search of anything that moves. Actively feeding fish are located by listening for sounds, from quiet slurps to astonishingly loud splashes. Nocturnal caddis hatches are entirely possible, so be prepared to cast high-floating dry flies in the direction of boils or splashes – and then hang on tight. ✄

Crystal Chenille Caddis Pupa
Hook: Mustad 9671, #8–10
Body: Pale olv. Crystal Chenille
Hackle: Dyed olv. speckled partridge/guinea fowl
Head: Peacock sword/brnz. peacock

Fishing Calendar

Hot Nights

July and August are the hot months. Full sinking lines are required as the trout seek deeper, cooler water along the edges of drop-offs where oxygen levels are higher. By mid-July the majority of aquatic insects have reached or passed their peak emergence.

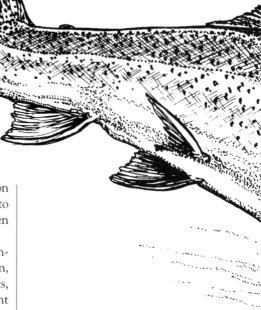

Night Time Matuka
Hook: Mustad 9671, #4
Body: Drk. olv. dubbing mixed w/Flashabou
Rib: Copper wire
Wing/Tail: 2 large multi-var. hen hackles fastened matuka style
Hackle: Nat. blk. hen hackle

Anglers must be prepared to fish bread-and-butter-type food sources such as shrimp, dragonfly nymphs and leeches. Retrieves must be just fast enough to keep the fly from snagging bottom vegetation. Depth sounders will help locate drop-offs and the critical depth zones preferred by feeding fish.

Fishing at night is an exciting alternative to the slow work of mooching deep lines during the daylight hours. Prime time is well after the sun has gone down and the moon has moved into the night sky. By then the water on the shoals will be cool enough to allow trout to feed in relative comfort. It is also the time when the largest fish in the lake are on the prowl.

Pre-trip preparation is essential. On pitch-black overcast nights with only a partial moon, a flashlight or headlamp is needed to tie knots, untangle leaders and point the boat in the right direction when it comes time to head home. Arrange the boat so fly lines will not catch on anything and ensure there is enough clear floor space to lay down retrieved fly line.

Ron Newman: Trophy rainbows often feed after dark, which explains why about 50 per cent of all large Interior rainbows are caught between 8:00 p.m. and 11:00 p.m. Night-feeding rainbows use their 'distant touch sense' to locate food. This touch sense allows them to detect minute vibrations in the water and then zero in on the prey. The lateral line and the supra- and sub-orbital lines on the trout's head are the organs which allow them to hunt at or after dark and without sight.

Water less than 10 feet deep is best for night fishing, making floating lines ideal. Leader tippet strength should be beefed up to at least eight-pound test so there is some chance of stopping big fish from running into cattails or bulrushes. Shorter leaders of between 10 and 12 feet are preferred – casting long leaders at night is asking for trouble; ditto for barbed hooks. ⌗

Fishing Calendar

Boatmen & Backswimmers

September and October mark the return of good fishing. Trout begin feeding aggressively in response to rapidly cooling water temperatures and shorter daylight hours. Soon their body metabolism will gear down to semi-hibernation in preparation for the four to six months they will spend under the cover of ice.

By mid-September the waters on the shoal zone are cool enough for trout to feed all day long. The fish will be looking for staple food items such as shrimp, bloodworms, juvenile damselfly and dragonfly nymphs, and leeches. When they encounter swarming and mating flights of waterboatmen and backswimmers, trout will eagerly take these protein-rich packages. As temperatures continue to drop, the trout will feed in progressively shallower water.

Floating fly lines and varying leader lengths are an ideal combination for shallow-water fall fishing. In clear-water lakes anglers will see trout tipping their heads into the marl bottom in search of Gammarus and Hyalella shrimp. The secret to catching these very focussed fish is to properly present a weighted shrimp pattern of the appropriate size and color. By anticipating a fish's travel path, it is possible to cast well ahead and wait for the fly to sink into the marl. Twitch the fly only when the fish is close by, within two feet or less. The trout will see the disturbance in the marl and hopefully will pounce.

Fall is also the time to fish amidst the bulrush and cattail patches that are ubiquitous along the shorelines of Interior lakes. Opportunistic to a fault, late-season trout will rarely pass on offerings such as small bead-headed damselfly nymphs or leeches. Don't be afraid to fish right into the openings in the mats of coontail or Potamogeton that cover the shoals. Fish feed deep in this dense vegetation; landing them is similar to pulling big bass out of heavy cover. Leader tippets should be between six- and eight-pound test; fall trout are rarely leader shy.

Fall fishing days are short and because there are few, if any, insect hatches, determining when the fish will feed is problematic. Normally the fish feed in several short spurts during the day. Anglers must spend the entire day on the water or risk missing the bite. Often fish are most active during the last hour before dark, but any indication of moving fish calls for immediate action. Even a single rising fish makes pulling the anchors worthwhile – chances are other fish will be feeding in the immediate vicinity. ◂

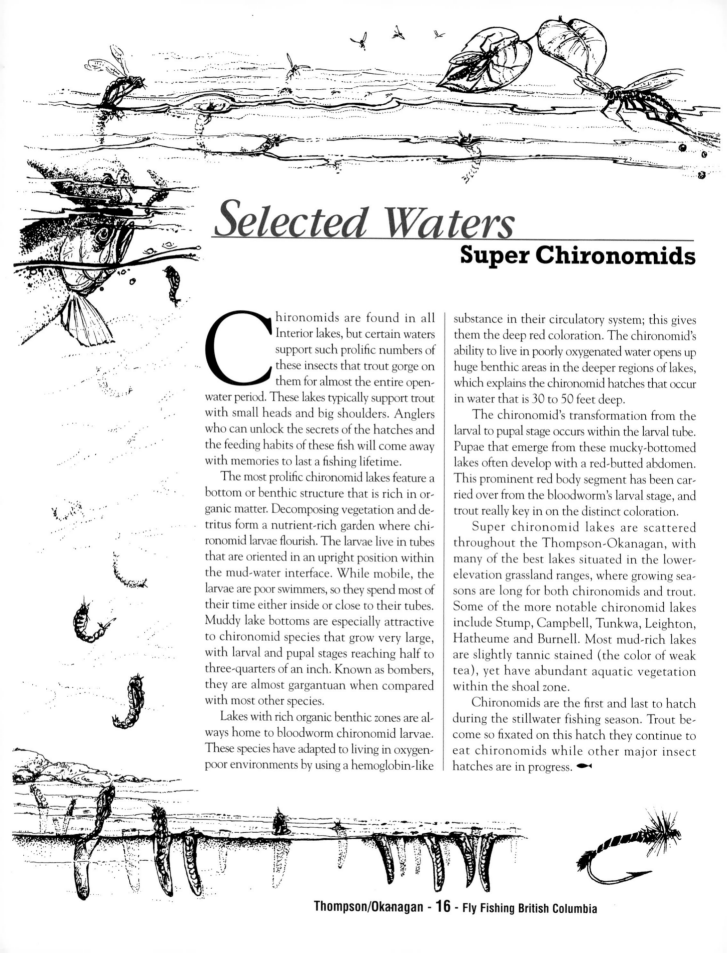

Selected Waters

Super Chironomids

Chironomids are found in all Interior lakes, but certain waters support such prolific numbers of these insects that trout gorge on them for almost the entire open-water period. These lakes typically support trout with small heads and big shoulders. Anglers who can unlock the secrets of the hatches and the feeding habits of these fish will come away with memories to last a fishing lifetime.

The most prolific chironomid lakes feature a bottom or benthic structure that is rich in organic matter. Decomposing vegetation and detritus form a nutrient-rich garden where chironomid larvae flourish. The larvae live in tubes that are oriented in an upright position within the mud-water interface. While mobile, the larvae are poor swimmers, so they spend most of their time either inside or close to their tubes. Muddy lake bottoms are especially attractive to chironomid species that grow very large, with larval and pupal stages reaching half to three-quarters of an inch. Known as bombers, they are almost gargantuan when compared with most other species.

Lakes with rich organic benthic zones are always home to bloodworm chironomid larvae. These species have adapted to living in oxygen-poor environments by using a hemoglobin-like substance in their circulatory system; this gives them the deep red coloration. The chironomid's ability to live in poorly oxygenated water opens up huge benthic areas in the deeper regions of lakes, which explains the chironomid hatches that occur in water that is 30 to 50 feet deep.

The chironomid's transformation from the larval to pupal stage occurs within the larval tube. Pupae that emerge from these mucky-bottomed lakes often develop with a red-butted abdomen. This prominent red body segment has been carried over from the bloodworm's larval stage, and trout really key in on the distinct coloration.

Super chironomid lakes are scattered throughout the Thompson-Okanagan, with many of the best lakes situated in the lower-elevation grassland ranges, where growing seasons are long for both chironomids and trout. Some of the more notable chironomid lakes include Stump, Campbell, Tunkwa, Leighton, Hatheume and Burnell. Most mud-rich lakes are slightly tannic stained (the color of weak tea), yet have abundant aquatic vegetation within the shoal zone.

Chironomids are the first and last to hatch during the stillwater fishing season. Trout become so fixated on this hatch they continue to eat chironomids while other major insect hatches are in progress.

Selected Waters

Super Caddisflies

Searching out B.C. lakes holding abundant populations of caddisflies, or sedges, will put anglers on the trail to some of the best stillwater dry fly action found anywhere. Even the largest trout will savagely attack newly emerged adults dangling in the surface film, making this hatch unmatched for nerve-tingling excitement and well worth the trouble involved in searching out just the right lakes to concentrate on.

While caddisflies are found in almost every small southern Interior lake, certain special waters are home to very large populations. Specific lakes include Hihium, Island in the Highland Valley, Knouff, Lac des Roches and Badger, but there are many other super caddis lakes in the southern Interior. Finding them is a matter of recognizing the specific biological features, or indicators, common to lakes of this type.

Look for the telltale signs of prime caddis larvae habitat – expansive shoal areas provide the best habitat overall. Larvae like both vegetation-covered shoals and those shoals which feature pale yellow marl bottoms. Marl occurs where calcium has precipitated out of the water and formed a particulate covering of the lake bottom. In good caddis lakes the marl areas are criss-crossed with trails left by the larvae as they crawl around in search of food.

Aquatic plants that make good caddis habitat include Chara, milfoil and Potamogeton. Shoreline areas with abundant long-stem bulrushes or cattails complement the rich nature of the shoal zone. Newly emerged caddis adults frequently crawl up onto the stems of these emergent plants either to rest or complete the reproductive process.

Generally, marl-bottom shoals and cattail riparian edges are associated with clear-water lakes. Lily-pad lakes are often tea colored, or tannic stained, and also have the potential to support abundant caddis populations. Regardless of lake type, the caddis life cycle and emergence process is similar. There are numerous different species of caddis found in B.C. lakes, and they differ in size and coloration. Caddis anglers learn the timing of the various species hatches and go prepared.

Take some time to inspect the shallow shoreline area when sizing up a potential caddis lake. It can be quite surprising to see the number of larvae clinging to the undersides of boulders or old tree stumps. Prime caddis emergence in the Thompson-Okanagan region occurs from the second week of June to about the third week in July. That should be enough time to plan at least one trip in search of this super hatch.

Selected Waters

Multiple Hatches

Aquatic insect hatches are directly dependent on water temperature. In most cases, nymphal and pupal development and subsequent emergence follow a logical sequence, starting with chironomids and followed by mayflies, damselflies, caddisflies and finally dragonflies. This natural progression of hatches is exactly what the fly fisher wants. Well-defined hatches allow the trout – and anglers – to focus on one particular food item at a time. While there are always natural overlaps of emergences, unusual weather patterns, such as a very early and hot spring, accelerate insect development and can result in several different insect orders hatching at the same time. These "multiple hatches" offer a new set of challenges, making it necessary to determine not only which hatches are in progress, but also which one the trout are keyed to for that particular day.

Multiple hatches require the angler to be prepared to use a variety of fishing techniques. Several different fly lines are required so that one can quickly change to fish a variety of different depth zones. The majority of insect hatches will occur on or at the edge of the shoal zone. This makes the floating fly line very important. Fishing the deeper depths of the drop-off requires slow- and fast-sinking lines so that flies can be presented as close to the bottom as possible.

Observant anglers catch more fish, and this is particularly true during multiple-hatch situations. Trout will often switch from chironomids to mayflies then back to chironomids during a two-hour morning feeding period. Watch the intensity or the relative abundance of adult insects on the water to determine which hatch is getting stronger or weaker. Be prepared to switch back and forth between tactics and hatches as there is a specific duration to any hatch encountered.

Having a second rod strung up and ready to go is a big advantage during these overlapping hatches. Have one rod set up with a floating line for use with nymphs, pupae or adults and the second one with a type I or slow-sinking line. The sinking line is ideal for fishing nymphs and pupae deeper in the water column, yet still over the shoal or drop-off zone.

Watch for feeding signs elsewhere on the lake and be ready to move around in search of a more prominent hatch of one particular insect. The bottom line in fishing multiple hatches is to be flexible in pattern selection and presentation.

Selected Waters

Late Season

Some of the most exciting action of the year occurs during the last four to six weeks of the Interior lake fishing season. With winter looming, the trout feed aggressively and, as a bonus, much of the activity occurs in shallow water.

By late fall the water is again cold and there are few insect hatches. The exceptions will be the small chironomid and mayfly hatches that emerge sporadically throughout the last month before ice cover. Rainbow, cutthroat and brook trout will focus in on these hatches, but most of the time these fish are looking for more abundant and larger food items, such as leeches, shrimp and damselfly and dragonfly nymphs. These invertebrates all over-winter in juvenile or immature stages and thus become staple food items in the late fall.

Since these food sources are most abundant in the shallow water of the shoal zone, most fishing takes place in water 10 feet deep or less; often fish will feed in water only three feet deep. Preferred areas of a shoal are those that have mats of aquatic vegetation covering the lake bottom. This thick

salad provides ideal habitat for all of the late-season insects. Casting into openings or channels in the thick patches of cattail and bulrush reeds can also yield results, as trout love to pick snails, leeches and damselfly nymphs off the stems of these emergent plants. Floating and intermediate or slow-sinking fly lines cover these shallow-water situations best.

Late fall fishing means a short day on the water. Be prepared to fish the entire day as trout can be moody at this time of the year. It is not uncommon to encounter two or three short (15- to 20-minute)

feeding periods during daylight hours. The rest of the day fish are not very active, and enticing them to bite often means using bright or flashy flies and changing regularly in hopes of triggering a territorial or aggressive response.

Fish will also move or feed in precise locations, with minimal action elsewhere in the lake. Anglers should always be looking for moving fish, even ones that are just jumping – at least those fish are active. Watch for flocks of coots and diving ducks; trout will follow them around and pick up shrimp and damselflies dislodged from the bottom vegetation by the birds.

Some of the better known late-season lakes include White near Salmon Arm, Tunkwa and Leighton near Logan Lake, Kidd near Aspen Grove and Roche near Kamloops.

Selected Waters

First Time Waters

British Columbia is blessed with such an incredible abundance of trout lakes that fishing new waters and unravelling their secrets is a big part of the fly fishing experience. Approaching these diverse waters from the perspective of the fish and knowing something of the requirements of their var-

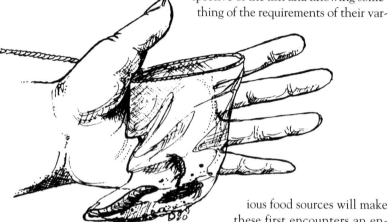

ious food sources will make these first encounters an enjoyable, rather than a frustrating, experience.

Background information on particular lakes is available from such sources as regional fisheries management agencies, lake guidebooks and hatch guides. These sources contribute basic information such as lake elevation and access, water chemistry, mean depth, and types of aquatic vegetation present. In conjunction, they provide a profile of a given lake which anglers can use to advantage. Knowing whether a lake is acidic (pH less than 7.0) or alkaline (pH greater than 7.0) is critical – alkaline lakes are far more productive. Similarly, TDS (total dissolved solids) gives an indication of the relative amount of dissolved nutrients in the lake – the higher the number, the more fish food the lake will produce. Knowing the different depth zones of a lake will help determine the amount of shoal area present and thus the extent of fish and fish food habitat. Combining this information with details of the types of aquatic vegetation present will indicate the diversity of aquatic insects to expect.

Time of year is critical as well. The majority of insect hatches occur in the spring to mid-summer months. Before or after this period, trout are limited to a much narrower menu selection, which can make for less complex angling. Let's assume a new lake is being explored during the third week of May. This is prime insect emergence time for Thompson-Okanagan lakes and for much of the province's southern Interior. Emergence charts will indicate heavy hatches of chironomids and mayflies. Knowing that the juvenile stages of these insects live within the shoal area of the lake provides a valuable starting point. Since chironomid pupae and mayfly nymphs will hatch from water that is generally less than 20 feet deep, it makes sense to concentrate fishing time on these shoal areas rather than in the deeper zones. Similar strategies can be worked out for each of the various hatches and annual seasonal cycles in the life of a lake.

The better stillwater anglers constantly scan for insect hatch activity. The observant angler will see chironomids or mayflies hatching or notice swallows or gulls working over a partic-

ular spot on a shoal. Anglers must be prepared to follow up on such visual clues, as the trout will be concentrated nearby. Taking the time to capture emerging insects with an aquarium net and then matching the size and color of the particular hatch that day will pay huge dividends. Tracking all this information in a diary builds a body of fishing lore that will quickly become the most valuable reference source for unlocking the various puzzles presented by old and new waters alike. ◄━

Selected Waters

Crystal Lakes

The crystal clear stillwaters of the Thompson-Okanagan region offer some of the most challenging yet rewarding fly fishing opportunities one will ever encounter. Many of these clear lakes are extremely productive, supporting excellent insect hatches and growing big trout. The combination of well-fed fish in a clear-water environment can be frustrating for the unprepared fly fisher. Developing a set of refined fishing strategies will yield rewards that can be built on during each successive outing.

A key to these waters is remembering trout have both excellent vision and hearing. Anglers can rest assured that when they see trout, the fish can see them as well. Trout, particularly the larger specimens, cruise a defined feeding territory, so it is possible to watch individual fish swim by regularly as if on a circuit. Even in flat calm situations, big rainbows will regularly be seen under the boat or float tube, but only if left undisturbed. This means not standing up and waving arms about or shouting to other anglers or dropping a fly box on the floor of an aluminum boat. Spooked fish will leave a telltale trail of dust behind when they depart, a sure sign that more stealth is required. Calm water makes spotting fish easier, but a slight riffle on the water is an angler's best friend in these gin-clear lakes. Polarized sunglasses will help to cut the glare on both calm and rippled water and are a tremendous advantage in such difficult angling conditions.

The majority of trout feeding occurs on the shoal, in water less than 20 feet deep. Floating fly lines and different combinations of leader lengths can be used to imitate almost all the important food sources. In fact, floating lines are ideal for clear-water lakes, affording good depth control and thus allowing the fly to remain in the feeding zone for longer periods – less time casting means more time fishing. Leaders are critical to this formula, obviously, and leaders in excess of 16 feet are regularly employed. The key to manipulating long leaders successfully is to ensure the butt section is stiff enough to turn over the entire leader and fly when casting.

Outdoor carpeting on boat floors will reduce noise levels and protect fly lines from abrasion. Simple anchor control systems at the bow and stern of the boat minimize the amount of movement required when pulling or setting anchors, but patience and persistence are the two mandatory requirements: A fish which earlier cruised the shoal and ignored all offerings could well be in feeding mode on the next pass through.

Clear-water lakes to sample include Peterhope, Roche, Alleyne/Kentucky, Lac des Roches, Big Bar and Island. 🐟

Dave's Damsel
(Contributed by Dave Connolly)
Hook: Mustad 94840, #10–12
Eye: Gold brass bead set on thread base
Tail: A few strands of olv. Diamond Braid (Flashabou dubbing)
Body: Roughly spun olv. Diamond Braid

Selected Waters

High Elevation Lakes

High-elevation lakes are generally described as those located over 4,500 feet above sea level. Lakes at this elevation and higher differ substantially from those found in lower grassland regions or in dense fir or pine forests. Perhaps the most significant difference is the reduced productivity of these lakes. Many high-elevation lakes are beyond the tree line, so nutrient input from the surrounding plants and soils is quite limited. Key basic chemicals, such as calcium and phosphorus, are scarce, thereby reducing the diversity and abundance of aquatic invertebrates. The growing or open-water period is also much shorter, so both fish food and trout growth are limited. The variety and abundance of aquatic vegetation are reduced, and the blue-green algae blooms that are so familiar on lower-elevation lakes are almost non-existent.

Many high lakes support self-sustaining populations of trout as a result of well-defined inlet and outlet creek systems. Each lake will vary in terms of fish size and abundance: some lakes will hold big fish, but fewer of them, while other lakes will have an over-abundance of small fish. Snowpack levels and the timing of the spring runoff can be critical factors determining fish size and abundance.

In general, high-elevation trout are easier to catch simply because the fish are more aggressive feeders. Matching the hatch often requires no more than a small dry fly to imitate any surface food and a small selection of basic nymphs to imitate any nymphal or pupal emergences. Don't forget, these fish see far fewer fishing flies and anglers than those in the popular lakes of the valley bottoms. Attractor fly patterns such as *Woolly Buggers*, *Muddler Minnows* and *Royal Wulffs* are proven favorites for high-elevation lakes.

Many high lakes are accessible only by foot or aircraft, so much of the fishing is done from shore or by wading short distances out from shore. A floating line and two sinktip lines, a slow and a fast sinker, will cover most situations. Sinktip lines allow better coverage of the drop-offs when casting out from shallow water.

Anglers approaching a high-elevation lake for the first time should locate any inlet or outlet streams, as flowing water tends to concentrate the food or insect drift which may be entering or leaving the lake. Scan the shoals for feeding fish and, if possible, watch the edge of the drop-offs for fish that may be leaving or just travelling to the shallow water.

Some good high-elevation lakes in the Thompson-Okanagan include those within Cathedral Provincial Park, Spruce Lake near Goldbridge and the Stevens lakes within Wells Gray Provincial Park.

Selected Waters

Brook Trout

First introduced to B.C. waters in the early 1930s, brook trout stocked in the productive lakes of the Thompson-Okanagan provide exceptional – if challenging – sport. Interior brook trout commonly attain weights in excess of five pounds, and lakes managed to support both brook and rainbow trout offer a range of intriguing fishing scenarios throughout the changing stillwater seasons.

While stillwater brook trout and rainbow trout target the same food sources, brook trout select the nymphal, larval or pupal stages of insects, rather than the adult form. Brookies also seem to prefer feeding lower in the water column, rarely showing on the surface, and are rather moody feeders; during a major chironomid or mayfly hatch they tend to feed heavily for only a very short time. A throat pump of a fish caught during one of these typical hatches would likely yield several live chironomid pupae or mayfly nymphs amongst a good number of live freshwater shrimp. This behavior may be a result of their preference for deeper water or their affinity for some form of cover, such as bottom vegetation or underwater structure, when feeding.

Moody brook trout can often be enticed into taking a leech pattern, notably during the hot summer months when few aquatic insects are emerging. Find some steep drop-offs or a rocky point dropping off into deep water, and fish leeches on a fast or extra-fast sinking fly line. Use a relatively fast three- to six-inch retrieve. Work the fly right up to the surface, as brookies will often follow their prey a long way before striking.

Late fall weather and cooling water temperatures bring brook trout back onto the shallow waters of the shoal zone. They often feed in water less than three feet deep, chasing down freshwater shrimp, damselfly nymphs and waterboatmen. In these situations an intermediate sinking or floating fly line works well, affording better depth control and allowing the fly more time in the feeding zone. If the fish are working over a weed-covered bottom, keep the fly just ticking over the tops of the plants. Brook trout spawn in the fall, and mature fish will cruise the shoreline zone looking for gravel areas to dig redds. Spawning schools of fish are followed by immature brook trout in search of a meal of newly released eggs.

Brook trout are a challenging alternative to chasing the more predictable rainbow trout. They are secretive fish, but once an angler figures out their feeding location and food preference, some very exciting fishing action follows.

Lakes supporting healthy populations of brook trout include Marquart, Upper and Lower Second, Edith and Horseshoe.

Thompson Okanagan Journal

The early July sun was painting the Copper Bluffs across the lake from Savona as I made my way along the north shore of the Thompson River. Footing was treacherous on the loose gravel and boulders six or eight feet below the river's high-water mark. Reaching the outwash below a series of swirling, rough-edged pools, I paused to set up my fly outfit and catch my breath. The cutbanks had become steeper and the rocks along the river's edge more hazardous over the years.

Heavy swirls close to the shore upstream marked spots where the occasional late-hatch stonefly skittered on the polished emerald of the most beautiful trout water I've ever known. I'd fished this stretch since 1933, even in those years when I had to travel days to reach it, but my excitement at knowing that I was here at the right time hadn't diminished over the years. My hands trembled as I fastened a #8 brown sedge to the leader. The stonefly hatch was ending and the big sedges were moving.

The weighted sedge suited their taste, and hefty Kamloops trout took almost every cast. But, all too soon, a late-morning breeze was strengthening, loosening rocks along the cutbank towering above my back. After a few head-sized cobbles had clattered and banged down to *whump* into the river close to me, I decided my reaction time had slowed too much to risk staying. I cleaned one big trout for a friend in Chase and retraced the careful steps I'd taken to reach 'my stretch'.

My van was parked high above, near the edge of the Pinecrest bench, at the same spot I'd started a steep trail many years before. My father and I had shared that trail with Bert Collins, who owned the TU Auto Camp at Cache Creek. We had it pretty much to ourselves those days, but times had changed. Putting the fish on ice, I sat down on the sand (carefully — that's prickly pear country!) and looked down on Skull Flat. The land was now being developed and I realized that this could be the last of such trips. I'd retired in '84 and was now revisiting old haunts. This was my first and most important stop.

The fish I had hooked differed in appearance. Many of them — bright, heavy-bodied rainbow — were actually young steelhead. They were mad fighters despite their relatively small size: around 12 inches, with the occasional fish reaching 14 inches. The fish I kept was a big resident Kamloops whose rosy-bright flanks showed just how good trout food still was in the Thompson. A few lanky, dark fish had probably just returned from spawning in the Deadman River, which joins the Thompson about a mile upstream from my 'private' stretch of river. This stretch is actually the property of the Skechesten band, although I was not aware of that then. To fish the area a $10 annual licence, obtained from the band office, is required.

There are many stretches of the big Thompson where fly fishing is still good, according to reports. The whole river is fishable right from Savona to Lytton. However, my 'sure-bet' stretch of river has not fared well over the years. The great swarms of stoneflies and sedges have been drastically reduced on the whole river, and along my part of the river have almost disappeared; with them, most of the resident fish, which wintered well in past years, have been reduced to almost nothing. The surviving fish are still lank and dark in July because there is not enough food to allow them to regain their beauty and power. I still fish that water occasionally, since I now live right above it on the Thompson River Estates. However, as I discovered, the loose Thompson River boulders have become a bit hard to handle. As I write this I am recovering from broken ribs and pulled ligaments (I used to fall, occasionally, but I don't bounce well now).

By noon on that beautiful July day I'd reached Chase to deliver the gift fish. I was actually Okanagan-bound when I set out from the Island. The Skull Flat stopover was well worthwhile, but I also wanted to fish Okanagan waters again. So I turned onto the Falkland road just west of Chase, passing Pillar and Joyce lakes enroute. I'd had good fly fishing in that water, although Pillar fish were a bit small. The larger fish in Joyce weren't easily fooled. At Vernon I took the Westside road, bypassing Kelowna and the numerous stops along the way.

I pulled into the OK Falls campground well before dark, had a bite to eat, then set out to try the Okanagan River below Vaseux Lake. In the early '60s, when I first fished this water, it was open to fishing year round and was loaded with rainbow trout in late winter and early spring. The really big trout were Oregon hybrids. I nearly broke my rod on some of those six- to eight-pound lunkers, but must admit that I've caught big squawfish that fought better. However, on this trip, after nearly 20 years or so of not stocking Oregons, all the fish I hooked were resident rainbow. None were large enough to be interesting. July trout fishing never was too great, so I turned my attention to bass.

Eurasian milfoil was becoming a nuisance in the valley lakes, but I managed despite this, using a 4X-long #6 fly I'd tied which worked well for largemouth in Creston waters. The big fly was my impression of a blue dragonfly and, although fly tying was not (and still isn't!) one of my great achievements, it had always taken bass very well.

I soon discovered that the fly still worked well for largemouth. At the time there were no bass above McIntyre Dam, just below Vaseux Lake, so I fished the downstream water right into Osoyoos Lake. I had tied my Sportspal onto the roof of my van and worked my way through the backwaters, which I reached by crossing the Road 23 bridge just upstream from the lake. Milfoil was a nuisance, but I fished openings at several bends, releasing a number of hefty largemouths. Just before dark I fished several different streamer patterns in the waters below Bridge 23, catching both trout and smallmouth bass.

I believe I was the first to discover smallmouths in this stretch, back in the '60s. It was in early May and I was drifting a big dry stonefly for rainbows in the outrace from the last drop-structure. When the four-pound-plus smallmouth bass hit, I really thought I'd tied into a big, crazy-fighting rainbow. Today the bass have somehow spread upstream, through Vaseux and (presumably) all the way to big Okanagan Lake. Skaha Lake in particular holds a large population of smallmouth bass, but at that time I had to take the fish into the Penticton Fish & Wildlife office to convince them that a new bass had been added to local stocks.

I moved on to revisit the Kettle River, then headed home to the Island.

Today I can sit out on the edge of my land and see 'my stretch' of the Thompson River. Heavy rockfalls have obliterated most of the good fly water and have restructured eddies and runs downstream. The terrific fly fishing of yesteryear has been greatly diminished and won't come back until clear-cutting scars along tributaries of the Thompson system have grown back sufficiently to maintain more regular fluctuations of the big river. This should revitalize the bugs which for millennia have provided a rich food source for Thompson River fish. It seems unlikely, at 80, that I will see that day, but it's good to know it will come, given half a chance. ><

— Dave Stewart

Cariboo Chilcotin Coast

Prospecting for trout in small, hidden lakes is what fly fishing the Cariboo is really all about. The southern Interior of British Columbia offers some of the best small-lake angling in the world and the Cariboo lies at the heart of that region. The magic combination of mineral-rich soils and nutrient-rich water extends throughout much of the region but, unlike the more famous trout waters to the south, huge tracts of Cariboo angling country remain undiscovered by all but a dedicated few.

This is not to say the Cariboo is bereft of angling meccas – far from it. Highway 24 is, after all, known as the 'Fishing Highway' and the Interlakes region it accesses boasts a legion of hall-of-fame-type lakes, Sheridan, Bridge and Lac des Roches being among the best known of the larger lakes. Surrounding those lakes and extending for hundreds of miles in all directions lie a multitude of more intimate waters, any one of which might yield quite spectacular fishing, yet few would perk an angler's ears the way mention of Stump or Tunkwa or Peterhope almost certainly would.

If the early gold seekers who blazed the Cariboo hinterlands were bewildered by the region's limitless possibilities, anglers prospecting for trout face a similarly dizzying dilemma. Just

where amidst the region's endless scattering of lakes does one start?

Roads of various kinds – paved, gravelled, rutted and combinations thereof – branch east and west from the Cariboo Highway to snake endlessly into a mix of ranch lands, angling resort areas, and miles and miles of not much of anything but more backwoods lakes, more rolling hills, scattered moose meadows, and always another series of lakes, on and on seemingly forever. Lakes with big-fish reputations draw the majority of anglers, so names such as Big Bar, Howard, Hammer, Fawn, Forest, Fir, Owen, Elk and Dragon (to reel off just a few) have their loyal following, but similar, and in some cases better, angling might be found at any number of lesser-known lakes.

Locating on one of the resort lakes is often a smart move, since lodge owners keep close tabs on nearby waters and are reliable sources of information. Most maintain boats on nearby walk-in lakes, and these can yield very good angling indeed. It is not unusual to fish a mix of lake types, from those offering slow fishing for large fish to fish-a-cast lakes with decidedly smaller trout forming the bulk of the population. Regional guides are available and the local Fisheries Branch office as well as area tackle shops, especially those catering specifically to fly fishers, are all good sources of information on the hot spot of the moment. But, really, fishing the small lakes of the Cariboo means boning up on lake reading

skills, being familiar with the various hatches and heading out, preferably with a high-clearance vehicle such as a pick-up or sports utility and as many regional maps as can be cadged (the Forest Service's East and West Cariboo maps, for starters).

Fly fishers tend to be serious about their sport, so most are familiar with the various indicators which provide invaluable clues to the quality of angling a given lake is likely to deliver. This becomes especially valuable in the Cariboo, where only a relatively few waters have known reputations. Fortunately, all the usual rules hold. For instance, lakes with extensive

Bead Head
Woolly Bugger

(Contributed by
Larry Pemberton)

Hook: Mustad 9671, #6–8

Tail: Med. olv. marabou &
4 strands of grn. myl. or
Krystal Flash

Body: Olv. peacock chen.

Hackle: Olv. saddle hackle
wrapped palmer style

Head: Gold (brass) bead

aquatic plant life, such as Chara or coontail, are most likely to offer quality angling. Add large areas of marl and the recipe is complete. Lakes sustaining only limited plant life and meagre shoal areas are much less likely to produce double-digit trout. So far so good, but one of the intriguing – or maddening, depending on the point of view – aspects of Cariboo lake life is the number of variations on these quite standard themes.

Boulder-strewn silt-bottom lakes with only marginal aquatic plants are not to be dismissed out of hand, at least not in the Cariboo where any lake slightly off the beaten track is likely to receive negligible angling pressure. Such lakes might well be in delicate balance, neither oligotrophic nor eutrophic but somewhere in between and entirely capable of producing trout of remarkable sizes, albeit in lower numbers. If spawning creeks are blocked or non-existent, anglers had best maintain firm grips on their rods: some of the Cariboo's largest trout come from precisely such waters.

A word or two on fish sizes seems in order, even if, as

most anglers are aware, such descriptions are generalities at best and can be entirely misleading. Anglers unfamiliar with the kind of trout small Cariboo lakes are capable of producing will in any case not become believers until confronted with the evidence for themselves. Ten-pound-plus rainbow trout exist in a surprising number and array of lake types. Fish weighing more than 20 pounds have turned up in net survey samples from lakes only slightly larger than small pothole ponds – hooking and landing such giants, however, remains an elusive achievement. Well-conditioned two-pound rainbow trout are quite standard, with fish between five and eight pounds considered 'nice ones'; it takes a double-digit rainbow to qualify as a true trophy.

Ron Newman: Larger Interior rainbow trout establish distinct feeding territories and tend to feed quietly in ones or twos, while smaller fish feed in splashy schools. Prior to feeding, larger fish chase smaller competitors from the vicinity, then patrol their territory while feeding. When fish are obviously active elsewhere on a lake, but an ideal-looking shoal remains devoid of activity, this often marks the exclusive preserve of only a few larger fish. Drop the anchor and try a few casts.

The larger fish are most often found in hard-water lakes with extensive plant life and marl shoals, just the kind of lake to quicken an informed angler's heartbeat, but again the Cariboo offers a variation on the theme. Quite a number of the region's crystal-clear lakes are too alkaline to sustain trout, although special strains of alkaline-resistant trout are being developed for these waters. On the other hand, lakes with plunging shorelines and little or no plant life might offer spectacular fishing, especially for those familiar with the stocking program involving Gerrard, Blackwater and Tzenzaicut rainbow trout. These native strains of highly piscivorous trout are being stocked in lakes with dense populations of coarse fish such as the redside shiner. Fishing strategies for these lakes differ radically from those employed on the alkaline and algae-type lakes – forage fish patterns worked in and around structure are standard – but for those in the know, an excitingly different angling experience awaits.

All the myriad complexities of lake fishing with a fly seem to coalesce in the Cariboo; this extends to the intricacies of hatch-matching as well. Aside from a very few variations such as the hatch of Hexagenia mayflies in select regional lakes, the aquatic insects found in Cariboo lakes, and in Chilcotin lakes for that matter, do not differ from the familiar handful already well known to B.C. lake fly fishers.

Chironomids kick off the season and peak from mid-May through to mid-June. Trout avidly take chironomids throughout this period and follow the emergence all the way, from bottom to top, becoming increasingly selective as the hatch builds, often maddeningly so. The damselfly emergence follows, normally through the month of June and overlapping with the dragonfly and Callibaetis mayfly emergence. The sedges, or caddisflies, are more important than either of the two latter hatches, and these insects normally emerge from mid-June through to the end of the month, tapering off during the first two weeks of July. Sedges provide the best dry fly action of the season and offer the best chances for taking large fish on the surface – the skittering surface dance of the naturals regularly proves irresistible even to the wariest trout. The egg-laying flight of the waterboatmen takes place in September and is often enthusiastically greeted by trout preparing for the long dark months ahead.

A nodding acquaintance with the various life cycles of these insects is certainly required and for consistent success anglers must be well versed in both the basics and the idiosyncrasies of aquatic insect behavior. This is not as daunting as it may at first appear. Most of the details are spelled out in various sections of this book. In combination with the patterns provided, it should be possible to prospect a given Cariboo lake with some measure of confidence. Hanging on to the often large trout found in these lakes is another matter.

Being on a Cariboo lake during a damselfly hatch will drive the point home in spades. Emerging damselflies swim shoreward just under the surface and the trout will follow them in. Often the heaviest feeding takes place amongst emergent vegetation, right next to shore in water so shallow the backs of large trout will be clearly visible above the surface. Here the nymphs crawl out of the water onto plant stems where they emerge as adults, leaving the nymphal shuck clinging to the stems. Given the small size of the naturals, light tippets are required to breathe life into imitations. Trout hooked amongst the ranks of plant stems will dash for deeper water, obligingly clearing the dangerous near-shore zone, but often stopping short of the drop-off to roll themselves in submergent plants such as Chara. There they lurk, unmoving, and so too does the angler. Given the light tippets involved, there is no horsing the fish out.

Most often such fish are lost, and even those which streak for deeper water beyond the drop-off must be handled most gingerly. Any slight glitch – a momentary pause in the rapidly disappearing fly line, for instance – will be enough to pop the tippet and truly large fish just keep going, running out first the fly line, then the backing and stopping only momentarily, if at all, when they come up against

Hexagenia Mayfly

Hook: Mustad 94838, shrt. shank, #8–10

Tail: Wood duck flank feather strands threaded into body

Body: Hollow tube, yel. wool built on needle, dipped in thinned Soft Body glue

Thorax: Amb. dubbing

Wing: Wood duck flank feather

Hackle: Gold. badger tied parachute-style or Forbes style w/thorax dubbing pulled under hackle

Ian Forbes: Many fertile Cariboo lakes get a plankton bloom in summer which may last through into the autumn. The plankton reduces visibility, making trout less wary. Fishing small flies becomes less practical, but large *Shaggy Dragons* and *Woolly Buggers* cause a disturbance trout can sense with their lateral lines, causing them to draw near and investigate. Trolling a bulky fly is one of the best ways of assuring success during plankton blooms.

the arbor knot. It is exciting, frustrating, exhilarating and highly addictive, precisely what lake fly fishing the Cariboo is all about.

For all that is made of hatch-matching, there will be many days when general-purpose searching patterns fished near bottom on full

the height of a strong hatch, the largest fish will rarely refuse a properly presented fry pattern, having imprinted on fry in the rivers and smolts in the lakes. Prospecting for Cariboo trout really ought to include an outing or two on flowing water, even if small lakes are the region's hallmark.

Chilcotin

The Chilcotin encompasses all the superlatives normally applied to B.C. in one grand sweep of country. Extending west from the Fraser River all the way to the coast at Bella Coola, the land rises gradually from the rolling Chilcotin Plateau until the towering backdrop of the Coast Range of mountains dominates the landscape. Quality angling waters abound, from such meccas as Puntzi, Nimpo and Anahim lakes alongside Highway 20 to the countless lakes and streams found to the north and south of the main road, reached either over a network of backroads or by air into the Chilcotin wild country.

While float planes will lift anglers to such wilderness destinations as Tweedsmuir Park's Eutsuk Lake, the remote headwaters of the Blackwater (West Road) River, or the farthest reaches of Chilko Lake in Ts'yl-os Park, backroads will take the adventurous to any number of remote waters, many of them offering angling to rival the best found anywhere in the province.

Nor is there any need to travel hundreds of miles to find exceptional angling. Lakes such as Fletcher, Mons, Willan and Kloacut, all within easy driving of Williams Lake on the Fraser, offer quality angling for large rainbow trout. Fletcher has a small lodge, and cabins ring the lake, while the other three are more remote. Mons, Willan and Kloacut are subject to periodic winterkill, but when the trout survive two or more winters, they grow to large sizes, especially in Kloacut, likely the richest of the three with dense gardens of Chara and coontail admirably suited to fly fishing.

The three large lakes of the south Chilcotin – Taseko, Chilko and Tatlayoko – are among the most scenic in the province, but their large size makes them daunting prospects for the fly. The Chilko River at the outlet of Chilko Lake rates as one of B.C.'s finest trout streams and is

sinking lines are entirely sufficient. Leeches and Gammarus shrimp, after all, are mainstays in the diets of these trout, and artfully worked imitations of these food sources, or any number of suggestive patterns, often prove highly effective. Still, successfully fishing general attractor patterns or working any fly deep is something of an art form. The fly must be worked just so, with pauses and twitches and subtle nuances of movement. Unvaryingly stripping the fly in standard six-inch pulls is not only mind-numbing, it also results in far

Tom Thumb
Hook: Mustad 9671, #8–12
Tail/Body/Wing: Nat. deer-hair

fewer hook-ups. At its best, this is a highly meditative form of lake fly fishing and real imagination is required to constantly picture the fly as it darts, pauses and alternatingly inches along in an intricate underwater dance designed by the angler.

Given the endless number and variety of lakes found in the Cariboo, it is easy to overlook the region's quality trout streams. This would be a mistake. Rivers such as the Horsefly and the Quesnel would be highly touted elsewhere but are rarely mentioned in the Cariboo where lake fishing casts such an immense shadow. Tumbling a stonefly nymph or drifting an adult imitation on the surfaces of either of these streams, or on any number of lesser-known waters, can produce exceptional trout. Spawning sockeye salmon lure large lake-resident trout into the streams and the emerging fry bring them back in the spring. Many of these trout will hold over in sockeye streams to take advantage of various insect hatches, but even at

readily accessible by road. Small lakes clustered near the big three provide the kind of waters most often sought by fly fishers. Stand-outs include Chaunigan, home to a native Chilcotin strain of rainbow trout particularly susceptible to

the dry fly; two hike-in lakes, Yohetta and Dorothy, both offering fast fishing for small rainbow trout in settings which must be seen to be believed; and the popular Horn, Sapeye and Bluff group of quality angling lakes.

North of Highway 20, Fir, Owen and a number of nearby pond-sized lakes offer challenging fishing for very large rainbow trout. Dead-drifting flies designed to 'breathe' with minimal movement under a strike indicator is often an effective way to fool wary trout in clear water. Even in the Chilcotin, lakes with big-fish reputations see a steady parade of anglers over the course of the season and the trout soon become inured to trolled fly patterns or flies which do not mimic the movements of the naturals. Only a short distance to the west but reached over the Alex Graham Road, Palmer Lake holds similar-sized fish which may not be quite as fussy. The lake has a nice mid-lake shoal and bays with patches of Chara that harbor good shrimp populations. Patience and skill are required to fish such lakes successfully.

As a general rule, the lakes of the Chilcotin Plateau can be divided into two broad categories: the eutrophic waters holding large but often exceptionally wary (read difficult) trout, and the less-rich waters which tend to hold legions of relatively small but incredibly feisty trout. Variations are ubiquitous, and large lakes such as Eutsuk are unique unto themselves, but as a rule of thumb, grouping Chilcotin lakes into these two distinct categories will help anglers form a mental fishing map of this vast sweep of country.

Gammarus shrimp and thick growths of aquatic plants are the two key indicators of quality Chilcotin angling waters. As always, any number of exceptions exist and waters which lack these two features should never be dismissed arbitrarily, not in the still-remote by-ways of the Chilcotin. Lakes such as Fish near Taseko, Tsuniah near the outlet of Chilko, and fly-in Eliguk in the headwaters of the Blackwater River offer exceptionally fast fishing for normally quite small native trout. Young, learning fly fishers dote on precisely such waters, but even those without children would be doing themselves a disservice by not stopping off at one or more lakes of this type.

Nor does maximum degree of remoteness necessarily mean teeming numbers of large trout. More often, remote Chilcotin waters deliver small, plentiful fish and owe their reputations to their spectacular settings. The fly-in Turner Lake chain of canoeing lakes in Tweedsmuir Park offers very fast fishing for small, colorful native cutthroat trout, but the Coast Range mountain setting is wild country writ large, and fishing is often only a handy excuse for lingering. Much the same can be said of the Blackwater River, although dry fly fishing for its small, aggressive rainbow trout quickly becomes addictive, not unlike the Chilcotin country itself.

This grand country ends at Bella Coola on the coast, but not so the fly fishing. Besides the coastal rivers which beckon here, promising wild steelhead trout and coho salmon, the coast itself offers fly fishers a relatively new frontier: open-water fishing for both coho and chinook salmon. It seems fitting that one of B.C.'s grandest landscapes should end in one of the province's greatest salmon fishing destinations, Hakai Pass. The world record open-water chinook was caught at Hakai, albeit not on the fly, but fish of similar size and even larger pass by each year, leaving the door open to what surely must be one of fly fishing's last great challenges. ✦

Glass Bead Chironomid
Hook: Mustad 94838 or Captain Hamilton, #14–16
Tail: Maroon marabou
Body: 3 glass beads: olv., grn. or red

Hakai Tyee

Popovic's Silicone Wool Head

(Contributed by Bob Popovic)

Hook: Stainless steel, Mustad 3407 or similar, #1/0–4/0
Tail: 12 strands prpl. Krystal Flash over #4–6 wht. saddle hackle
Collar: Shrt. clump of white lambswool, either side of tail
Body & Head: Wht. lambswool spun into thick chen. then flattened & smoothed back w/thinned solution of clear silicone glue; before gluing mark back w/drk. blu. & grn. Pantone pen
Eyes: Plastic stick-on, glued later

Situated at the north end of Calvert Island near the entrance to Rivers Inlet, Hakai Pass encompasses a stunning marine wilderness long known for its incredible chinook salmon fishing. Here homeward-bound chinook linger, having come by way of the open North Pacific and the Gulf of Alaska. Rivers Inlet is home to the largest chinook in British Columbia and these fish, as well as those from countless southern streams, touch down at the Pass in water that is difficult, but not impossible, for the determined fly fisher. Those who require further inducement need only consider that the world record open-water chinook, a fish weighing 85.5 pounds, was caught at Hakai's Odlum Point in 1987.

Odlum, with the Pacific on one side and the splintering of wind-carved, rocky islets which mark the entrance to the Pass on the other, is a choice location for those who would tempt the largest of the Pacific salmon to the fly. Incredible catches have been made at this one-of-a-kind spot, but the tyee (chinook salmon over 30 pounds) remains an elusive goal for the fly. The technicalities have certainly been mastered – suitable rods, reels, lines and fly patterns are there in plenty – so it only remains to put the last element together: the hooking, playing and landing of these magnificent fish.

A series of shallowing rock ledges step their way to Odlum Point, much like a giant underwater staircase. Each step acts like a bench which

holds and concentrates prey fish, and there the salmon feed. Small patches of bull kelp cling to Odlum Island and the small string of it is the vanguard, surviving the crash of ocean swells and providing shelter for schools of herring. These open waters can appear daunting to the fly fisher, but traditional 'cut-pluggers' fish these

Barry Thornton: To reach salmon in these waters it is vital that your fly line sink quickly to those magic depths of between 20 and 50 feet. These are the depths where salmon feed and often travel when they are near the surface. Eight-, nine-, or 10-weight outfits are necessary for the large salmon encountered in these waters. Flies should be weighted so they quickly reach the salmon depths. Colors should include the three principal salmon attractors: pink, silver and chartreuse.

same locations with six- and eight-ounce weights at between 12 and 25 'pulls', depths readily reached with type V or faster shooting tapers (preferably coupled to 100 feet of running wet line and 300 yards of backing spooled on large-arbor reels).

Anchored fly fishers may in fact have a slight advantage over conventional trollers when fishing along Odlum's rock ledges. Trollers must line up just so and hope their cut-plugs sweep over the shelves as they turn out and away; fly fishers can set anchors so their flies fish precisely over a given shelf, provided sea conditions are right. Ideal shelves are in water between 40 and 50 feet deep (depth sounders are definitely required), but strong

Karl Bruhn: The Hakai Land and Sea Society has been operating in the Pass for more than 25 years, and right from the earliest days members recorded their catches on the plywood walls of the cookhouse. Besides chronicling absolutely incredible catches – many individual entries show one-day catches of four or more fish, each weighing between 40 and 60 pounds – they also leave no doubt as to trip timing. Decidedly, the best fishing each year occurs between July 15 and August 15.

tidal currents and breaking waves require
anchors be set with long leads if they are
to hold. Casts are made upstream and
the fly line should be allowed to sink
as it swings under the boat. Retrieves
are started once the fly reaches maximum depth. Late strikes are common as salmon
will often follow a fly to the surface and take only at the last possible moment. Anchor
lines are released on a float and the boat is used to give chase
when large fish are hooked.

Tying off to bull kelp is also possible, either
right at Odlum (there is a largish patch
off the east side) or in any of the more
protected waters nearby. Flies are cast
out and retrieved back to
the kelp, but as sur-
rounding waters are rela-
tively deep, even weighted
patterns and fast-sinking
lines must be given maximum
sink time before retrieving.
Innumerable black sea bass
will be caught as the fly closes with the kelp.

Fly fishing for large chinook salmon is still in the
experimental, even pioneering, stage. Fish are caught
each season, but consistency remains elusive. So the
game is wide open and perhaps a pivotal round
will be played at Hakai Pass. With its striking
setting, diversity of waters and legendary
runs of chinook, it would be entirely
fitting if the first tyee to be caught
on a cast fly were taken in the
open waters surrounding
Odlum Point. ✜

Sockeye Systems

Sockeye salmon and rainbow trout in combination produce some of the finest fishing in British Columbia. The Babine, the Chilko, the Horsefly, the Stewart and the Adams all produce heavy, superbly conditioned trout, and sockeye salmon are a key reason why. Their spent carcasses

Matuka Sockeye Fry
Hook: Mustad 9671, Eagle Claw D1197N, #2–4
Body: Flat silv. tinsel
Rib: Fine brass wire
Tail & Wing: 2 large gold. badger saddle hackle tied matuka style & held in place w/brass wire
Throat: Small clump of hot orng. steelhead wool

fuel the food chain at its most elemental levels, while their eggs provide trout with a rich pre-winter harvest. In spring, emerging fry are the first serious protein boost of the year. The more famous of these wild trout fisheries all have other factors going for

them – the bonanza of golden stoneflies on the Babine, for instance – but sockeye provide the solid baseline from which all else flows.

Anglers who seek sockeye systems will be amazed at the trout they find. Prime wild trout, whether trophy sized or smaller, tend to leave an indelible impression. Finding these fish and learning the secrets of their seasonal movements means knowing the ways of sockeye salmon, so intricately are the lives of these trout entwined with that of the sockeye.

Sockeye require rivers with lakes in their headwaters, usually quite large lakes. Sockeye feed on plankton, and because the fry spend two years or more in fresh water, they require lakes large enough to produce vast quantities of this food source. Typically, the fry emerge from river gravel in early spring and quickly migrate to the nursery lake. Trout will congregate where such rivers meet the lake, providing one of the few times each year when the free-roaming trophy trout of large lakes are concentrated. Fantastic fishing results.

Returning sockeye usually reach their home streams in September, with spawning often completed by mid-October. In most instances the salmon travel through a lake and ascend various tributaries. Such streams can be difficult for anglers to reach, but in some cases, as with the Chilko River profiled below, sockeye spawn below the lake, with the fry ascending in the spring. Again, large, lake-resident trout will congregate, in this case in the various rivers to feed on eggs.

Both of the two sockeye systems profiled here have the advantage of offering relatively easy access, and while they differ widely in character, both yield exceptional trout to anglers familiar with sockeye salmon habits and associated fishing strategies.

pools exceed 20 feet. The glaciers surrounding the western end of Chilko Lake provide the river with a constant supply of cold water, while the suspended glacial solids tint the water in both lake and stream a lovely cerulean blue.

Egg Fly
Hook: Mustad shrt. shank 9479, #4
Body: Small clump of hot orng. steelhead wool sandwiched between clumps of salmon-pink steelhead wool, spun on dubbing loop & packed into ball, then trimmed to shape

> ***Ian Forbes:*** When trout start feeding on salmon eggs they will seldom take anything else. At such times, pattern color becomes important. Sockeye and coho eggs are brighter red than those of chinook or chum salmon, but all loose eggs turn peach pink when washed out for a while. Experiments have proven a #4, 5X short-shank hook with a down eye is the most effective. The flies are easy to tie: a dubbing loop spun with a piece of orange wool sandwiched between two pieces of peach-pink wool. A few egg flies should be tied weighted to be used with a floating line. Unweighted flies are fished off weighted leaders or fast-sinking lines.

Chilko River
The Chilko is a big, fast river pouring out of spectacularly beautiful Chilko Lake. Most of the river's depth is over four feet and some of its

Only the upper few miles of the Chilko River are of real interest to anglers. Below its junction with the Taseko River the Chilko turns milky with glacial silt. Upstream from there the river is a wild torrent, but the first three miles below the lake feature a smooth, even current and provide some of the best fly fishing for large trout found anywhere. Rainbow trout and Dolly Varden char up to 10 pounds are taken each year in this section.

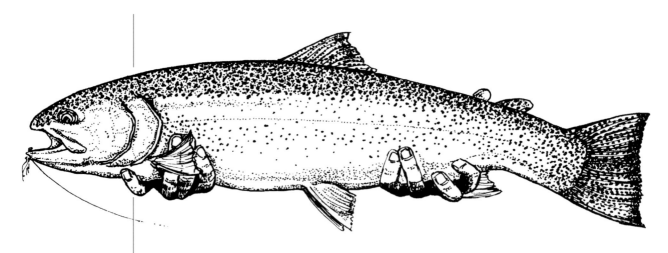

Sockeye spawn in September near the outlet of the lake. Trout hold behind the spawning salmon and dart in to take the eggs. Anglers fishing at this time use pink and orange egg pat-

terns, and while the action can be non-stop, flies must drift drag free. In water less than four feet deep a floating line with weighted fly is cast upstream so the fly has time to sink. Frequent line mends are required to keep the fly drifting naturally. In water between four and six feet deep, a sinktip line is fished in the same manner.

In fast water more than six feet deep, heavy sinking heads will be required.

Sockeye fry and smolts offer trout a year-round food supply; hence, minnow patterns will work at any time of year and at times are the only flies that will attract notice.

A canoe or rowboat is adequate to fish the first mile below the lake, but motors of 10 horsepower or better are required to properly fish the faster water below (see regulations). Boats are anchored in the current and casts are made to the side and downstream. Guides run their boats upstream, then drift down while clients cast flies quartering downstream.

Horsefly River

The Horsefly River is an anomaly; trout fishing can vary from spectacular to terrible depending on the area fished, the time of year and even the year itself. Maddeningly, success can also vary from day to day during the same trip. While the river opens June 1, high runoff lasts until about mid-June, which coincides with the first major insect hatches of the season.

Large Quesnel Lake rainbows enter the Horsefly with returning runs of sockeye in September. The salmon come to spawn, the trout to feed on eggs. Sockeye runs traditionally alternate between major and minor years. It follows that in years with abundant sockeye, more trout will take up temporary residence in the river.

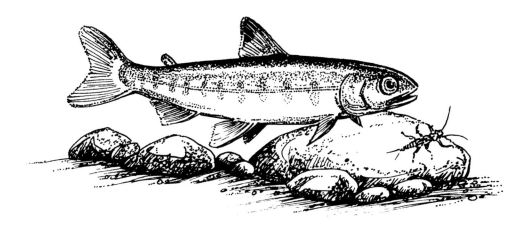

Rainbow trout ascend the river in spring on their own spawning run, and some of these fish will hold in the river all summer awaiting the sockeye. In minor sockeye years the trout migrate back to Quesnel Lake.

While there are always numerous small rainbows resident in the river, the 20-inch and better fish can be difficult to find and even harder to fool. Most often they ignore smaller flies and are lured from tight cover only by properly presented minnow/fry patterns. It is not unusual to find no fish in a series of beautiful pools, then locate all the trout in one run. The best fishing is often in fast-water runs with boulder-strewn pockets.

Quesnel Lake's unique strain of large, aggressive, late-maturing rainbow trout was under considerable pressure at the time of writing and new management policies were being developed. Angling pressure on the lake was surveyed at 25,000 angler days each year over a two-year period. Juvenile production had plummetted and the numbers of large fish showing up in the catch declined enough to raise serious concern. Managers were optimistic that Quesnel Lake stocks would rebound within three to four years following implementation of new regulations – possibly size slot limits and/or temporary closures.

Visiting the river when the fish are in can be deceiving as anglers are still likely to encounter good numbers of large Quesnel trout. This is a function of the sockeye run which concentrates trout, otherwise scattered far and wide in the big lake. The aggressive nature of the fish means mortality rates among released trout are higher than average; anglers are urged to play fish deftly and practise careful release techniques.

With the exception of a few rapids, the river is navigable by canoe or raft from Mckinley Creek to just below the village of Horsefly, downstream of which there is a series of small waterfalls. A gravel road follows the river for more than 30 miles, and while there are a number of places where a raft can be put in or taken out, foot trails are abundant and boats are not strictly necessary to fish the river. A small Forest Service campsite about 20 miles east of the village of Horsefly makes a good starting point. ✂

Ian Forbes: Rainbow trout lured from Chilko Lake to the river by sockeye often hold over to take advantage of the river's great insect hatches. Chilko River stoneflies are huge, requiring #4 long-shank hooks to imitate. Golden stones dominate, but there are also some huge black stones, several grey and brown species and the ever-present small green stonefly. Weighted nymph patterns are required in the river's fast current. Abundant caddis hatch on most summer evenings and deer or elk-hair patterns with brown, yellow or green bodies will cover most situations. Mayflies are plentiful, but the trout don't seem to key on them as much as the larger caddis or stoneflies.

Ian Forbes: The Horsefly has good insect hatches throughout the season; mayflies, caddis, and stoneflies are all abundant. Small stoneflies are the first to hatch, followed by the larger stones. Mayflies and caddis come next. Evening hatches of caddis can be great; a small deerhair pattern will work wonders.

Orange Heron
(Contributed by Syd Glasso)
Hook: TMC 7999, Partridge Wilson, Bartleet, Alec Jackson
Body: Rear 2/3 orng. floss, front 1/3 orng. seal fur
Rib: Flat silv. tinsel
Body Hackle: Blu. heron or blu. eared pheas.
Throat Hackle: Nat. teal or pintail flank feather
Wing: 4 matching fluor. orng. hackle tips tied low
Thread: Red

Dean River Steelhead

D ischarging into the head of remote Dean Channel north of Bella Coola, the Dean River attracts fly fishers from around the globe who come to test their skills against the river's fabled run of summer steelhead. A fly fisher's dream, typical Dean River summer-run steelhead weigh about nine pounds with a length of 29 inches. Ocean-going smolts will have spent three years in fresh water and return to the river after two winters at

sea. About 10 per cent of the run consists of fish which spend three winters at sea and grow to lengths of 35-plus inches and weights of between 15 and 20-plus pounds.

River water temperature during the mid-July to mid-September season ranges from 50 to 60 degrees. Fish will rise to the surface to take flies throughout that temperature range, provided the water is clear. The Dean is glacial fed and that fact, above all, influences fly fishing technique.

The Dean's location at the head of a long inlet means summer temperatures regularly soar into the 80s and 90s. The warmer it is, the more glacial melt descends and the less clear the water becomes. With visibility often reduced to between three and four feet, sunk-line techniques employing looped-on sinktips (or manufactured lines with high-density tips) are required. Fly size also must be varied to suit water and light conditions.

Visibility of about two feet calls for flies such as a four-inch-long 5/0 *General Practitioner*. Fortunately, water clarity is usually more than

two feet, so smaller sizes may be used, but old hands will rarely use a *General Practitioner* dressed on a hook smaller than a #2. When the river is clear and visibility increases to four feet or more, a surface presentation and floating line become the method of choice.

For the waked fly technique, a #4, #6 or #8 *Bomber*-type pattern works well, as does a *McVey Ugly*, but any wake-producing fly will suffice. Both the *Bomber* and *McVey Ugly* flies can also be used for the natural-drift dry fly technique. Some fly fishers like to cast more upstream and allow a portion of the drift to fish dry, then put the fly into tension and wake it for the remainder of the cast. Throwing a half hitch around the head of the fly will ensure the waking action.

For the floating-line technique, fly size must be matched to both water clarity and light conditions. A #2 black *General Practitioner* has proven successful fished with a floating line during poorer light and water clarity. In such marginal conditions, some prefer to use the sunk line, which is the staple technique on most steelhead rivers. As the water clears and the light becomes more direct, sparsely dressed patterns such as a *Black Spey* or *As Specified* in #6 through #4 are suitable. Other sparsely dressed, dark-bodied winged patterns will also work.

When fishing deep runs, a *Woolly Worm*, *Black GP* or *Cowichan Special*, swept deeply using the nymphing technique, often produces results.

Although the Dean River has a June to end-of-September season, most anglers plan their trips for the period between mid-July and mid-September. Angling effort is concentrated on the lower part of the river during the early part of the season, as the fish are fresh from the ocean. As the season advances and the steelhead populate the river, fishing waters expand to include the full 32-mile section from the mouth at Dean Channel to Craig Creek, the upper boundary.

There are no roads to the Dean; access to tidewater is either by personal boat or by aircraft to the landing strip. There is a road from the airstrip above the canyon to the five-mile landing, which the guides use to ferry their clients to upstream lodges. For a fee, someone from one of the camps near the airstrip will usually taxi camping anglers as far as the five-mile landing. Others arrange to be taken by helicopter to the area they plan to fish, flying either direct from Bella Coola or upriver from the tidewater airstrip. Travel arrangements should not be left to chance. ➤

Dean River Lantern
Hook: TMC 7999, Partridge Wilson, Bartleet, Alec Jackson
Tail: Blk. squirrel tail
Body: Fluor. orng. Edge Bright over silv. tinsel
Hackle: Nat. blk. hen saddle hackle

Aquatic Plants

Cattail

Being attuned to the aquatic environment is the first and most important step on the road to becoming a competent fly fisher. Recognizing this truth, growing numbers of anglers pursue entomological detail with scientific zeal. Fish biology too has come under microscopic study, with any number of anglers able to speak knowingly of such obscurities as orbital and sub-orbital lines. Aquatic vegetation, on the other hand, still languishes as mere 'lake weed' for a majority of anglers. Yet understanding the relationship between fish, fly fishing and aquatic plant life provides a unique window on the aquatic environment. Knowing the role played by aquatic plants allows anglers to hazard informed guesses, thus increasing success ratios.

Aquatic plants can be divided into two general categories: submergents and emergents. The emergents are those plants with some structure emerging above the surface of a lake. Key emergent plants for angling purposes are cattails and bulrushes which surround lakes, and lily pads which float on the surface. Submergent plants are those whose whole structure remains below the surface. Submergents of interest include vascular plants such as milfoil, pondweed and coontail. They also include Chara, which is actually a true algae and thus not a vascular plant.

Chara

The prime function of aquatic plants in relation to fly fishing is they harbor aquatic insects. Aquatic insects use these plants for several purposes including shelter, as a food source and even as a source of building material for their homes. Since aquatic insects spend much of their time in weedy areas, these are the sites where fish will congregate.

Of all the plants important to anglers, Chara ranks near the top. Chara looks superficially much like a vascular plant. It is typically found in the shoal areas of productive lakes, covering the bottom like a luxuriant lawn. All species of aquatic invertebrates can be found in Chara beds, so a good rule of thumb when fishing a lake is to scout out the Chara regions – the fish are sure to be nearby. Since it requires sunlight to survive, Chara will be present only to the depths where light can penetrate.

Sedge

Aside from revealing potentially productive fishing areas, Chara also gives anglers a clue to the water chemistry of a lake. A plant of highly productive alkaline waters, Chara is found only in lakes with a high pH and suitable nutrients. Many lakes in the Cariboo-Chilcotin do not have the chemical make-up necessary for Chara growth. The characteristic brown water of the dystrophic

dragonflies, but most aquatic invertebrates use these rich beds. Mapping out a lake's Chara beds and storing the information for future use is good practice since, overall, these areas will have the best fishing.

Numerous submergent vascular plants are common to Cariboo-Chilcotin lakes, and anglers will be familiar with at least some of them. Introduced Eurasian milfoil (Myriophyllum) is commonly identified. Through sheer size and volume it has negatively impacted trout populations by choking out spawning gravel, but it is an indicator of productive waters – those lakes with higher pH, alkalinity and hardness. Unfortunately, it has the ability to remove nutrients through its root system, including those deposited over the centuries. A North American species of milfoil which is beneficial to fish also occurs in B.C. lakes. This plant provides habitat for aquatic insects, concealment areas for young trout and prime feeding areas for larger trout.

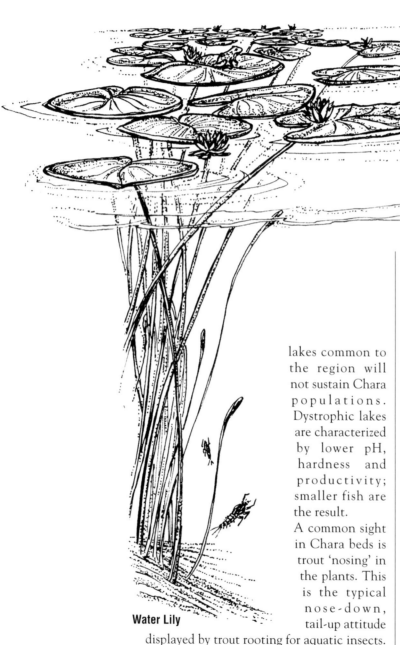

lakes common to the region will not sustain Chara populations. Dystrophic lakes are characterized by lower pH, hardness and productivity; smaller fish are the result.

A common sight in Chara beds is trout 'nosing' in the plants. This is the typical nose-down, tail-up attitude displayed by trout rooting for aquatic insects. Major insect species associated with Chara beds include mayflies, shrimp, damselflies and

Water Lily

The common coontail (Ceratophyllum) is similar to milfoil. The two known species which occur in British Columbia waters are common to Cariboo-Chilcotin lakes, but they are more prevalent in lakes with higher alkalinity, pH and hardness. Growing profusely in waters high in organics and dissolved nutrients, their presence can be taken as a tip-off that a lake is productive with a good likelihood of larger fish.

The common pondweed (Potamogeton), with some 20 different species in B.C., is an important aquatic plant because it can be found in a wide assortment of lakes. It supports numerous aquatic insects and supplies shelter and feeding habitat for trout. As with coontail and milfoil, it is found in greater profusion in productive, alkaline waters. Generally, the larger a lake's pondweed production, the better the odds that larger fish will be present.

Observing and comparing the extent of submergent aquatic plant growth to the quality of the fishing encountered will show a direct correlation between trout numbers and size, and the extent of submergent plant growth. Taken together, these factors allow anglers to hazard shrewd guesses about the water chemistry of a given lake and thus the quality of angling likely to be encountered.

Emergents are the lake margin and floating plants common to most Cariboo-Chilcotin lakes. Fly fishers will be familiar with the bulrushes and cattails which surround many lakes, but only more experienced anglers will know them as prime trout-feeding sites. Bulrushes are found in slightly deeper water than cattails and, while both thrive in more chemically productive waters, they can exist in nutrient-poor lakes as well.

During certain times of year, these plants become extremely important to both trout and several key aquatic insects. Dragonflies and damselflies require vertical structures to hatch from the nymphal to the adult stage. When hatching times draw near, these insects migrate from their normal underwater habitat to the weedy lake margins. There they climb the cattails and bulrushes, upon which they transform from nymph to adult.

Trout follow this migration into the reeds – often into mere inches of water. The fishing then becomes nothing short of spectacular. At times the trout will actually try to dislodge the clinging nymphs or newly hatched adults from the reeds; at other times they chase swimming nymphs through the reeds. Fishing a dry line and a dragon or damsel pattern in amongst the reeds can be deadly. The fun begins when trying to move a hooked trout out of the maze. The end result often leaves the water littered with uprooted reeds and cattails.

Water lilies tend to be synonymous with lower pH and less productive waters, although they can be found in productive lakes as well. They prefer very organic substrates with lower dissolved oxygen levels, conditions often found in the less productive brown-water lakes. Aquatic insects abound in water lily patches, so this is where the trout will be concentrated. One observation showed that when water lily pads die and sink to the bottom, freshwater shrimp are attracted to the decomposing vegetation. This is not lost on the trout, and anglers prepared to take advantage will have some pretty exciting fishing.

When fishing in water lily growths, it is important to cast directly amongst the pads. Many more trout feed deep in the cover than along the outside edges. ➤

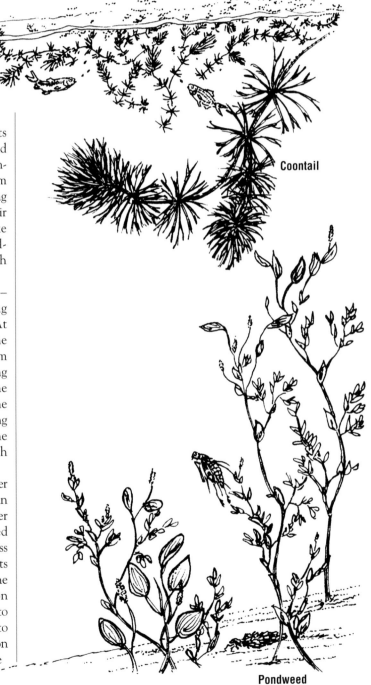

Coontail

Pondweed

Blackwater &
Tzenzaicut Trout

Marabou Dace
Hook: Mustad 9671, #4–8
Body: None or silv. tinsel
Wing: Dark olv. marabou
over pale yel. marabou
over red marabou over
wht. marabou
Eyes: Plastic stick-on eyes
glued in place w/epoxy or
Soft Body

Long the bane of some of British Columbia's most hallowed waters, the much vilified redside shiner now plays a key role in an exciting new rainbow trout fishery. Prolific in nature, shiners have successfully mated with dace, peamouth chub and even squawfish. Moving and feeding in vast schools, they displace juvenile trout from prime habitat and reduce the number of trout which can be produced. In the past, many lakes were poisoned and subsequently stocked with trout, a practice which proved expensive, unpopular and not particularly successful. More recently, highly piscivorous native rainbow trout strains have been stocked instead. These aggressive trout not only propagate amid shiner populations, they also provide a new and uniquely different challenge for anglers.

Three native strains are being stocked in lakes with shiner populations: the already well-known Gerrards and the less well-known Blackwater and Tzenzaicut strains. All three are piscivorous, but it is the highly aggressive Blackwater strain which has captured the imagination of anglers, at least in part because Blackwaters differ so markedly from the finicky Kamloops insectivores.

Originating in the wild waters of Tweedsmuir Park's Blackwater (West Road) River, the strain evolved with a host of in-water predators, including lampreys, dace, squawfish, whitefish, chub and shiners. Not only did they survive this school of hard knocks, they thrived. Provincial fisheries literature describes them as follows:

"The Blackwater rainbow trout have a heavier spotting pattern than the Pennask or Tzenzaicut rainbow trout. The spotting pattern tends to occur from head to tail with a heavier concentration above the lateral line. The Blackwater rainbows prefer larger prey items such as dragonfly nymphs, snails, mollusks and small fish. These fish begin feeding on small coarse fish as early as age one and are highly piscivorous at maturity. These fish can be quite active during daylight hours and prefer to forage in the shoal habitat of lakes. The high growth rates seen in the Blackwater rainbows indicate that these fish are far more active feeders than a slower growing strain. Their aggressive shallow water foraging behavior enables anglers to target these fish easily. Considering the above, the Blackwater rainbows have the potential to become one of the most sought-after strains by 'knowledgeable' anglers."

Exceptionally shoal oriented, the Blackwaters' aggressive disposition makes them ultra-competitive, especially in waters containing other fish species such as shiners. Much the same can be said of the equally piscivorous Tzenzaicut strain, although these fish, originating in Tzenzaicut Lake (25 miles southwest of Quesnel) where they co-exist with longnose suckers and redside shiners, prefer open waters to near-shore shallows. Officially, they are described as follows:

"The Tzenzaicut rainbow trout have a characteristic spotting pattern where the spots are large, concentrated towards the posterior end of the fish, above the lateral line, and on the caudal fin. The body spots are generally larger and more

sparse than those on a Pennask or Blackwater rainbow trout. The wild Tzenzaicut rainbow trout prefer to forage in open water habitats where there is less competition from the large populations of suckers found in the benthic environments of Tzenzaicut Lake. Although the Tzenzaicut rainbows have similar foraging habits to the Pennask rainbow trout, they tend to be far more piscivorous. The Tzenzaicut rainbows can be caught using a wide variety of prey imitation lures (chironomids to minnow patterns). Anglers will come to recognize these fish for their exceptional leaping abilities when hooked. These fish fight very hard and recover very well upon angler release."

Catching either of these exciting strains presupposes at least some knowledge of their prey. Conditions permitting,

Redside Shiner
Hook: Mustad 9671, #4–8
Body: Silv. myl. tinsel
Wing: Dark olv. polar bear hair over pale yel. hair over red hair over wht. hair
Eyes: Plastic stick-on eyes glued in place w/epoxy or Soft Body

redside shiners prefer to forage in water from two to 12 feet deep and, depending on water temperature, migrate from deep to shallow water throughout the year. In lakes the smaller shiners will be higher in the water column and closest to shore, a point to bear in mind when choosing fly patterns.

Like many schooling fish, shiners find security and food in and around structure such as weedbeds, rocky outcroppings and fallen timber. During the heat of summer they ball up in large schools, a trait more common in deep than in shallow lakes. Juvenile shiners feed primarily on copepods, diatoms and other zooplankton; as they mature their diet turns to insects and small fish, including immature trout. Left unchecked, their incredible feeding efficiency will harm both trout and insect populations.

At maturity shiners range from three to five inches in length with a broad body profile and prominent silver to gold sides (*Zonker*-style patterns do a good job duplicating this profile). Their backs range from a dark peacock olive to brown, depending on location. Shiners have prominent yellow eyes with black pupils; forage fish imitations should incorporate this important trigger. Both male and female shiners display vivid colors during spawning. The male's red- to orange-colored lateral stripe intensifies during courtship.

Structure, such as sunken debris, deadfall and weedbeds, acts as a magnet for schooling shiners. Steep shorelines with fallen trees along their banks are great locations. Seeing a Blackwater or Tzenzaicut trout vault out of the depths to chase shiners amongst fallen limbs is a thrilling experience. Anglers must be prepared to probe such structure, even at the risk of losing the odd fly. As with any structure, try to fish parallel to the edge so the fly has maximum exposure.

In shallow lakes, work the shoal edges and well into the tules. Piscivorous trout will chase and herd shiners against the weeds in shark-like fashion. Since the trout never linger long in shallow water, casting becomes frenetic the moment explosive shoreside rises are seen. Listen, too, for commotion in shoreline weeds – it may well be ducks or coots making a fuss, but in lakes stocked with Blackwaters it is just as likely to be an aggressive trout.

When shiners are being taken at the surface, an intermediate or dry line works best. Density-compensated sinking lines, such as the Uniform Sink or the new SLS (Straight Line Sink), offer superior bite detection when fishing deep. To improve hook-up ratios when fishing down, strike the fish with a combination pull of the stripping hand and a sharp, lateral motion of the rod. Also, weighted flies should be considered when probing deeper water. Too often fly fishers work the upper columns of stillwater lakes and ignore the lower columns that hold concentrations of fish at certain times each day.

The list of lakes stocked with Blackwater and Tzenzaicut rainbows grows each year. Updated stocking reports are available through regional Fisheries Branch offices, but following is a list of lakes, by region, stocked with 10,000 or more of these native strains (releases consisted of adults and yearlings, as well as fry):

Cariboo-Chilcotin – 108 Mile, Blue, Chimney, Cuisson, Dewar, Dragon, Earle, Felker, Fir, Greeny, Gustafsen, Howard, Lorin, Marmot, McLeese, Nazko, Owen, Paddy, Palmer, Rail, Sheridan and Yimpakluk lakes. Dragon, Jim, Ruth and Watch lakes each received 10,000-plus Tzenzaicut trout.

Thompson-Okanagan – Birch, Crystal, Elbow, Hammer, Lac des Roches, Niskonlith, Paul, Allison, Jewel and Pinaus lakes, as well as 10,000-plus Tzenzaicuts for Garcia Lake.

The North – Tyhee, Cluculz, Eulatazella, Heather, Morfee, Nadsilnich, Naltesby, Norman, Purden and Tachick lakes, as well as Hart Lake, which received 10,000-plus Tzenzaicuts.

The Rockies – Columbia and Edwards lakes.

Vancouver Island – Elk and Quennel lakes. ➤

Selected Waters
Super Damselflies

A super damselfly hatch will see literally hundreds of mature nymphs swimming mere inches below the surface of a lake as they head towards large bulrush patches to emerge. Big rainbows regularly interrupt this peaceful scene, shouldering through the bulrushes and rolling on their sides to knock plants over and dislodge nymphs, partially emerged adults and the adults themselves. The fish then slash through the hapless insects in a feeding frenzy. Trembling-handed anglers will want floating fly lines and floating nymph or adult patterns to ply amidst the mayhem.

Super damselfly lakes are those with their shores surrounded by long-stem bulrushes or cattails. Often these emergent plants extend well out into the shoal zone, providing even more habitat. Mature damselfly nymphs crawl up onto the vegetation to complete emergence into adult form. Anglers will know a damselfly hatch is in progress by the number of nymphs they see swimming close to the surface of the lake and heading towards shore.

There are numerous damselfly species in the lakes of the Cariboo-Chilcotin. All juvenile damselfly nymphs spend their time amongst the lush vegetation covering the bottom of the shoal and drop-off zones. Ideal juvenile habitat consists of lush beds of Chara weed, sago pondweed or coontail. All three provide good hiding areas, as well as excellent habitat for shrimp and mayfly nymphs, which the damselfly nymphs eat.

Damselfly nymphs take on the coloration of the water and habitat they live in. Examining a small mat of bottom vegetation will reveal nymphal color and size range. Trout will often feed on the very small juvenile nymphs – it is not uncommon to see nymphs just over three-eighths of an inch in length crammed into the gut of a big rainbow. Late fall seems to be a preferred time for the trout to feed on juvenile nymphs. Small nymphs should be fished as close to the cattail or bulrush patches as possible. Better still, cast offerings right into openings in the reeds and retrieve back out. Fairly stout tippet material should be used in order to wrestle fish through the reeds.

Super damselfly lakes also provide trout with the opportunity to feed on the adult stage of the insect. After major hatches, adults will congregate in large numbers and hover just above the surface of the water. A strong gust of wind will push adults into the surface film, thus providing cruising trout with an easy meal.

Some excellent damselfly lakes include Dragon, Forest, Nimpo and numerous waters in the Interlakes area of the southern Cariboo. ✒

Selected Waters

Hexagenia Mayflies

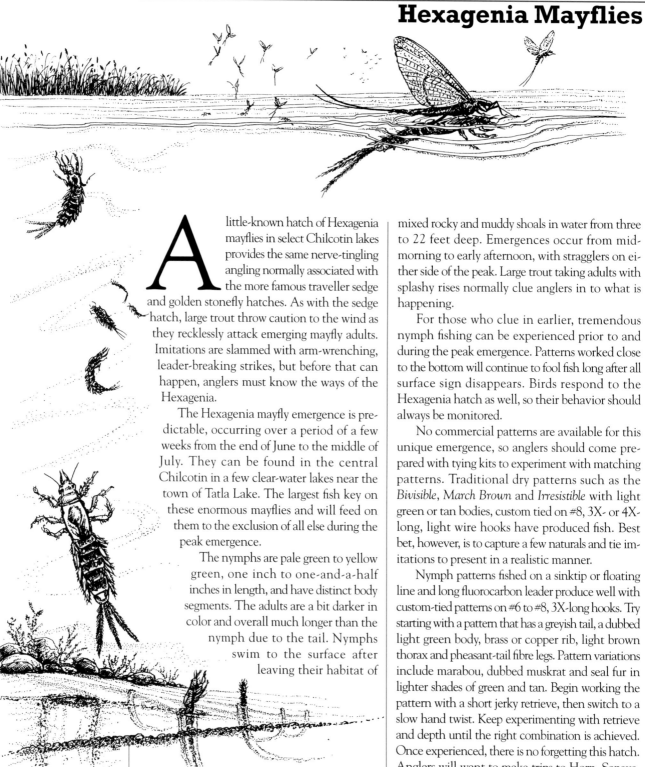

A little-known hatch of Hexagenia mayflies in select Chilcotin lakes provides the same nerve-tingling angling normally associated with the more famous traveller sedge and golden stonefly hatches. As with the sedge hatch, large trout throw caution to the wind as they recklessly attack emerging mayfly adults. Imitations are slammed with arm-wrenching, leader-breaking strikes, but before that can happen, anglers must know the ways of the Hexagenia.

The Hexagenia mayfly emergence is predictable, occurring over a period of a few weeks from the end of June to the middle of July. They can be found in the central Chilcotin in a few clear-water lakes near the town of Tatla Lake. The largest fish key on these enormous mayflies and will feed on them to the exclusion of all else during the peak emergence.

The nymphs are pale green to yellow green, one inch to one-and-a-half inches in length, and have distinct body segments. The adults are a bit darker in color and overall much longer than the nymph due to the tail. Nymphs swim to the surface after leaving their habitat of mixed rocky and muddy shoals in water from three to 22 feet deep. Emergences occur from mid-morning to early afternoon, with stragglers on either side of the peak. Large trout taking adults with splashy rises normally clue anglers in to what is happening.

For those who clue in earlier, tremendous nymph fishing can be experienced prior to and during the peak emergence. Patterns worked close to the bottom will continue to fool fish long after all surface sign disappears. Birds respond to the Hexagenia hatch as well, so their behavior should always be monitored.

No commercial patterns are available for this unique emergence, so anglers should come prepared with tying kits to experiment with matching patterns. Traditional dry patterns such as the *Bivisible*, *March Brown* and *Irresistible* with light green or tan bodies, custom tied on #8, 3X- or 4X-long, light wire hooks have produced fish. Best bet, however, is to capture a few naturals and tie imitations to present in a realistic manner.

Nymph patterns fished on a sinktip or floating line and long fluorocarbon leader produce well with custom-tied patterns on #6 to #8, 3X-long hooks. Try starting with a pattern that has a greyish tail, a dubbed light green body, brass or copper rib, light brown thorax and pheasant-tail fibre legs. Pattern variations include marabou, dubbed muskrat and seal fur in lighter shades of green and tan. Begin working the pattern with a short jerky retrieve, then switch to a slow hand twist. Keep experimenting with retrieve and depth until the right combination is achieved. Once experienced, there is no forgetting this hatch. Anglers will want to make trips to Horn, Sapeye, Bluff and Cochin lakes an annual event. ⌖

Selected Waters

Dragonflies

Dragonfly nymphs are high on the list of preferred trout food items and suitable imitations have long been recognized as key searching patterns. Available to fish throughout the open-water season, the nymphs are most vulnerable during their spring and fall migrations, and again during the mid-summer emergence.

> **Ron Newman:** Although normally nocturnal, dragons will sometimes migrate en masse during the daylight hours of a spring migration. After a hard winter the fish go crazy when this happens and it is a dream come true for the fly fisher who has deciphered what is happening. Use large to moderate-sized imitations on the shoals. Fall migrations are generally more drawn out and call for much smaller imitations, retrieved from shallow to deeper water.

Beginning within a few days of ice-off, many of the larger second-year nymphs migrate from their deep hibernating waters to the shallows where they will feed and grow. In late fall, smaller yearlings and newly hatched nymphs migrate back to deeper water in preparation for hibernation. Fly size should be varied accordingly (larger in spring, smaller in fall) and fishing effort should be concentrated during evenings and after dark.

During daylight hours dragonfly nymphs remain inactive. Imitations are best fished on or near the bottom, preferably over a drop-off in water between 15 and 25 feet deep. Slow retrieves or even a sta-tionary fly will work, but an occasional fast pull will attract cruising fish.

As darkness approaches, dragonfly nymphs come out of hiding in search of food, and this is when the trout will actively seek them out. Imitations can then be fished on the shoals and higher in the water column. Using a dry line, allow the fly to sink for at least 10 seconds before retrieving. In the poor light conditions of evening, the pause gives trout time to locate the fly. Dusk is always a good time to try dragonfly imitations; retrieves can be quite fast during this more active time in the nymphs' daily cycle.

Emergence from nymph to adult peaks about mid-July and takes place amidst shoreline vegetation. The nymphs congregate in deeper water during the day in preparation for their trek to shore and their late-night emergence to adulthood. For these hatches, use very large imitations. The best direction to retrieve is towards the shoreline.

Dragonflies prefer water that is free of pollution, has a good supply of oxygen and is somewhat alkaline. Cover must be sufficient to allow the nymphs to escape predation and to launch their own ambush attacks on unsuspecting prey. The water should be deep enough to not freeze entirely during the winter months. Good dragonfly populations will be found in waters balancing these attributes. Lakes to try include Big Bar, Helena, Hen Ingram, Elk, Fir, Owen and Palmer. 🐟

Floating Dragon

Hook: Mustad 9671, #6–8
Tail: 1/2 lngth. of hook; dyed brn., soft marabou-style body feathers
Under-Body: Warmed & flattened Friendly Plastic molded onto length of hook & tapered at each end
Over-Body: Closed-cell foam cut in thin strips & wrapped around hook, then colored w/Pantone pen
Hackle: Dyed grouse or partridge body feather
Wing Pad: Trimmed piece of closed-cell foam

Big Darner Dragonfly Nymph

Hook: Mustad 9671, #4–6
Tail: Marabou dyed red. brn.
Body: Spun, packed & trimmed deerhair dyed brn.
Rib: Sparse dubbing loop of red. brn. seal fur
Wing Pad: Glued & trimmed grouse feather
Legs: Speckled guinea fowl dyed olv.
Head: Spun, packed & trimmed deerhair dyed brn.

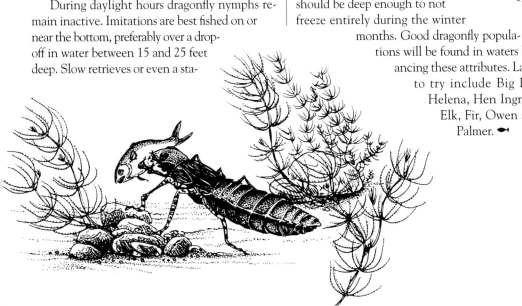

Waterboatmen

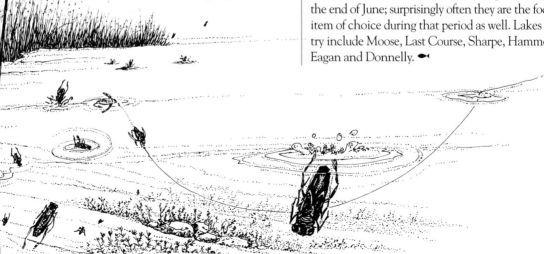

Waterboatman
(Contributed by Harold Lohr)
Hook: Mustad 9671, #14–16
Body: Syn. dubbing mixture of brn. wool w/bits of olv. Flashabou dubbing mixed in (Dragonfly sparkle dubbing)
Legs: Shrt. section split from Super Floss & tied in near hook's centre
Over-Wing: Brnz. turkey tail or irridescent grn. feather strip

Unlike other members of the order Hemiptera (the water bugs), waterboatmen do not bite or sting, and hence rate quite high on the menus of Cariboo-Chilcotin trout, notably during their spring and fall mating flights. Successfully fishing boatman patterns is quite tricky and quickly becomes an exercise in frustration for those not familiar with the boatman life cycle and habits.

Some species (there are more than 100) have one generation per year while others have two, which explains why anglers often see both spring and fall post-mating swarming flights. Those which mate in the spring average about half the size of fall-swarming boatmen, a point to bear in mind when selecting patterns. On emergence, newly hatched boatmen must swim to the surface to capture a bubble of air. Carried by specially adapted legs, the air bubble acts somewhat like a modified gill, making boatmen less reliant on atmospheric oxygen. Still, they make periodic trips to the surface to replenish their air supply.

Trout key on the silvery sheen of the air bubble, but for some reason seem to prefer boatmen when they are diving, as opposed to rising to the surface. Prime fishing times are during the spring and fall flights, but trout will take boatmen at any time, leaving anglers with two interesting challenges: learning when boatmen are present and figuring out how to fish appropriate patterns to mimic the top-to-bottom swim.

Boatmen are not easy to spot, but careful observation will provide clues. Watch for dimples on the surface that appear to be air bubbles rising. Often these are boatmen retrieving air bubbles. They will dive in alarm when a boat or float tube comes too close and will thus tip anglers to their presence. Boatmen have been found in feeding samples during every month of the open-water season, so there is reason to persevere.

To mimic the downward swim preferred by trout, anglers use buoyant patterns fished on sinking lines. The fly remains on the surface while the line is allowed to sink. The moment the weight of the line pulls the fly under, the 'boatman paddle' is imitated by a series of very short pulls. Combined with some variations and rest stops, the technique is repeated through the dive, across the bottom and back to the surface. This U-shaped retrieve imitates the full variety of boatman movements. Take note at what point during the retrieve a fish strikes, then adjust the technique accordingly.

Trout consume more boatmen from September through October than during all other months of the fly fishing season combined, so that is the time to concentrate effort. For all that, it would be a mistake to ignore the smaller boatmen which are most available to the fish from mid-April through the end of June; surprisingly often they are the food item of choice during that period as well. Lakes to try include Moose, Last Course, Sharpe, Hammer, Eagan and Donnelly. ⌐◄

Selected Waters
Sight Casting in High pH

Crystalline blue water and bleached shoal formations are the hallmarks of classic alkaline lakes. Possessing a higher-than-normal calcium carbonate content, their chemical evolution was a function of local geology. Typically formed without significant inlets

or outlets, most of these lakes were devoid of trout for generations. Stocking hatchery-raised trout into alkaline or high-pH lakes initially results in high mortality, but the fish which acclimate normally do exceptionally well.

Ongoing Fisheries Branch research examining wild trout stocks better suited to these environments is of major import to anglers. Hardwater lakes are significantly more fertile than soft-water lakes and produce large, superbly conditioned trout. The super-clear water makes it possible to watch such fish as they browse the chalky shoals, foraging for shrimp, caddis larvae, dragonflies, leeches, or chironomids. As the trout 'fossick' for bottom fauna, or rise for surface invertebrates, a rare opportunity to sight cast to stillwater trout results.

This adds the drama of hunting to the sport of fishing and the size and condition of the quarry ups the intensity yet another notch. Anglers must search for individual or schooling fish in shallow water, then manoeuvre to within effective casting position. For lake fly fishers these conditions provide the ultimate challenge in presentation. The quarry must be stalked and the cast must be delivered just so as the angler watches the fish either respond or deliberately swim away.

Gin-clear, high-pH lakes make it easier, but foraging trout can be difficult to spot. There will be times when the fish are discernible, usually as dark silhouettes, but more often anglers must look for indirect signs of feeding and moving fish. These take the form of subtle surface disturbances, or an upheaval of bottom material marking the passing of a 'fossicking' trout. Polarized glasses are essential equipment; success can hinge on being able to spot approaching trout in time to determine the direction of travel before laying a trap in their path.

Flies rising up from bottom anywhere near feeding trout normally bring results. As the fish approaches the area, a short strip of the line will pop the fly from the mud. If the fish sees the fly move or sees the small disturbance the fly makes in the mud, attack-mode behavior normally kicks in. It is important to watch the initial response closely. Fish that miss on the first pass often turn to strike repeatedly, provided the fly remains within their field of vision. Takes can be very subtle; flies are regularly inhaled and rejected before the angler realizes what happened. Waiting until resistance is felt is to have waited too long. Paired or multiple trout feeding together almost always result in a display of competitive behavior. A properly presented fly will normally result in a vicious strike and a sizzling run for deeper water.

Werner Shrimp
Hook: Mustad 9671, #6–12
Body: Syn. seal fur, olv. or orng.
Hackle: Sparse brn. tied palmer style
Back: Nat. deerhair pulled over top of body
Head: Deerhair stubs cut from back

Feather Wing Caddis
Hook: Mustad 9671, #8–10
Body: Olv. dubbing
Wing: Grouse body feather smoothed w/glue
Hackle: Multi-var, trimmed on bottom
Head: Spun deerhair

Selected Waters

Kokanee

Micro Caddis

Hook: Mustad 9671, 94840, #16–20
Body: Sparsely tied drk. olv. or brn. dubbing
Wing: Zing Wing (myl. string material)
Hackle: 3 wraps of furnace or gold badger

Fly fishers have long despaired over the Cariboo's kokanee, with many considering them impossible to take with a fly. They are, admittedly, a difficult fish for the fly, but far from impossible. Inventive anglers have found ways to lure these silvery fish, some exceeding two pounds in weight, with traditional flies.

Pelagic feeders, kokanee cruise in schools feeding on plankton found in mid-lake zones. Phytoplankton blooms in the late spring create great feeding for the kokanee as their favorite zooplankton (Cladocera and Copepoda) become

remain on the outside edges of the school. Spooking them is decisive, as the entire school will disappear, sounding to the depths. Long casts just to the edge of the school will allow anglers to catch numbers of fish without disturbing the rest of the group. Effective patterns include #12 to #16 *Adams*, *Griffith's Gnat* in #16 to #18 or *Micro Caddis* in #12 to #16. *Rolled Muddlers* in #10 to #14, *Gold Ribbed Hare's Ear* in #12 to #18 and *Pheasant Tail* nymphs in #14 to #18 have also proven effective.

Kokanee often gather where inlet streams enter a lake. They will hang just on the edge of the drop-off looking for small morsels. In this

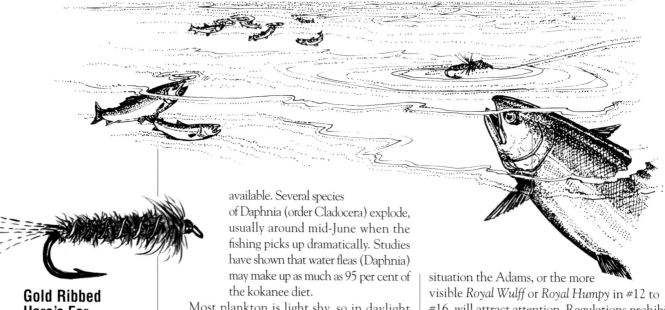

Gold Ribbed Hare's Ear

Hook: Mustad 9671, #12–16
Tail: Gry. speckled partridge
Body: Brn. and gry. hair from near ear of wild hare, tied sparse at rear of hook & tapered fatter towards head; leave in guard hairs
Rib: Oval gold tinsel

available. Several species of Daphnia (order Cladocera) explode, usually around mid-June when the fishing picks up dramatically. Studies have shown that water fleas (Daphnia) may make up as much as 95 per cent of the kokanee diet.

Most plankton is light shy, so in daylight hours the kokanee and their food are often too deep for the fly rod. The only time kokanee are reasonably available is when the plankton is close to the surface, so the best fishing occurs at night, on cloudy days or very early in the morning and late evening.

Why kokanee should take a fly remains a mystery, but they do, and at times quite readily. Fly rods should be rigged and ready when searching for schools of wandering kokanee. Once spotted, it is important to approach with maximum stealth (electric motors are ideal) and

situation the Adams, or the more visible *Royal Wulff* or *Royal Humpy* in #12 to #16, will attract attention. Regulations prohibit taking kokanee in streams throughout British Columbia.

In their fourth year, kokanee lay their eggs in gravel beds along the lakeshore, or ascend a stream, spawn and die. The availability of food and nutrients determines how big the kokanee will grow. Nutrient-poor lakes may have kokanee reaching only eight inches in length. Cariboo-Chilcotin lakes that produce kokanee to two pounds and better include Puntzi, Lac la Hache and McLeese. In the Omineca, try Cluculz, Bobtail and Cunningham lakes.

Cariboo/Chilcotin Journal

The rain continued pounding on the roof of my ancient travel trailer. It had been unrelenting in these first three days of my week-long holiday. I had read the novel I brought along and had cast aside old, weary fly patterns from my boxes, replacing them with new ones I hoped would be more productive. As I stared out across the grey mist to where my boat was pulled up on the beach, slowly filling with water again, my thoughts returned to the winter months and the hours spent watching fishing videos depicting anglers in shorts under bright blue skies, catching and releasing fish after fish. Rarely had I experienced that type of fishing, as evidenced by entries in my diary over many seasons. I picked it up and began to browse to see what forgotten wisdom I had chronicled on those coffee-stained pages.

One thing about being an experienced fly flinger is that even after graduating from Humility 1A, there are still lessons in frustration to learn. At least my graduate degree has provided a number of quirky responses to use whenever fate deals me a blank hand. At these times I would return to the beach well after dark, ego wilted, and hoping everyone else would be inside and too weary to ask how my day might have gone. When cornered, I would un-hesitatingly respond with a litany of prepared excuses: a cold front put all the fish down; I accidentally spilled gas on my hands and the scent repelled the fish; I had the wrong color (or size) of fly; the wind was from the north (or east); the water was too cold (or warm or calm or rough). There are many more, but these, when properly used, are among my most effective. Feel free to try them.

I never see anglers on videos getting skunked, yet it happens to me quite often. My diary is full of similar excuses, based on my expert evaluations and observations of what went wrong. Here are some examples.

July 30: Mons Lake. Upon launching the boat I noticed a large number of immature back-swimmers along the weed line in less than three feet of water. I recall thinking how unusual it was to see them in such large numbers at that time of year. The lake's contingent of ex-perienced anglers were trolling high-density lines in 30 feet of water and catching more than the odd fish on leech patterns.

I anchored in 25 feet of water and tried leeches, sedge pupae, chironomids, even dry sedges (I had seen a few rises even though I had seen no insects). Nothing. The hours passed. I consumed copious amounts of water from my cooler to counter the heat and continued relentlessly casting, hoping each time that the next would produce a strike. Still nothing.

After three applications of sunblock and numerous anchoring depths, I decided to move into shallower water where some trollers were picking up the occasional fish. The day was almost over and I had nothing but a weary casting arm and a frustrated look to show for my efforts. I noticed the odd fish still dimpling the surface and remembered the backswimmers I had seen when I launched the boat. I chose a ragged-looking fly of the same general size and color and, using my floating line, cast it towards the shore. Zip. I started with a slow hand-twist retrieve and gradually worked up to a full quick strip. A subtle resistance. Was it a take?

I cast again and repeated the retrieve. Bam. A take. After seven hours of fruitless fishing with the wrong flies in the wrong place, I finally had a fish on. It jumped and threw the hook.

Oh well, at least I had finally figured it out. A few more casts, and one more half-hearted hit, and it was time to pack it in. Another fishless day and another valid excuse for my diary. Pay attention to what is happening. Don't overlook the obvious.

June 20: Palmer Lake. I had arrived in hopes of finding the sedges on the rocky shoals near the centre of the lake, but there were none showing. I cruised the marl flats to see

if any fish were in on the shrimp, but couldn't locate any. I saw a few fish dimpling the surface in about 20 feet of water and anchored nearby.

I had seen a few small green chironomids on the water, so decided to start with a dry line and #12 green fly. The fish continued to move occasionally near my fly, but no takes. I changed sizes, from #14 to #16 and back to #12, from black to grey to peacock herl. Still nothing. By this time the day was nearly over and the fish had stopped moving. I decided to head home.

While loading my boat, I mentioned to an angler who was camped that I had not touched a fish. He said he had had a great time fishing the damselfly emergence in the next bay. I shook my head with realization, but it was too late to do anything but make another entry in my diary. What I should have done: Talk to other anglers to find out what has been happening on the lake. Never assume anything!

April 2: Crater Lake. The fish were in three to six feet of water, feeding on small chironomids, the first hatch of the season. They could be imitated with a #14 peacock herl pattern fished on a dry line and short leader. The fish, though small, were eager to take after being subject to foraging on whatever insects, leeches or crustaceans they could find in the weeds all winter. The hatch lasted for about an hour, with fast and furious action. Then, as if someone had thrown a switch, it stopped. The fish were still moving as before, only now they were completely ignoring the peacock fly.

I changed from pattern to pattern, trying to solve the mystery. Only when, in desperation, I tied on a small white chironomid did I begin to catch fish again. Stomach samples (in the old days I didn't have sophisticated pumps and probes and relied on the kill-and-gut method to determine what was happening) indicated that the earlier emergence had been replaced by a second species, this time all white. I was fortunate enough that time to have a fly in my box which worked. Keep trying until the right pattern is found.

The rain continued and I kept reading entries in the diary from days long past. I realized that written words differ from memories, which are more like videos in that we choose to replay the sunny days when things all come together and the fish keep hitting no matter what fly is used. The diary is reality, recording not only those rare days, but also the fishless ones with rain, snow, hail, storms and wind. I think I'll go rent another fishing video. 🐟

— Doug Porter

The North

Chapter

3

G iven a lifetime to spend casting flies to northern waters, an angler still would achieve no more than a nodding acquaintance with northern British Columbia. Encompassing fully half the province's land mass, the North's angling challenges are so diverse and take in such an overwhelming variety of waters that even the most dedicated are unable to form anything approaching a comprehensive picture. In this lies a good measure of the North's allure, the famous spell of the North long celebrated in poetry, prose and song. Always there is more to see, another bend in the river, another turning of the trail, a byway yet unexplored or a wilderness that beckons.

Arctic grayling somehow embody the essence of the far North, perhaps simply because an angler must travel a good ways north just to find them, but Skeena steelhead are the fish that most often lure southern anglers north. These are incredible fish and they cast a spell in their own right. The Kispiox River, where the world record fly-caught steelhead was taken in

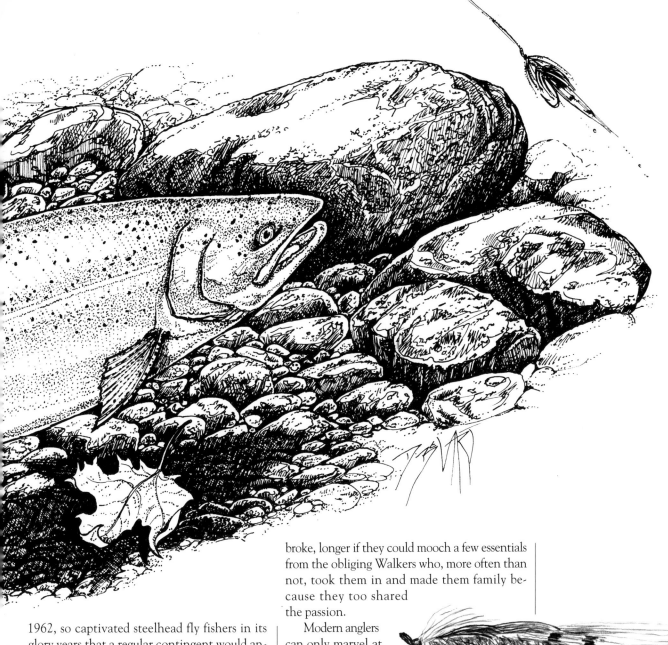

broke, longer if they could mooch a few essentials from the obliging Walkers who, more often than not, took them in and made them family because they too shared the passion.

1962, so captivated steelhead fly fishers in its glory years that a regular contingent would annually forsake jobs and families to spend the entire season camped beside the banks of the river they loved so well.

While no official record of those early steelhead fanatics exists, their names and records of their catches (a number of which clearly dwarf the official world record fish) remain in the unofficial log kept by Olga Walker at Kispiox Steelhead Camp. Reading through those tattered pages, the picture that emerges is not so much one of fish caught and good times had, but of a certain type of angler so addicted to northern steelhead that not much else in life seemed to matter. They stayed until they were

Modern anglers can only marvel at the catches made in that now-lost era, and while steelhead numbers may never again rival those in the heyday, much of the old passion lingers, and for good reason. The steelhead still arrive each year, not just in the Kispiox, but throughout the vast and complex Skeena system. Sensitive system-wide management practices which evolved through the 1990s augur well for continued and increasingly strong runs of these exceptional fish. Each year during the key Skeena steelhead angling months of September and October, droves of dedicated fly fishers venture north to any number

General Practitioner

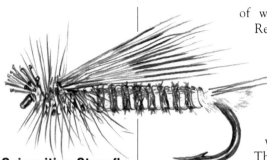

Ovipositing Stonefly

Hook: Mustad 9672 or similar, #4–6
Tail: Goose flight wing biots on either side of dirty orng. wool
Under-Body: Packing foam strip wound on hook & protected w/Soft Body glue
Over-Body: Dirty amb. fur wrapped in dubbing loop over packing foam but leaving bands of the silv. packing foam to show thru
Wing: Nat. deerhair
Thorax & Head: Spun deerhair
Hackle: Multi-var. wrapped over thorax, trimmed on bottom

of world-famous streams. Renowned for their willingness to rise to the fly, Skeena steelhead remain the sole reason many anglers ever wet a line in northern waters.

These steelhead are, beyond doubt, everything a fly fisher could ever hope for in a quarry, but they represent only one dimension of the North's diversity, a fact which in itself speaks volumes. Many of the same flows home to steelhead also offer chinook and coho salmon, and there are any number of remote (boat or charter air access) mainland coast and Queen Charlotte Island streams with good runs of both species. Stream strategies for these fish are well known (see Chapter Six), while open-ocean fly fishing for Pacific salmon is only just emerging from the pioneering stage.

Tactics for taking ocean coho on the cast fly are proven beyond any last shadow of a doubt, a fact many fly fishers are only beginning to discover. Fly fishing for coho salmon at such 'exotic' destinations as the Queen Charlotte's Cumshewa Inlet or Chatham Sound's Dundas Island, which lies far enough north to be within sight of Alaskan waters, has all the potential for international renown, but for now still languishes on the brink of discovery. When the runs are in, and they linger for some months in these northern waters, the fishing can be unbelievably good. Coho frequent Chatham Sound from mid-July through to the end of September and the kelp-bed strategies developed further south suit the region's kelp-strewn islands to perfection. Patterns such as *Shim's Sardina*, the *Chartreuse Clouser* or a *Flashy Glow* (see Selected Patterns for Chapter Five) will take coho on virtually every cast if they are worked by knowledgeable hands.

Bruce McLeod: The riffle hitch is great when fishing a waked fly for steelhead, but after prolonged casting the resulting leader twist is exasperating. To get around this problem, eliminate the riffle hitch and use a curve cast combined with an upstream reach mend. After casting across and downstream, reach upstream to bring the belly of the line parallel to the current. Allowing a slight belly to form at the tip of the fly line makes the fly ride broadside to the current. To create a slight wake as the fly is pulled toward you and downstream, follow with your rod tip downstream. To slow the wake of your fly, simply swing your rod downstream quicker. To speed up the swing and create more wake, slow the downstream swing of your rod. With a little practice you can fish a fly broadside to the current, giving the fish more opportunity to see and react to your fly.

Open-ocean tactics for chinook salmon are not proven, meaning while numbers of fish are taken each season, consistency remains elusive, but B.C.'s far northern waters offer one of the best opportunities anywhere to take trophy-class chinook on the fly. Prospecting such renowned waters as those found in any number of spots in Chatham Sound or off the Queen Charlottes,

Ian Forbes: The golden is the most important of the stonefly species in British Columbia, but the small green stonefly (*Lime Sally*) and some of the large brown stoneflies can be almost as vital. Found only in well-oxygenated, fastwater streams, stonefly nymphs crawl along the bottom to feed and onto rocks to hatch. They seldom swim, so nymph imitations must be fished close to bottom. The golden stone has a bright yellow belly and an olive brown back, colors which must be reflected in any imitation. Size can be matched with #6 long-shank hooks. Egg-laying adults can be imitated with appropriately colored elk hair caddis patterns and should be presented drag free with only an occasional flutter.

and closely following the fly fishing strategies used at Hakai Pass for deep water or those for kelp forest chinook in shallower areas, allow the angler to cast a fly with some confidence. Chinook in northern waters tend to hold and travel in water between 20 and 60 feet, depths easily reached by quick-sinking fly lines or shooting heads, and are often concentrated in sufficient numbers for the fly fisher to know beyond doubt the fly is being presented to fish during the retrieve. The key, as when fishing for coho, is knowing where to set the anchor, or precisely where in the kelp maze to tie off.

Being on the leading edge of a new fishery brings its own unique rewards – not the least of which is the chance to take part in a piece of unfolding fly fishing history – but the salty environs of the coast are, like the steelhead and their streams, evocative of only northern B.C.'s Pacific character. Further inland, lakes begin to dominate, most notably in the swath of country between Houston and Prince George.

Lakes to the north and south of Highway 16 between these two centres abound in such numbers they splash blue across even the tourist road maps. Venture off the main paved road and onto the network of backroads which lace the area (using maps substantially more detailed than highway maps), and it soon becomes obvious this is lake fishing country writ large. Babine, Takla and Stuart are among the lakes enriched by runs of sockeye salmon and everything that means for lake-resident rainbow trout. Quite a number of small lakes at no great remove from the main paved roads have been stocked and are groomed to provide angling not dissimilar to that found in the fertile waters of the southern Interior plateau. On such waters all the rules of stillwater hatch-matching and demanding angling hold, while a lake no farther away than the next Forest Service campsite might hold only wild fish, the rainbow trout and lake char that live a true northern eat-or-be-eaten existence.

Wild waters in this area of northern B.C., meaning those lakes which have not been enhanced and are entirely self-sustaining, do not necessarily mean gullible fish and easy angling. On the larger waters, merely finding the fish can take a fair bit of sleuthing. In many instances the dynamics at work in a given lake are complex, involving two or more strains of rainbow trout, each specifically adapted to take advantage of different lake zones and food sources. It would not be unusual to spend a day catching quite small rainbow trout on nymphs and surface flies while the lake's larger piscivorous trout go entirely unnoticed.

The presence of kokanee or large schools of other small prey species often means a lake holds rainbow trout adapted to these food sources, but not necessarily. Rainbow trout quite regularly make surprising adaptations to northern environments and even the largest piscivorous strains will curtail their free-ranging habits and feed in shallow water should a strong hatch, or the right hatch, emerge. Having a huge, large-mawed rainbow trout quietly surface to suddenly sip a midge pattern which previously had drawn notice only from tiddlers is entirely within the realm of possibility. It happens, but predicting when and where is just about impossible. There are rare exceptions, Stuart Lake's blizzard mayfly hatches for instance, but for the most part there are no generalities which apply to these waters. Anglers must take them as they find them and go home knowing the next visit might produce radically different fishing, either because something fundamental in the lake has changed, or simply because specific conditions on a particular day resulted in quite fabulous fishing. Just don't expect the same conditions to hold next week or next year at the same place, same time. Change is constant, and in the North it seems to happen quicker than just about anywhere else.

Southern lake fly fishers make a serious game of finding fertile waters, or the 'hot' lake of the moment,

Latex Stonefly Nymph

Hook: Mustad 9671, #6–8
Tail: Dyed yel. goose biots from flight feather
Under-Body: Warmed & flattened Friendly Plastic molded onto hook length & tapered at each end
Over-Body: Latex rubber cut in thin strips & wrapped around hook, then colored w/Pantone pen; yel. belly, brn. back
Thorax & Legs: Dyed amb. rabbit hair spun on dubbing loop, trimmed top & bottom
Wing Pad: Latex rubber strip pulled over fur dubbing & marked w/brn. Pantone pen

Lime Sally

Hook: Mustad 9671 or similar, #14
Tail: Goose flight wing biots
Body & Head: Deerhair dyed chartreuse grn. folded along & around hook shank, then held in place w/bright grn. tying thread
Wing: Zing Wing or section of thin, clear plastic string mat.
Hackle: Griz. dyed bright grn. w/lime Koolaid
Thread: Bright grn.

and while similar waters exist in the North, usually in the form of managed lakes near population centres, it would be a missed opportunity not to search out one or more wild lakes. Management is increasingly sensitive to such waters – Kazchek Lake north of Fort St. James offers quality angling for wild northern rainbow trout, but access has been purposefully left as a portage, for instance – making local Fisheries Branch offices good sources of information. Regional angling guidebooks will point the way to many more waters than a visiting angler could reasonably hope to cover and, of course, staff at area fly fishing shops will be steeped in local lore. They are normally quite open to those who speak the same language and share the release ethic that is increasingly pervasive in fly fishing circles.

While it would be entirely possible to spend an angling lifetime roaming between the Lakes District south of Burns Lake and the backcountry waters surrounding Fort St. James, perhaps stopping to fish such renowned streams as the Nation, Stellako and Upper Babine, fishing the North inevitably means moving on, if for no other reason than the fact there is no end of country to move on to.

The waters discussed thus far have focussed on the near north, the relatively known areas of the region's southern extremity, which have their loyal following of local anglers and substantial numbers of annual rod-in-hand visitors. Finding true northern fish such as Arctic grayling and northern pike means heading a good ways further north on one of only three main roads. The Cassiar Highway branches into far north country at Meziadin Junction, but does not touch on Arctic waters until it reaches Dease Lake, the headwaters lake of the Dease River. The

Alaska Highway wends its way north through a landscape dominated by rivers, a sprinkling of far-flung lakes and the fabled Northern Rockies, awe-inspiring country which will have anglers thinking seriously about charter float plane costs. In between these two main north-running arteries, the lakes and streams of the Omineca Mountains are accessible over a network of industrial roads reached either from Fort St. James or from near Windy Point on the Hart Highway. That's it. Branch roads are almost nonexistent except in the Peace River country/Fort St. John area, where industrial roads provide access to a handful of mostly managed and/or stocked lakes.

Driving into the Omineca means leaving certain securities behind. There are limited services only at Manson Creek and Germansen Landing. Otherwise there are logging camps, which may or may not be able to sell fuel. Anglers must not only be self-sufficient, they

must also be seasoned industrial road travellers. The compensations take the form of the wild Mesilinka River's grayling, the Omineca River's rainbow trout and the all-but-unknown angling to be had on the Osilinka and Ingenika rivers. Ingenious anglers with the requisite boating smarts will find remarkable angling for large predatory bull trout near where any of these rivers enter Williston Reservoir, but be warned there are no put-ins and the reservoir's debris-

Mary Lou Burleigh: My background is in fly fishing for Bulkley and Kispiox river steelhead. For wet flies, I carry black and purple leeches, black and grey articulated leeches, black and orange *Squamish Poachers* of all sizes, a wonderful little pink and orange chenille fly my husband ties, which we call a *Happy Hooker*, and, most importantly, I carry *Skunks*. For dry flies, I carry variations of the *Bulkley Mouse*, a few *Sofa Pillows* and, most recently, some *Bombers* in different colors. The flies that I tie on most often are the *Skunk* and the *Bulkley Mouse* for wet or dry fly fishing respectively. I like the traditional black and white *Skunk*, or a green-butt *Skunk*, tied on a #4 Tiemco, larger in colored or changing water conditions. My favorite dry fly is the *Bulkley Mouse*. I like Andre Laporte's little fat mouse, tied on a #4 or #6 Tiemco, or a larger, sleeker version my husband ties on a #4 Partridge Wilson. The bottom line is that I have faith in these flies. I try many others, but I always come back to these.

choked waters can be dangerous. The Mesilinka River is the subject of a unique fertilization project, holds good numbers of grayling, rainbow trout and bull trout, and is the only river in the area with guide services. Tom Gratton, a fly fisher and nearby resident, offers jet boat excursions and knows every grayling run intimately. Those not inclined to northern backroad rigors might sample the Nation River's grayling and rainbow trout or the comparatively civilized comforts at Carp Lake, which continues to offer good fly fishing for larger rainbow trout.

The North's Cassiar country embodies much of what true northern angling is all about and services of various types are never far away. The exception comes with float plane travel, which can whisk anglers into the heart of the northern wilds where the fishing is everything southern anglers imagine when they picture northern waters. The Iskut lakes lie alongside the main road and offer quite exceptional angling for typical northern rainbow trout – relatively small, silver-bright fish with almost clear fins. Forming the headwaters of the Iskut River, a tributary of the Stikine, the last lake in the chain, Natadesleen, is reached by trail and consequently offers larger fish and more secluded angling, but the fishing is surprisingly good even adjacent to the provincial park at Kinaskan Lake. Further north yet, small lakes associated with the Dease River offer roadside angling for pike, grayling and lake trout. To either side of the road lie countless fly-in lakes, not the least of which are those found in Spatsizi and Tatlatui wilderness parks.

Further north yet, shimmering Atlin Lake acts as a gateway to yet more spectacular north-country settings and any number of remote, lightly fished waters. Those with sufficient time will want to explore the Taku country west of Atlin or the remote reaches of Teslin Lake and its grayling-rich streams. Arctic grayling are known to reach maximum sizes in these waters, so the next world-record grayling might even now be quietly finning in some remote, untouched reach of a river draining into Teslin Lake. ⌖

Lake Char Minnow
Hook: Eagle Claw D1197N #1–2, or Mustad 9671, #2–2/0
Tail & Under-Wing: 2 large multi-var. saddle hackle tied in matuka style
Body: Pale yel. dubbing
Rib: Flat silv. tinsel
Over-Wing: Pearl grn. & Baitfish Angel Hair tied sparsely over matuka hackle wing
Eyes: Plastic stick-on glued w/Soft Body

Kelp Forest Chinook

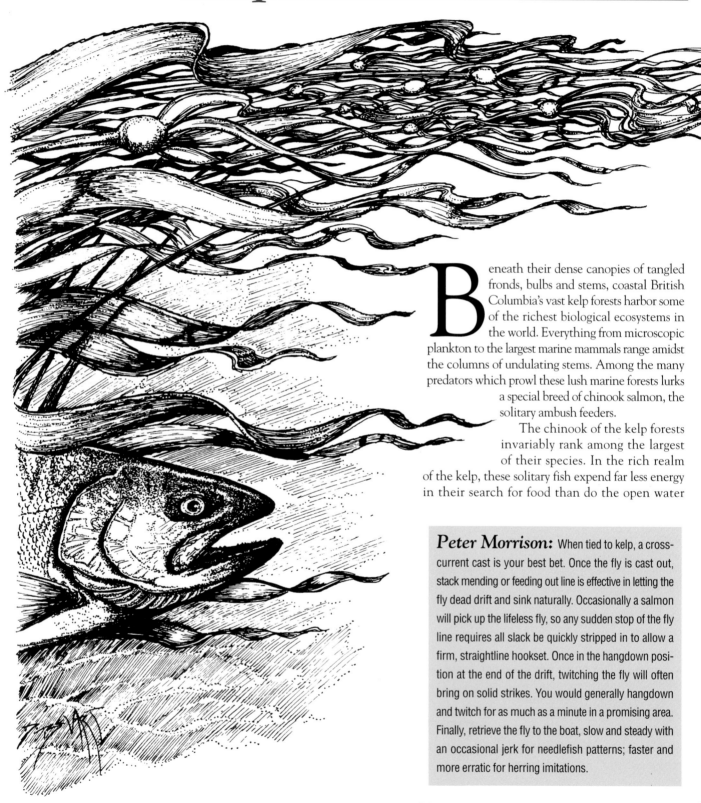

Beneath their dense canopies of tangled fronds, bulbs and stems, coastal British Columbia's vast kelp forests harbor some of the richest biological ecosystems in the world. Everything from microscopic plankton to the largest marine mammals range amidst the columns of undulating stems. Among the many predators which prowl these lush marine forests lurks a special breed of chinook salmon, the solitary ambush feeders.

The chinook of the kelp forests invariably rank among the largest of their species. In the rich realm of the kelp, these solitary fish expend far less energy in their search for food than do the open water

Peter Morrison: When tied to kelp, a cross-current cast is your best bet. Once the fly is cast out, stack mending or feeding out line is effective in letting the fly dead drift and sink naturally. Occasionally a salmon will pick up the lifeless fly, so any sudden stop of the fly line requires all slack be quickly stripped in to allow a firm, straightline hookset. Once in the hangdown position at the end of the drift, twitching the fly will often bring on solid strikes. You would generally hangdown and twitch for as much as a minute in a promising area. Finally, retrieve the fly to the boat, slow and steady with an occasional jerk for needlefish patterns; faster and more erratic for herring imitations.

salmon, and consequently devote more protein to sheer weight gain. Consummate hunters, they lie in wait for the schools of prey fish which seek shelter from both predators and tidal currents in the swirling back eddies of

the kelp forests. In this enclosed world, the sleek, silver-sided hunters easily corner their concentrated prey and it is this concentration of predator and prey in relatively confined areas which gives the fly fisher an edge, albeit a slim one.

Whether in the kelp forests off the Queen Charlotte Islands, among the byways of Chatham Sound or in any of the hundreds of more southerly destinations, two key methods are most often used: anchoring to the kelp or drifting along its open face.

Anchoring or tying to the kelp requires anglers to first locate concentrations of prey fish such as herring or needlefish. These fish gather in tight-packed masses during maximum tidal flows in the shelter of kelp-formed eddies or backwaters. The salmon's hunting area is then limited to very narrow feeding corridors or lanes, and these are readily explored with the fly.

Look for any irregular jut of kelp out into the current, or any depression, bay or opening large enough to provide shelter from the tidal stream. Tie the boat mooring line to one or more bulbs of kelp (enough to hold the boat in place) in a position that will allow the fly to be presented effectively and naturally near the school of prey fish. Most often this requires the boat to be positioned slightly up current and inshore of the school. Salmon usually attack stragglers on the outside edge of the school.

To dead drift along the kelp face, position the boat close enough to be within easy casting range, but out far enough to avoid tangling either boat or fly lines in the fronds which extend out from the fringes of the dense canopy. This method is an effective way to prospect for prey fish or salmon activity in the kelp.

Important points to consider when calculating the drift include the flow of the currents, and wind strength and direction.

Big chinook hooked along the face of the kelp or down one of the open lanes deep in the forest are very difficult to land. Capable of extremely long, powerful runs, there is every likelihood the fish will dash headlong into the kelp and be lost. Counter measures are few, limited in most instances to immediately disconnecting any mooring with the kelp and manoeuvring as far away as possible. Once in open water, the angler's odds increase dramatically, but even so, deft handling is required. Any momentary glitch can be enough to break the tenuous connection between fish and angler.

To successfully hook and land one of these solitary kelp hunters on a cast fly would be a crowning achievement for any angler.

Saltwater Squid

Hook: Mustad 3407 S.S. or similar, #1/0–4/0
Tail: 4–6 wht. saddle hackle; spots marked w/Pantone pen
Collar: Wht. saddle hackle
Eyes: Glass beads on mono.
Body & Head: Wht. lambswool spun into a thick chen., flattened & smoothed back w/thinned solution of clear silicone glue

Chartreuse Clouser

(Contributed by Peter Morrison)
Hook: Daiichi 2546, TMC 811S or similar, #2–3/0
Thread: Clear, fine mono.
Body: (Optional) Fluor. gry. Diamond Braid (behind eyes)
Over-Wing: Chartreuse bucktail or substitute
Under-Wing: White bucktail or polar bear, etc.
Lateral Line: 2-3 strands each side Krystal Flash or Angel Hair
Eyes: Medium plated or painted lead eyes w/prismatic stick-on eyes

Skeena Steelhead

Steelhead anglers the world over are drawn each fall to the rivers of British Columbia's justly famous Skeena watershed. Rivers such as the Kispiox, where the world record fly-caught steelhead (33 pounds) was taken in 1962, leave an indelible impression, but there are many more where steelhead in the 20-plus-pound range regularly to Skeena steelhead waters do so in those two key months. The first frosts normally arrive about mid-September and by mid-October temperatures hover near or at freezing through the day. On high elevation rivers such as the Sustut and Babine, the freeze will set in even earlier. By the end of September snow is not uncommon, especially at higher elevations.

Orange Marabou
Hook: TMC 7999, Partridge Wilson, Bartleet, Alec Jackson
Tail: Fluor. orng. marabou, same length as hook
Body: Blk. seal fur
Rib: Flat silv. tinsel
Wing: Fluor. orng. marabou tied on either side of hook

come to the fly. Waters such as the Zymoetz (Copper), Bulkley, Morice, Suskwa, Babine, Sustut and the mainstem Skeena itself provide unmatched fly fishing for steelhead in a range of settings and river types, from small wadeable streams through to huge flows that dwarf the angler.

Most of the fishing takes place during the popular prime time period between September and the end of October. Some rivers fish earlier in August and some will fish longer than October 31 if the weather is agreeable, but most journeying

Skeena steelhead enter the mainstem river at Prince Rupert as early as late June, and continue through early September, with the bulk of the run going through in mid-August. On average, it takes the fish from three to five weeks to journey from tidewater to the headwaters of their natal streams.

The Copper River near Terrace, a heavily glaciated stream, has steelhead from August through until the snows of late fall, or until the cold drives anglers from the river, usually in mid- to late October. Copper River steelhead are of a good average size, with some fish in the 20-plus-pound range.

The Kispiox River sees its first fish in late August, but the bulk of the run arrives later in September and October. Of all the Skeena watershed rivers, the Kispiox has a higher proportion of larger fish, with steelhead of 15 to 25 pounds quite common. Some of its fish reach 30 pounds and larger, so this is definitely the river for those looking for huge fish. Its long-standing international reputation, coupled with easy access, mean its pools and runs are often very crowded.

The Morice will fish through August and go into late October or later, depending on

The Suskwa, entering the Bulkley upstream of Hazelton, does not have a big run of steelhead, but those entering the river are quite large, regularly pushing the scales over the 20-pound mark. Suskwa fish can be found in the river as early as mid-August. It is one of the Skeena's smaller tributaries and is best fished as it drops after a good rain.

General Practitioner

(By Colonel Esmond Drury)

Hook: TMC 7999, Partridge Wilson, Bartleet, Alec Jackson
Tail: 10 hot orng. polar bear hairs w/gold. pheas. neck feather flat over top
Body: Pink-orng. seal fur
Body Hackle: Hot orng. saddle hackle palmered sparsely
Wing: A series of gold. pheas. neck feathers tied flat on back; gold pheas. tippet feather w/a "V" cut out & the black bars extending to either side of hook

weather. This river holds a large number of small fish in the five-pound range and some in the 15- to 20-pound category. Fish of 20-pound weights are rare – a 15-pound steelhead from the Morice is considered a good fish.

The Morice flows into the Bulkley at Houston, so all ascending Morice River fish must first travel the Bulkley, which explains why the Bulkley fishes well in August, water conditions permitting. The bulk of fish homing in on the Bulkley arrive through September and October. Bulkley fish are of a higher average size than Morice fish, with steelhead in the eight- to 12-pound range quite common and some chances of larger fish. The Bulkley's character makes it an excellent fly fishing river.

The Babine fishes best from mid-September through October, but has some fish showing as early as late August. Aside from the Kispiox, the Babine has the next largest average-size steelhead, with many fish in the 20-plus-pound range and some going into the 30s.

The Sustut has some early fish running through August bound for the river's upper

Ian Forbes: All Skeena tributaries are crowded during steelhead season. A steady stream of boats will come drifting down and guides will be running the rivers in jet boats. All obvious runs will have anglers on them. Search for the little pockets that often get overlooked. If the water is three to six feet deep, steelhead often hold close to shore, especially on rivers with overhanging vegetation. Early-run steelhead are more receptive to flies than fish that have seen a constant stream of traffic. Quite often, fly fishing will be better early in September than later in the month, even though more fish are in the river.

Scott Baker-McGarva: Anyone hoping to catch steelhead on a fly would be well advised to abandon their single-handed rod for a spey rod. There are two basic reasons why double-handed rods have been embraced by those who seek these magnificent fish. First is line control. Rods of 12 to 16 feet give better reach, accommodate more effective mending, and provide powerful line pickup. The other advantage lies in the weight-forward fly lines now used by most anglers. The belly portion of the line is shortened to around 20 feet and is two line weights heavier than the rod it matches. This allows for the use of far heavier interchangeable sinktip systems than the rod could normally manage without compromising pleasure and effectiveness.

watershed. Fish migrating to those portions of the river below the Bear River confluence usually arrive through September and October. Although the run is not as large as other Skeena tributaries, the river has a good average size, with a reasonable number of fish weighing 20 pounds and better.

As the steelhead make their way up the Skeena, provided the mainstem is clear enough, there are fishing opportunities on some Skeena bars, mostly in the Kitwanga to Kispiox area, but even the reaches lower down towards Terrace produce steelhead as long as the river water is reasonably clear. Rain frequents this watershed during the fall, and it can be intense enough for all the rivers to go out. The Skeena is probably the last to go, but it will also be the last to recover after a big storm. Anglers fortunate to be there at the right time will experience catching large fish in huge pieces of water – in itself a thrill.

A unique characteristic of Skeena watershed steelhead is their enthusiasm for rising to flies fished on or just below the surface in much lower water temperatures than elsewhere. River temperatures will vary through the season, but hover in the mid- to low 50s in the early part of the season, decreasing to about the mid-40s by mid-October. This varies considerably with elevation and during years with cold fall weather. The free-rising nature of Skeena steelhead may be explained by their multi-year fry-to-smolt residence in fresh water and the relatively short freshwater growing season. Every feeding opportunity is taken, including the late-hatching Diptera flies common to most streams, so Skeena fish imprint on surface fare early on. Whatever the reasons, fly fishers can consider themselves fortunate. There are few more thrilling experiences in steelhead fly fishing than presenting a fly on or just below the surface and having a fish rise and take that fly.

Even though the fish are eager to rise to a fly, the sunk line is still a staple technique. To be

successful, flies and sinktips need to be matched to water depth, flow and color. Big flies between two and four inches long or even longer are required. Flies such as the *Egg-Sucking Leech*, *General Practitioner*, *Woolly Bugger* or the popular *Popsicle*-type flies all work well. Usually the darker-toned wet flies produce better than brighter colors, but much of fly selection is based on personal preference.

The waked fly is one of the most thrilling techniques for taking steelhead on the surface and is quite effective on most Skeena system rivers. The technique is worth a try through water temperatures down to the mid-40s. Flies such as the *Bomber*, *Muddler Minnow* and *Grease Liner*, as well as newer flies of foam-body design, will all produce. The choices are literally endless, but the important thing is that the fly leaves a wake as it comes across a run. Flies ranging in size from #8 through #2 are needed to cover the various water and light conditions.

The Skeena's free-rising steelhead also provide opportunities for the traditional dry fly technique. Any fly that floats well in sizes #8 through #4 is appropriate, but patterns that wake well are a bonus as it is then possible to fish the two techniques on one drift – both dry and waked.

The floating line technique, where the fly is fished just under the surface on a floating line in a down-and-across cast, is a very popular method on many Skeena tributaries. Fly size, as well as degree of dressing or sparseness, needs to be adjusted to match conditions such as water temperature, clarity, velocity and light conditions. Darker patterns seem to produce better than those of lighter tones. For glacial streams or those colored by rain a large *Black GP* or *Woolly Bugger* works well, especially in poor light. A variety of flies in #8 to #2 are needed to cover the wide variety of conditions. The *Black Spey*, *Skunk*, *Woolly Worm* and *Doc Spratley* are a few of the traditional flies, but there are myriad choices.

The nymph-type presentation is used mostly for skittish fish in low, clear water which is best not approached with the usual down-and-across cast. For example, when the water is low and clear in the Kispiox or the Upper Copper and the fish can be readily spotted, casting a fly upstream and letting it sink to near bottom often produces results when nothing else will. An egg-type pattern fished with a floating line and strike indicator works as well as anything. ❧

Cold Water Realities

Northern British Columbia is cold enough for otherwise rule-abiding game fish to adopt a host of odd behavioral traits. Winter begins in late September on some northern plateaus, and even in the larger coastal valleys like the Skeena the ice can take hold in October and stay until March. This reality dominates the lives of northern fish, inducing a lethargy for much of the year that borders on piscine hibernation. The warm summer months consequently spur the kind of ferocious feeding that is the stuff of angling legend.

When they do feed, northern fish are less particular and more aggressive, striking at garish attractor patterns just as readily as they do the most realistic imitations. This can be a bonanza for anglers, leading novices to vast catches and the illusion of fly fishing mastery. For more experienced anglers, it is the zest with which northern fish feed and the unlikely prey they often target that bring a new and intriguing dimension to angling in the far north.

At almost four inches in length, the northern water shrew (Sorex palustris) does not look like trout prey. Snaking along the river's edge as it searches for its meals, this tiny shrew might even eat small trout. In southern waters it might live without fear of aquatic carnivores, but not so in the north. Carnivorous bull trout can weigh more than 20 pounds and have no trouble handling the shrew. As mammals go, water shrews are exceptional swimmers, but they are no match for salmonids.

Like their terrestrial cousins, water shrews prefer to feed at night, when most predatory birds are roosting and bull trout lie motionless on the bottom. For the attentive angler, dusk and dawn provide narrow windows of opportunity when the shrews still swim and the bull trout begin to prowl. The enormous splashes heard at deep dusk might be a cold-blooded char taking in a hot meal before settling into deep pools for the night.

Zonker
Hook: TMC 9394 or Mustad 9671, #1,2,4
Body: Crystal Chenille, various colors including silv.
Wing/Tail: Thin strip of rabbit hide w/fur attached, nat. or dyed

Buried in the mud of the river bottom lives another unlikely prey for trout. The Pacific lamprey is an anadromous fish that spawns in fresh water, migrating to and from the sea. The young are called ammocoetes and they live for up to six years in rivers before their seaward migration. At up to four inches in length, they look like tough-skinned earthworms. Rarely seen by anglers, ammocoetes are found in most rivers and while not unique to the North, they are perhaps more important there because of a lack of other food.

Living most of the time within a muddy burrow, ammocoetes are rarely seen by trout and form only an occasional part of their diet. Despite this, their shape and movement have an innate predatory appeal to trout. The frantic wriggling motion of the ammocoete is irresistible, arousing the same ancient behaviors that lead steelhead to swallow rubber worms and marabou. The rippling, rhythmic motion of the tiny lamprey appeals equally to 20-pound steelhead in the 30-degree water of the Sustut River and to feeding trout in Morice Lake.

Ammocoete patterns should not be overly large since adult lampreys suck the flesh of salmon and trout and have a distasteful compound in the skin that keeps them off the menu of larger fish. Ammocoetes enter the water column only during the annual downstream migration, and then only at night and during the freshet, so matching the 'hatch' is not part of the equation. Nonetheless, northern fish will rarely refuse such a morsel.

When sockeye salmon spawn along beaches, such as in Tahltan Lake, sometimes they dig up each other's redds, sweeping the eggs into the water column and sending them adrift in the current. From there the eggs might be swept up by waves and carried onto the gravelly shore, rolling up and down the beach like marbles, giving rainbow trout an unusual feeding opportunity.

Salmon eggs provide an incomparable feast for northern rainbows each September. Patrolling the shore in as little as three feet of water, the trout are easy prey for ospreys, but the lure of fat-rich eggs seems to justify the risk. Several rainbows may swim along together, actually riding the waves up the beach to grab eggs. The concept of imitation is valid here, though it can be applied loosely as any egg pattern will be equally well received. The rainbows, like so many northern fish, are understandably indiscriminate: there won't be much to eat for the next six months. ❧

Two Northern Trout Streams

It is said in the North when the Sleeping Indian is visible at daybreak over Rainbow Alley, it will be a blue-sky day. For the fly fisher, a blue-sky day spent under the Sleeping Indian will be a day never forgotten. Framed by the Babine Range to the west and the Frypan Range to the east, the short stretch of river draining vast Babine Lake offers some of the North's finest dry fly fishing for wild rainbow trout.

In a land of breathtaking landscapes, Rainbow Alley stands apart and it is perhaps the setting as much as its trout that will have anglers planning to return long before their trip to this one-of-a-kind northern destination draws to a close. The trout are there, though, and anglers being anglers, it is the promise of large, well-conditioned northern rainbows that will be the true lure.

The classic dry fly water extends over a 12-mile stretch starting near Fort Babine at the outlet of 110-mile-long Babine Lake. The first four miles of broad, even-flowing water mark the start of the Babine River and are known as Rainbow Alley after the concentration of fish found over the course of its many fine runs and classic holding water. Rainbow Alley spills into seven-mile-long Nilkitkwa Lake, a shallow, heavily weeded lake made to measure for the stillwater fly fisher. Where Nilkitkwa necks down and the flowing water resumes, there is a one-mile stretch of river which ends at a salmon-counting weir. The water flows faster here than at Rainbow Alley, making the drift quicker and the need for fast, accurate casts to rising trout more pressing.

The large, free-ranging trout of Babine Lake congregate at Rainbow Alley in the spring, gorging on newly emerged sockeye salmon fry, whose numbers receive a boost from the spawning channels on the Fulton River and Pinkut Creek. The fry frenzy starts about mid-May and continues through to about mid-June. Traditional strategy calls for anchored boats, floating lines and fry patterns. Quartering casts and dead drifts requiring two or more mends are standard, but loafing is possible too: feeding line out downstream behind the boat and searching by lifting the rod tip, then allowing the fly to drift back down, will do the trick as well as, and sometimes better than, more active methods.

Prolific golden stonefly hatches come on just about the time the fry 'hatch' ends. This hatch must be seen to be believed, making for pure, high-adrenalin angling. The even current at Rainbow Alley makes it possible to freewheel, with just the odd stroke required now and again to correct the course, freeing anglers to cast to rising trout as they drift by. There will be times when the entire river is pockmarked with rising trout, but the better fish naturally take the best lies, so it becomes possible to target specific fish during the drift. The one-mile section of river below Nilkitkwa ups the intensity level both because the water is faster and because the stonefly hatch is heaviest here – truly a 'blizzard' hatch.

Ian Forbes: There are any number of fine trout and grayling streams in the North. On the B.C./Yukon border, the Swift River is a fine grayling stream, as is the Dease and its tributary, the Cottonwood. The Tanzilla, which flows into the Stikine, has both grayling and rainbow trout. Coastal streams that flow into the Skeena, such as the Lakelse and upper Gitnadoix, have good fishing for migratory cutthroat. The Crooked River, north of Prince George, is a good trout stream in areas where springs seep in, often marked by a sandy bottom. The Parsnip has two excellent tributaries, the Table and the Anzac, both noted for their grayling. The Pine, Murray and Sukunka have good grayling and bull trout fishing. The Burnt River is a great little grayling stream. Along the Alaska highway, there is the Beatton, the Sikanni Chief and the Buckinghorse. All have fine grayling fishing.

Stellako Adams
Hook: Mustad 94838 or Partridge Captain Hamilton, #14
Tail: Moose hock or stiff hackle barbules
Body: Dubbing mixture of tan, gry. & olv.
Wing: Griz. hackle tips
Hackle: Multi-var. or 1 griz. and 1 brn.

The hatch of the big golden stones is followed by a hatch of small green stoneflies, which is heaviest at Rainbow Alley proper, as opposed to the faster water below. Where the flow enters Nilkitkwa Lake, cutthroat trout are often taken, as well as rainbows, and this is one of the best areas to anchor for evening fishing. The lake itself sees intense mayfly hatches in June and its complex mix of shoals, islands, drop-offs, winding channels and extensive reedbed flats makes for intriguing angling as well as providing the ideal nursery habitat for juvenile salmon. Take note: Some of the largest

rainbow trout ever landed in the Babine watershed were taken in Nilkitkwa Lake.

The hatches slow in late summer and the fish become much more difficult to find. Some will certainly disperse over the long length of Babine Lake, but others remain and good anglers will find them, even if the frenzied spring and early-summer action has slowed.

Stellako River

The Stellako is a freestone stream ideal for the wading fly fisherman. The first quarter mile below Francois Lake is a superb piece of flat pocket water with excellent fly hatches. Trout lie close to the bank under brush and out in the middle in rocky depressions. Downstream from the flats, the valley narrows and the river picks up speed, forming a series of runs, pools, and rapids.

The river can be drifted by experienced rafters. At one point it constricts into a rapid that can be tricky and dangerous, but it is possible to walk around this difficult stretch. Below the rapid is what is known as the Millionaire's Pool. After the Stellako leaves the narrow valley, the current slows down, becoming almost placid

by the time it reaches the Highway 16 crossing. The lower section is on private land, which is off limits to anglers.

The Stellako is about seven miles long and the best of the fishing water has been purchased by the Nature Conservancy. Trails follow the river downstream from the bridge at Francois Lake, where a sign and map provide information. Otherwise, there is very little access except through private property and a couple of steep, unmarked trails.

The best insect hatches occur from mid-June to mid-July. Trout will almost always rise during a big golden stonefly hatch. Imitations of these insects require a long-shank #6 hook. The slender, small green stonefly is important and can be matched with a #14 *Lime Sally*. The color is a bright chartreuse green. Trout can be very selective to them and refuse anything but a drag-free drift. Casts need not be long, but they must be accurate and line control must be good. This is also important during the mayfly hatch. Most of the mayflies are #14 or smaller and come in shades of tan and grey. Only the larger mayflies bring big trout to the surface.

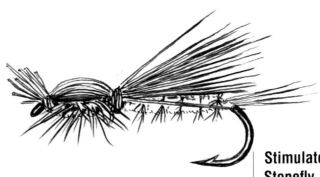

In September, sockeye salmon arrive and large trout follow them up from Fraser Lake. Smaller trout from Francois Lake also move downstream for the feast. During the sockeye spawn, a weighted egg pattern is the only fly needed to catch rainbows and whitefish.

The average resident Stellako rainbow is from 12 to 16 inches, but there are many trout over 20 inches during the spring insect hatches and the fall salmon run. During the heat of summer most of the larger trout return to Fraser Lake. ⬦

Stimulator Stonefly

Hook: Mustad 9672 or similar, #4–6
Tail: Deerhair clump
Body: Pale yel. wool
Body Hackle: Brn. saddle wrapped palmer style & clipped short
Thorax: Dubbed amb. fur
Hackle: Brn. wrapped over thorax
Wing: Nat. deerhair tied in behind thorax & at head
Head: Deerhair wing stub trimmed evenly
Thread: Yel.

Waked Fly Steelhead

Telkwa Stonefly

(Contributed by Mike Maxwell)

Hook: TMC 7999, Partridge Wilson, Bartleet, Alec Jackson

Tail: Goose flight wing biots tied on either side of amb. wool ball

Body: Moose body hair folded along hook shank & held in place w/yel. floss ribbing

Wing: Elk hair tied on hook top, NOT stacked; flare the butts & hold in place w/spun brn. dubbing

Antennae: Goose flight wing biots

Few angling experiences compare to seeing the shadowy form of a steelhead materialize from the depths to gently pluck a waked fly from the surface – suddenly the fly is gone and the fish is on. Other steelhead come mouth agape, violently taking the fly with considerable surface disturbance and noise. The violent-taking ones make fishing the waked fly a truly nerve-tingling experience, but luring any steelhead to the surface is always exciting.

Dating back at least to 17th-century Britain, the waked- or skated-fly presentation has had a variety of names attached to it over the centuries. Dibbling, skimming, skittering, waking, riffling, dry fly fishing and surface lure fishing are some that come to mind. All except dry fly fishing are proper terms used to describe the method in which the fly is brought across the surface of the water, causing a wake. This last point – the fact that the fly must leave a wake – cannot be over-emphasized.

Many of the flies developed in recent years incorporate materials such as foam bodies to increase flotation, or have wings flaring from the sides at an angle to the body. Others have oversized heads of clipped deerhair or appendages of foam or deerhair at the front of the fly to facilitate waking. Many of the older patterns, especially those dressed with deerhair (such as the *Bomber*), continue to work well, provided a half hitch is used behind the hook eye. The half hitch ensures the fly will wake, even in the calmest of waters.

To successfully fish the waked fly requires optimum light conditions with alert fish in water of suitable depth and temperature, usually in the 50- to 60-degree range. Skeena steelhead have been taken on a waked fly with water temperatures in the high 40s and lower, but only under optimum light conditions. On bright sunlit days, fish the waked fly at those times when poorer light prevails, or look for shaded pools and runs. On overcast and rainy days the waked-fly technique will take fish at any time, provided the angler can find them.

As much as the waked-fly presentation brings some spectacular rises, false rises and misses are all too common when using this technique. To the fish, the dominant target is the apex of the V at the end of the hook, which is what they key on. The result, alas, is many flashy, exciting rises with no corresponding hook-up – the fish simply

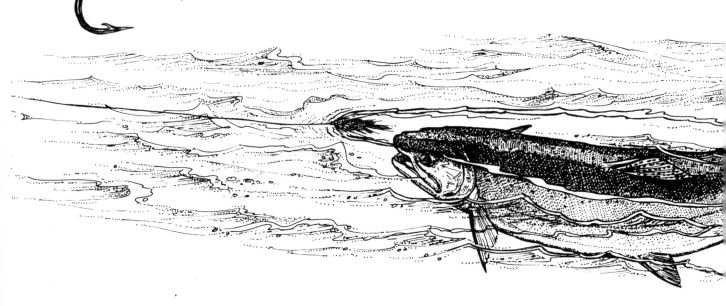

miss the hook. Typically, for every 10 fish that rise to the waked fly, as few as three might actually get the fly into their mouths, and of those it is just as likely the angler will miss one, lose the second and, with luck, beach the third.

While it is true that a fish must take the fly into its mouth before it can be hooked, the waked-fly technique does provide some of steelhead fly fishing's greatest moments whether fish are hooked or not. One great benefit is the fact the waked fly will attract attention from travelling fish, and some very large fish at that. Those showy non-taking rises alert the angler to the fact a steelhead has moved to the fly. Just as many fish may come to subsurface flies and not take them, but the activity is unseen and so remains one of steelheading's imponderables. We do know that changing to a subsurface fly on a floating line will often produce fish following a number of refusals or misses to the waked fly.

The traditional cast is quartered downstream, with the cast angle just below the angler to about 45 degrees down and across. The cast needs to suit the piece of water fished, and some fly fishers like to have the fly drift naturally through the upper part of the cast in the hope of attracting a fish to the fly fished 'dry'. Working a piece of steelhead water is best done methodically, starting at the head and working to the bottom. Using the waked fly, it is entirely within the realm of the possible to work all day for a single rise.

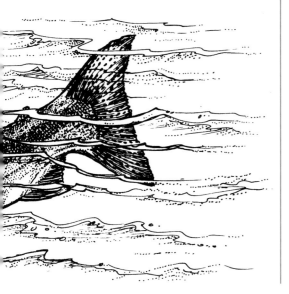

When a fish does finally respond, the action can be instantaneous and the take furious, which underscores the need for safeguards against over-reacting. A natural reaction when fishing a rod low to the water with a tight line is to strike immediately on feeling the fish take the fly. When fishing a waked fly, even experienced anglers will still periodically pull the fly from the mouth of a fish, particularly when taken by surprise, or perhaps by being distracted or by letting the rod drop too low. Holding the rod in a more vertical position provides a cushion against over-reaction. This puts a belly in the line, and by dropping the rod down when a fish takes, the fish has a chance to get the fly in its mouth and start back down before the strike.

On large pieces of smooth-flowing water where long casts may be necessary to cover the lie, some mending may be needed and the rod should be held somewhat upright. On turbulent waters, the cast must be long enough to cover the lie, and the rod held high enough to keep excess line and leader off the water while the fly swings over the lie. The more turbulent the water, the more control is needed. Control is obtained by making shorter casts with the rod held high. On small pieces of pocket water, the rod position will be almost vertical.

Flies ranging in size from #8 up to #2 cover most situations. Smaller patterns suit clear, slow-flowing and warm water, but a number of things must be taken into account. For instance, fly size should be increased based on water turbulence, velocity, clarity, temperature and light conditions.

The waked-fly presentation has become a popular way of fly fishing for steelhead on many summer-run steelhead streams, not because it produces more fish but because it is one of the most exciting ways of catching a steelhead on a fly. Once sampled, it is hard to return to more conventional methods, especially when light and water conditions oblige. ✦

Skeena Skater
Hook: TMC 7999, Partridge Wilson, Bartleet, Alec Jackson
Tail: Light tan elk hair
Body: Dyed amb. deerhair folded around & along hook, held in place w/yel. thread
Hackle: Light tan elk hair flared towards front & either side
Wing: Nat. deerhair w/butts cut long & flared into a flat head then held in place w/Soft Body

Grease Liner
Hook: Partridge, single low water
Thread: Blk. Monocord
Body: Blk. seal or seal substitute
Wing: Extra-long deer or elk hair, leaving trimmed butt fibres intact for waking

Grayling Waters

Arctic grayling are found only in pure, cold northern waters amidst settings lifted straight from the pages of a storybook. Small wonder they are a fish of legend. The rivers they inhabit drain distant valleys home to Dall sheep, grizzly bears, northern moose, elk, caribou and the last of the great wolf packs. Fishing for Arctic grayling inevitably means touching on such northern wonders and this, above all else, is the grayling's gift to the angler.

The classic image pictures a float plane beached on the shores of a lonely northcountry lake with grayling dimpling at the outlet stream, the mountain backdrop ablaze with fall color. While grayling do in fact inhabit lakes, they are many times more likely to be found in streams draining the faraway lakes. In those glass-clear northern flows, grayling have distinct preferences and so will not be found over the length of the river,

Karl Bruhn: The Arctic grayling of the Stikine have established themselves in the upper reaches of the river, from below Laslui Lake down at least as far as the Spatsizi River junction. The water they like best lies between Laslui and the Chukachida River, which is the clearest on the entire river. In the swift flow of the Pink Canyon they stage across the breadth of the river, but hug the many small eddies and never hunt far from the current seam. In this type of water, accurate casts must be made to the seams and deft fish handling skills are needed as the grayling 'sail' across the river.

but concentrated in certain pools where the flow is to their liking and the depth just right.

Most often they are found in the main body of clear-water pools with medium flows and with depths of between three and six feet. They like this open water, and it is breathtaking to watch them tip up to sip a fly from the surface. Some hiking may be needed to find any numbers of fish. For reasons known only to the grayling, some waters that look ideal may yield nothing, but when the right pool is found, it is

not unusual to have half a dozen or more come to the fly before the action slows. Recent studies have shown that the largest grayling tend to school together in the upper waters of a given river system.

Grayling average between 12 and 16 inches, so any fish approaching 20 inches is definitely a trophy (the Canadian record grayling measured 30 inches and weighed almost six pounds), but size seems irrelevant in a fish made as if by design to dazzle the eye. With their large sail-like dorsal fin, tarnished silver and gold coloring, and scattered black spots along the purple iridescent back, they are true marvels, in every way a reflection of their wild northern settings.

For the fly fisher, they are a dream come true: strikingly beautiful fish that readily rise to

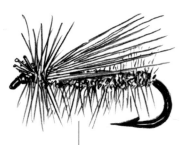

Elk Hair Caddis
Hook: Mustad 94840 or 9671, #14
Body: Blk., ol. or drk. brn. dubbing
Hackle: Furnace tied in at tip, then wrapped sparsely palmer style along body
Wing: Natural elk w/butt stubs left as a head

any appropriately sized fly pattern. This naive innocence has been the grayling's undoing in those northern waters easily reached by road.

Extremely vulnerable to overfishing, grayling have been managed on a catch-and-release basis in most regions since 1995. In rivers draining into Williston Reservoir, grayling are red-listed, meaning they are endangered. Fishing remains good in such Williston drainages as the Mesilinka or Nation, and with release now mandatory there is room for cautious optimism, even if the network of backcountry roads continues to expand each year.

Grayling can be found north of Prince George in the streams of the Parsnip River drainage, and those waters draining into Williston. The Pine, Murray, Sukunka, Peace and many of their tributaries contain grayling. Most streams crossing the Alaska Highway hold reasonable grayling populations, but anglers must be prepared to leave the roadside pools. North of Dease Lake on the Stewart-Cassiar highway grayling abound, but again, it is necessary to leave the roads behind to find the best fishing. ◄

Bob Melrose: Beautiful, colorful fish deserve a beautiful, colorful fly. A well-tied *Royal Wulff* fits the bill perfectly. Easily visible to the angler, it is an offering few grayling can resist. *Adams, Wulffs, Humpys* and *Elk Hair Caddis* in #12 to #16 complete the fly selection. Flatten the hook barb beforehand to facilitate quick, safe releases.

Selected Waters

Wild Stillwater Trout

Competing fish species, low fertility, winter or summer kill and regular spawning failure would seem to negate the possibility of large trout in small northern lakes, but some of British Columbia's best trout endure despite such drawbacks. These are wild trout which have evolutionarily developed ways to overcome handicaps.

Competing fish species are the norm for wild stillwater trout. This reduces the potential biomass of trout, but it can increase average size. Resident coastal cutthroat in generally infertile lakes would average far smaller without stickleback and sculpin. By feeding on those fish, cutthroat often grow larger than trout in fertile lakes. Some northern rainbow trout races have evolved the same approach for dealing with shiners, chubs and even squawfish. More often, though, these trout either force competing fish from preferred areas or develop efficiency about harvesting food in areas naturally avoided by other species. They are very good at this.

Winter and summer kills make many lakes barren, but periodic and partial kills can produce exceptional trout lakes. Partial die-offs prevent overpopulation of both trout and competing species, permitting sometimes explosive growth for the surviving trout. Complete kills are mitigated by young trout holding in feeder creeks.

When those creek trout move down to a 'killed' lake, they have no competition from older trout or coarse fish. Tiddlers can become three-pounders in one season; they may approach 10 pounds the next year.

Regular spawning failure can produce similarly outsized trout. Lakes with marginal spawning streams may produce virtually no fry for any given season and sometimes for several seasons. If trout are present, they will generally be rugged and long-lived enough to survive unsuccessful spawning to try again the next year. They will also be large enough to drop a good payload of eggs when conditions are right. Trout that genetically lacked those traits did not survive – simple as that.

Most of these lakes have no angling fame. They are found away from roads, and those near roads regularly have a 'fished out' reputation. As roads are developed, anglers naturally flock to the newly accessed lakes and tend to hit these large-trout lakes especially hard. Fishing nosedives. In some cases, killing too many trout tilts a delicate coarse fish/trout balance, or trout populations fall below their genetic brink. That's fatal, but often anglers abandon the lake – and spread word of its demise – before things get that bad. Keep in mind that this fishing is seldom easy and may exist only in some years. For those who know these waters, fishing may remain quite good even when it seems barren to others. And – protected by a bad rep – the trout often bounce right back. Anglers who know such places seldom talk about them except, more and more, to request restrictive kill regulations.

Areas to prospect for these exceptional fish include the Lakes District south of Burns Lake, and those waters reached over the network of logging roads branching from Fort St. James, particularly near lakes such as Great Beaver, Kazchek and the Grassham group. ❧

Humpy

Hook: Mustad 94840 or 9671, #14
Tail: Nat. deerhair
Body: Blk., olv. or drk. brn. dubbing
Back: Nat. deerhair tied in at hook bend & pulled over body
Wing: Nat. deerhair tied in upright & divided into "V"
Hackle: Furnace, brn. or griz.

Selected Waters

Bull Trout

While it is difficult to distinguish between the two, bull trout (*Salvelinus confluentus*) were recognized as a separate species from Dolly Varden trout in 1978. The taxonomic distinction between the two char species was made after identifying the morphological differences resulting from gene-pool isolation during the last ice age. Bull trout have an extensive range, from northern California to Alaska, but northern British Columbia qualifies as one of the last remaining strongholds of the huge, predatory bull trout of legend.

Although declining over much of its range, bull trout inhabit most major northern B.C. rivers and tributary lakes. Conservative regulation and a wild fish management priority augur well for bull trout, but they remain a slow-growing species, maturing only in five to seven years and with a life span of about 14 years. Optimum incubation and early rearing temperatures are critical to their survival, so environmental changes which alter water temperature can seriously impact populations. Overfishing, however, poses the greatest threat to bull trout, due to their aggressive feeding habits and slow growth.

The upper reaches of feeder streams which provide the spawning grounds for the migratory bull trout produce the smallest resident fish, while lakes produce the largest specimens. This is mitigated by the fact bull trout are system-wide migrants, readily travelling between lake and stream and roaming extensively within the river. In the fry stage they feed mostly on terrestrial and aquatic insects, switching to fish surprisingly early in the juvenile stage. Rivers and lakes home to salmon runs generally produce the largest bull trout, but even systems without migrating salmon smolts will produce impressive char. Opportunistic to a fault, bull trout will prey on any species smaller than themselves.

Often caught incidentally by anglers when fly fishing for rainbows, bull trout are increasingly becoming a specific target for fly fishers. The aggressive strikes for which they are justly famous rate as one of the true thrills of northern angling. Fishing large, buoyant minnow patterns where major rivers enter large northern water bodies such as Williston Reservoir makes for nerve-tingling angling. Bull trout charge the fly, executing a lunging head turn as they strike. The resulting crescent-shaped boil of water and attendant noise easily paralyzes awestruck anglers; hooks are regularly left unset.

Dark patterns seem particularly effective and while stonefly or other larger insect imitations will be taken, bull trout prefer a good mouthful – a *Bulkley Mouse* skated on the surface will almost certainly receive attention. The fish generally hold in slower eddies, deep pools or slicks close to the bottom, but might be found anywhere in the stream as they relentlessly forage.

Bull trout should be handled with the respect they deserve. Heavy rods and tippets help minimize stress and allow for quick release of these aggressive northern predators. ✒

Teal & Silver Smolt
Hook: Mustad 9671 or similar, #4–6
Tail: Gold. pheas. tipped feather strands
Body: Flat myl. silv. tinsel
Throat: Orng. breast feather from gold. pheas.
Wing: Drk. barred teal/pintail flank feather

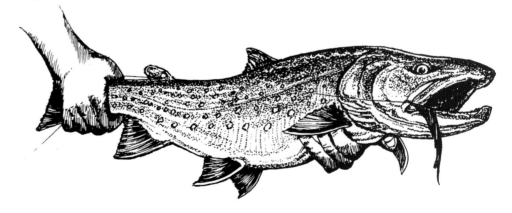

Selected Waters

Arctic Lakes

Arctic waters invariably conjure images of remote northern wilderness, but there are many Arctic-flowing lakes and streams in British Columbia which can be reached by road. North of Dease Lake, the gravel Cassiar Highway follows the Dease River valley and provides ready access to waters holding such northern species as pike, grayling, bull trout and lake char. Adventuresome anglers might sleuth out off-road oxbow lakes formed by the Dease River and experience wilderness-style fly fishing for large northern pike, but lakes such as Joe Irwin, Boya and Wheeler offer northern angling within hailing distance of the road. The point to bear in mind is the fact the 'highway' is no more than a thin scratch across hundreds of miles of still-remote wilderness.

Joe Irwin Lake, like Pinetree Lake a few miles farther north, is a widening of the Dease and may be used by those contemplating a drift down portions of this fabulous river, but the lake is a superb angling destination in its own right. Set against a mountain backdrop, Joe Irwin is one of only a very few lakes known to hold Arctic grayling. More often found in streams than lakes, grayling can often be seen rising where the Dease flows into the lake. A well-presented dry fly such as a #12 or #14 *Adams* or *Deerhair Caddis* is normally sufficient for these opportunistic fish.

Boya Lake Provincial Park is situated in rolling hill country and the lake is marked by crystal clear water and huge marl shoals. Lake trout (char) are the main species, but they can be difficult fish for the fly. In spring and fall the char are in shallow water and will readily take suitable forage fish patterns, but from June to September they go deeper and sounders will be required to pinpoint the precise locations they prefer. Char will take a fly if it can be presented to them, which often means going deep with set-ups such as heavy shooting heads (six feet of 850-grain looped to running line). Leaders can be as short as three or four feet, but for pike a short wire leader should be added.

Farther north, the country continues to flatten out, with dozens of ponds visible from the road and many more just out of sight behind the stunted forest. About 25 miles from the Yukon border, the cold, clear waters of Wheeler Lake beckon. A modest campsite provides easy access to the lake's pike-laden waters. Typically weighing between two and six pounds, these northern pike will provide fast action for those searching the edges of the lake's many shallow, reed-filled bays. Pike patrol the reed edges, and a large fly retrieved in foot-long strips will receive steady attention. For the few larger pike which inhabit Wheeler, probe the deeper water of the drop-offs next to the shoals. ❧

Parachute Black Fly

Hook: Mustad 94840 or 9671, #14
Body: Back 1/2 hook none, front 1/2 hook fine blk. dubbing
Wing: Plastic strip cut from "Waffle" section of Glad bag
Thorax: Blk. or drk. brn. Sparkle dubbing
Wing/Hackle: Drk. furnace wrapped parachute style around closed-cell foam post

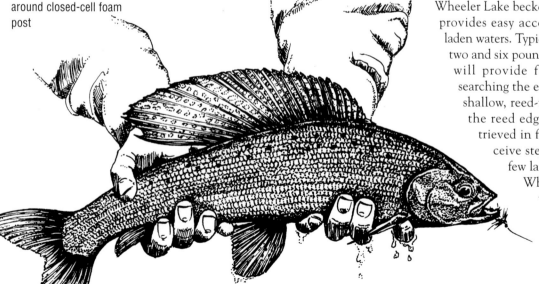

Selected Waters

Northern Pike

Aggressive, voracious feeders, mature northern pike live at the top of the food chain and easily fulfil all the qualifications of a classic gamefish. Extremely powerful and with an incredible ability to accelerate to top speed, pike have a nasty disposition and will slam any likely looking offering with determination. With large specimens weighing more than 40 pounds and average fish coming in at between 15 and 20 pounds, they are in many respects the true trophy fish of the North.

Common in the shallow lakes of British Columbia's Arctic watersheds, pike congregate in shallow bays at the windward ends of these lakes early in the spring. Seeking the warmest water in preparation for spawning, they feed most aggressively at this time. Wading the shallows and stalking individual fish in early spring can be dramatic, as even the largest pike will be visible to anglers sporting polarized glasses. Look for them in the heaviest cover, often in flood water no more than ankle deep, and be prepared for very aggressive strikes.

Often pike will track behind the fly, then quickly accelerate to engulf the offering. Takes at or near the surface will generally result in the fly disappearing suddenly in a turbulent whirlpool of water. Heavy shock tippets of braided or solid stainless steel wire (or very heavy mono) are required and the ensuing battle will be hallmarked by long, fast runs, violent head shakes and occasional 'greyhound' type leaps.

Pike will run the fly line around weeds, snags, partially submerged bushes and the like, so heavy equipment is necessary. Quality reels with reliable drag systems capable of holding the fly line plus 200 yards of 30-pound test backing make sense, as do short-tapered, weight-forward fly lines, necessary to turn over the extremely large 'flies' often required for this fishery.

Pike eat just about anything they can swallow, including shrews, mice, voles, lemmings and even small muskrats. Large pike have been known to take ducklings and goslings, but most often fish such as chub, perch, walleye, trout and grayling form the bulk of their diet. Several suitable patterns are included among the Selected Patterns for this chapter, but most prey-fish-type flies will work, particularly those incorporating red and white.

For the fly fisher, pike represent a relatively new and challenging quarry; it would be a mistake to venture north and not plan on seeking out these most predatory of Arctic fish. ➤

Weedless Pike Spook

Hook: Eagle Claw D1197N #1–2 or #2, Mustad 9671, 2/0

Tail: 2 griz. saddle hackles dyed red and 2 dyed yel.

Body: Rear 1/2 pearl mylar tinsel over packing foam then glued w/Soft Body for protection, front 1/2 wht. lambswool smoothed flat & shaped w/thinned silicone glue

Eyes: Plastic stick-on glued into place w/silicone

Weed Guard: 30-lb. test mono.

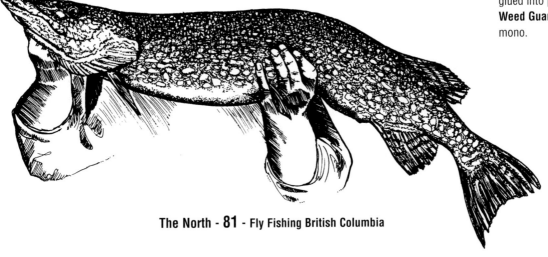

Selected Waters

Lake Trout

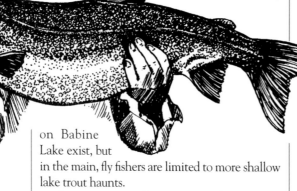

Lake trout are pelagic fish and consequently may be found almost anywhere in a given lake, but the big char most often dwell in precisely defined deep-water locations. Wire-line trollers, the true lake char devotees, ferret out such locations and zealously keep them secret, but these 'char holes' are in any case beyond the reach of fly lines. Exceptions such as the 20-foot-deep char hole near Smithers Landing on Babine Lake exist, but in the main, fly fishers are limited to more shallow lake trout haunts.

Growing to weights in excess of 60 pounds, with fish in the 20- and 30-pound range common, lake trout are a worthy quarry and, contrary to popular belief, can be caught on a cast fly, even if consistency remains elusive. Even the largest char occasionally venture into the main rivers that either feed or drain the large, cold-water northern lakes they prefer. Concentrations of char, however, will only be found during the fall spawning season and when they forage for schools of prey fish.

Shoal areas on the approach to lake inlet and outlet streams are always worth prospecting. Lake trout often mill where the current starts to pick up speed before flowing out of the lake. They also gather near deep-water edges surrounding inflow areas. Both locations are magnets for smaller fish seeking food items either washed into the lake or drawn by slow currents to the outflow.

Char lurk in deeper waters near these areas, moving in to feed on their unsuspecting prey. Casting into the depths and retrieving toward the shallows is standard practice. Imitating dead or wounded prey fish by casting into the current and allowing the fly to drift lifelessly to the depths can be effective. Voracious char readily consume such items.

The tendency of lake trout to hang just below the edges of drop-offs also can be used to advantage. From below the edge of the lip, they have ready access to the shallows and the smaller species which live and feed on the shoal. High-density sinktips or full-sinking lines are required to present the fly in a natural manner. Casts are made into deeper water; allow the fly time to sink deep before retrieving up to the drop-off contour.

Lake trout can be extremely difficult to land, partly due to their large size, but also because of their unusual fighting tactics. Quite often hooked char roll on the line as a means of escape. Unfortunately, this can result in well-tangled fish, making release difficult. Keeping maximum pressure on a taut line helps forestall the line-rolling tactic.

Heavily weighted *Clouser Minnows*, bucktails and polar bear streamers will all produce. Nine-weight and heavier outfits are required to turn over the large flies and to muscle large fish to the boat. ➤

Northern Journal

In its uppermost headwaters the river the ancient Thloadenni and Sikanni peoples called the Schadzue – the Great River – is but a winding alpine brook. The mighty Stikine of deep green waters and boulder-heaving strength awaits below, many long river miles away, but even here in its mountain-meadowed birthplace there is a palpable sense of greatness, of something extraordinary taking shape.

All those who came before and left a record of their passing sensed this feeling of something great impending, as if the world were holding its breath, waiting. Even the hard-bitten explorers of the fur trade, men who had surely seen their share of wilderness wonders, were awed and held spellbound by the land we now call Spatsizi.

It is no different for us, having arrived not by pole and paddle and towline, but by air, dropping from a cloudless sky to the black sand shores of an alpine tarn called Happy.

With the Beaver a mere silver speck, high and rapidly fading, and our outfit – all the sundry bags and packs necessary to a month-long adventure by canoe – yet scattered along the beach, we stood transfixed, more dazed, perhaps, than happy.

So we remained, too, for quite some time, two lonely figures on the shores of a mountain-ringed lake locked deep in a wilderness of mountains and plateaus and breathtaking alpine meadows. Now, quite suddenly it seemed, all this was spread before us in one grand panoramic vista.

The venture had been planned for more than a year and the 1,000-mile drive north from Vancouver to the float plane at Eddontenajon – Sikanni for Lake-Where-the-Little-Girl-Drowned – was allotted 10 days. Time enough, or so we thought, to take a measure of the wild northwest we were intent on exploring. Instead, the 10-day journey merely taught us what all northerners well know. Southerners don't know beans about the North and those who think they can take its measure in 10 days are the worst of the bunch.

It took a blast of frigid air, slamming down from the snowfield on 7,275-foot-high Mount Umbach directly behind us, to break the reverie. We watched the gust williwaw across the lake and then lose itself in the mix of meadow and stunted conifers, trees which might be several hundred years old yet barely thicker around than my wrist, which marked the far shore and its upland.

Time to rig camp was the message in that snow-cooled wind and so the mundane tasks that were to become so intimately familiar over the next weeks took hold. Even so, when by some chance the eye was distracted by blue water or meadow green, one or the other of us would stop and stare, ensnared again by wonder.

Six full days we spent among the three headwaters lakes – Happy, Tuaton and Laslui – and vowed on each one of them that someday we would return. In that time we experienced many hours of wilderness fly fishing for wild northern rainbow trout, silver-bright fish typically 14 to 16 inches. They came to the dry fly in droves near where any small flow entered the lakes and when finally they refused to rise to the dry, any simple nymph would bring again the sharp, urgent tug of fish feeding in a limited season of plenty.

It was absurdly simple fishing and the fish were so plentiful my companion, in casting to where I had just hooked yet another rainbow, once actually lassoed a bull trout with his leader. The char had been hammering the sides of the fish I had hooked, apparently attempting to steal my catch, and in the ensuing melee was ensnared by my friend's leader. I doubt this could have happened anywhere else but in the North, the land of tall tales, even if this one is gospel.

Below Laslui Lake the Stikine changes character. Gone is the idyllic alpine stream and with it go the meandering, easy-paced days. With a roar and a spectacular, sliding drop over a long, sloped ledge, the Stikine announces itself a full-fledged river, albeit a young river of the mountain stream variety.

Below the tumultuous cascade of the Fountain Rapids (the portage is an easy half-mile walk through open parkland), the river debouches in a wide, flat pool, as if to draw breath and regroup before embarking on the next stage of its journey, a 50-mile headlong dash to the Chukachida River junction.

We took our cue from the Stikine and pitched a camp to overlook the sunlit pool.

In a world of high-tech tents and space-age materials, the lean-to is an anachronism, no doubt, but the classic Canadian northwoods shelter has its advantages, too: sipping morning coffee from the comfort of one's bedroll while watching the rippling river and the first tentative riseforms of still lethargic trout, for instance.

Recalling that R.M. Patterson of *Dangerous River* fame had once shot a moose on the Nahanni River without leaving the comfort of his lean-to, we idly pondered the odds of reaching the trout below us with a dry fly cast from the luxury of our beds.

It was just morning silliness, but it did have the benefit of focussing our attention on the fish, and suddenly it struck us both that something was out of kilter here.

The fish were surfacing in the neat, tucking head-and-tail rises characteristic of Arctic grayling. The Stikine empties into the Pacific near Wrangell, Alaska, so the grayling, a fish of the Arctic drainages, had no business greeting the day in the Pacific waters below our camp.

Rigging the fly rod was the work of a few minutes and the tiny dry fly disappeared in a swirl the moment it kissed the water. Sure enough, Arctic grayling inhabit the Stikine. How they got there remains a mystery, but whatever the specifics, their presence underscores one of the primary wonders of this headwaters region.

Six major rivers find their headwaters at no great distance from where our lean-to was pitched on the upper Stikine and one of them, the Finlay, drains to the Arctic, all the way to the Beaufort Sea by way of the Peace and the Mackenzie.

Two of the others, the Spatsizi and the Klappan, we would meet further on, as both are tributary to the Stikine. The Nass and the Skeena find their headwaters less than 50 miles from Happy Lake as the crow flies, so it might rightly be said this land of wonders is, on top of everything else, also the birthplace of some of British Columbia's mightiest rivers.

To understand the scale involved, consider that the Skeena is B.C.'s second largest river after the Fraser, and the Stikine is the province's third largest Pacific drainage, encompassing 12,500 square miles. Then reflect for a moment on the fact that all the country taken in by these mighty flows doesn't amount to even half the area we call the North in British Columbia.

It took us three weeks in a canoe just to paddle from the Stikine's headwaters to its junction with the Cassiar Highway. There have been many trips North since and we still don't know beans. ◄

— Karl Bruhn

The Rockies

The Rockies are to the east (it's hard to miss them), and the entire region is spined with lesser mountains divided by river valleys. There's a good highway, backroad and trail system, population is sparse, vast areas of wilderness still endure, and there are all manner of lakes, rivers and smaller waters. End of geography lesson, but let's add that elevation, climate and water fertility just happen to ideally suit trout. The world's largest rainbow trout and bull char strains evolved here, native westslope cutthroat have survived better than anywhere else, and introduced brook char and exotic rainbow trout strains have thrived. This is trout fishing country.

The Elk and St. Marys rivers draw the bulk of visiting anglers (word is definitely out), but these are good-sized, exceptionally productive waters and the fishing remains excellent from July (after spring runoff subsides) through October. That was much less true just a decade back, but catch-and-release regulations and ethics have dramatically increased trout populations. Regulations were applied in 1985 and within six years improvement was obvious, with further improvement each year thereafter. Fishing is now splendidly reliable, and rafting and drift-boating – with or without a guide – have spread out angling pressure and opened up previously unfished water.

Wild westslope cutthroat trout in the 12- to 16-inch range are the norm – lots of them – with fish in the 20-inch class possible. Rainbow trout are also present. Covering a lot of water with general-purpose floating flies

is the standard approach, but it is possible to concentrate on a short stretch of river and fare just fine – presuming anglers have the requisite patience and do things right. This can be very demanding fishing.

There are other rivers though, and streams that range from almost river size down to mere trickles, which really shouldn't support trout but do. They are little touted and some of them (the Bull River is a good example) have a 'fished out' reputation which modern, restrained harvest regulations have made quite false. The exploring fly fisher can definitely find solitude and just might find larger trout or faster action than that on the Elk or St. Marys. Or not. There are dud waters out there and many of the streams are right only for those who can appreciate them.

The Moyie River, for example, has too many coarse fish and warms too much in summer, but it is classically Traveresque – with long placid stretches of water ideally suited to contemplative, slow-paced fishing. Hit it with the right medicine at the right times (which can be any time, even during the early season runoff) and the action can be very fast for rainbow, brook or cutthroat trout of at least respectable size, with five-pound rainbows definitely possible. More often though, anglers must be content with a standard-sized trout or two taken from especially pleasing water. Anglers with itchier feet might prefer certain stretches of seemingly unproductive riffles and rapids on the Goat River. The trick is to keep moving, covering every bit of pocket water

Black Stonefly 'Salmonfly'

Hook: Mustad 9671, #4–6
Tail: Dyed blk. goose biots from flight feather
Under-Body: Warmed, flattened Friendly Plastic molded onto length of hook, tapered at each end
Over-Body: Latex rubber cut in thin strips, wrapped around hook & colored w/Pantone; blk. w/thin orng. stripes
Thorax & Legs: Dyed blk. & orng. rabbit hair clumps spun on dubbing loop then trimmed top & bottom
Wing Pad: Strip of latex rubber pulled over fur dubbing

with short upstream casts. The cutthroat average smaller than Elk or St. Marys fish but, boiling up to a fly little more than a leader-length away, they seem larger.

Move down to the smaller waters and variety increases even more. Everything from boggy, weed-filled flows demanding the casting and imitative skill of a Marinaro to creeks that schuss down mountains in a series of waterfalls and pools is available. Those pools can be the stuff of high drama – both the business of getting to them and what happens when a fly, any fly, hits the water. Watch for beaver ponds, too. Beavers are abundant and their work creates trout water that maps don't show and few anglers discover. Beaver dams almost always hold trout (usually native westslope cutthroat) and provide distinctive fishing for trout that sometimes reach large size.

Fly fishers generally ignore the larger rivers and that makes a certain sense. The Kootenay, for example, runs intimidatingly high and thick all summer with glacial silt. This is bait-plunking water, but places where clear-water streams enter can be a very different story, and from fall to spring

the whole river changes. Flows are well below those steelheaders expect, water is clear, and anglers working steelhead-type flies or large streamers take good cutthroat and some enormous bull char and rainbow trout. The whitefish action is dynamite then too. Drifting a nymph below a strike indicator is the key and we're talking fish-every-cast action.

Don't write off the Columbia either. Much of it is of no fly fishing moment, but the stretch of that river near Castlegar is regarded by many serious anglers as just maybe the best piece of fly water anywhere. The rainbow trout average large and the fishing is regularly of the match-the-hatch, dry fly persuasion.

Kootenay Lake gets little ink for its fly fishing, and the outdoor press ink on it has mostly concerned the various environmental manipulations that all but destroyed its once world famous reputation for outsized rainbow trout and bull char. There's good news here though. No, things aren't as they were in 1940, but the big Gerrard rainbows have endured and, pursued by fewer and far more restrained anglers, produced some absolutely incredible fishing in 1998. One local highliner released nine trout in a day – all of them approaching or exceeding 20 pounds. A 27-pounder was kept and carefully weighed.

Savvy anglers in fact expected to take several coho-sized trout each day – particularly in the fall, winter and spring. This might seem of ho-hum fly fishing import, but a lot of those fish were taken on trolled bucktails fished just below the surface. A cast fly could have fared as well, maybe better. It may be too that the various more insectivorous races of Kootenay Lake trout are coming back. Older hands may recall that those fish once provided epic surface fishing (being in the Balfour area for June 'mayfly time' was dream stuff), so reports from trollers of 'small' (i.e., under five pound) trout obviously taking surface insects are definitely worth some investigating.

Trout Lake and the Arrow Reservoir offer some fly fishing, but the area's smaller lakes are a more likely fly destination. Fertility in some is equal to the better Kamloops lakes, fishing pressure is lower and the lakes tend to offer unusually common surface fishing. Don't leave the sinking lines at home and do bring a selection of the standard subsurface imitations and attractor flies, but do expect to see rising trout, some of them larger than seems plausible.

Premier, Whiteswan and Whitetail are the classics: all set in heavily forested mountain environs, several miles long and endowed with good basic fertility and extensive shoals. There really are no more perfect stillwater fly fishing locales. Severely limited kill restrictions and careful management have maintained a healthy population of rainbow trout and brook char, with fish over five pounds a distinct possibility. The fishing can be anything from extraordinarily demanding surface or sunken imitation action to trolling or chuck-and-chance-it sunken attractor fly work. The only flaw is the numbers of people who come here each summer. Things can get a tad hectic.

Hundreds of other lakes exist, most under a mile long – many mere ponds that appear only on the more detailed maps. The region west of the Radium-Golden Highway has perhaps the densest cluster of them, but lakes of this ilk exist all through the region. They vary in their basic fertility, depth, littoral area, invertebrate life forms, trout population size and species, ice-out and freeze-up times. They also range aesthetically from swamps to alpine jewels but, all that aside, anglers here generally expect adult trout of at least two-pound size and fish under five pounds are just 'nice ones'. An 18-pound Gerrard-strain rainbow was taken just a few years ago from a lake no more than a half-mile long.

Many lakes (Premier included) are ice-free and producing fast action by May. Some lakes produce a month earlier: Summit Lake (near Nakusp) even has a special April season of catch-and-release fly fishing. High summer action tends to slow at the lower-elevation lakes, but fall fishing is good everywhere and trout average especially large. Best bets for larger trout tend to be those lakes with restricted kill regulations, but some of the best big-trout waters have no special protection, either because they are hard to reach or because the fishing is especially demanding.

Alpine hike-in lakes deserve a special commendation. They are gorgeous and, thanks largely to an active stocking program, many contain thriving trout populations. The trout tend to be diminutive, but exceptions are common. That's particularly so of the larger lakes – some of them regularly visited by float planes – but a few quite tiny tarns produce consistently large trout, and all of these lakes hold a few trout that outlive their peers and reach at least double the lake's standard size. They seem enormous.

Largemouth bass might seem an implausible possibility, but they've found their way to several valley-floor lakes and provide some outstanding fishing. Duck Lake is about as good a bass lake as found anywhere, and fly fishing there is especially effective. Largemouth are also found in several small lakes, co-existing surprisingly well with planted rainbow trout and brook char.

There are no steelhead and, except for kokanee, no salmon. That's about all a fly fisher might miss hereabouts.

Deerhair Caddis
Hook: Mustad 94840/9671, #8–14
Thread: Match body color
Tail: Deerhair, 1/2 body lngth.
Body: Spun fur dubbing; color choice – olv., yel., brn., blk., orng.
Wing: Deerhair tied low, atop dubbed body
Hackle: Med. brn. or ging. var. wrapped over head
Head: Spun deerhair

Ian Forbes: Bass bugs can vary from poppers to divers to chuggers or sliders. It depends on the face of the lure. Poppers have a flat face, divers have a slanted-up face, chuggers have a slanted-down face and sliders have a smooth, rounded face. Each style gives a different action. Bass bugs can be made from spun and trimmed deerhair or from carved and sanded balsa wood or foam. When deerhair is used, the face is hardened with glue to maintain its shape. A thinned solution of Goop can be used, but the new Soft Body glue is better. Rubber legs can be threaded through the bug for added action and the tail consists of saddle hackles. Green, yellow, red and white are all popular colors.

Columbia Dry

Despite the dam degradation heaped on the Columbia from all sides, what angling water remains is second to none. Large and swift flowing, the river offers classic dry fly fishing for brilliant rainbow trout of exceptional size and stamina. At least two rainbow strains inhabit the river: the predominant silver fish with pale fins and a blush of pink on their cheeks, and the more heavily spotted trout with yellow-tinged fins, believed take advantage of the abundant insect populations for which the river is justly famous.

The best trout water is found downstream from the junction of the Kootenay and Columbia rivers at Castlegar and extending to the U.S. border at Waneta. Water levels fluctuate dramatically when adjustments are made at the seven Kootenay River dams and the Hugh Keenleyside Dam on the Columbia, but the river is intimidating in its own right by dint of its speed and size. To find the fish it is necessary to

break the river into separate components; slower currents, current seams and back eddies mark the prime water. Feeding trout travel in loose schools and hover just under the surface to pick off insects caught in the river's eddies and current seams. Reaching mid-river eddies is impossible without a boat.

Incredibly rich in insect life, the river's silt-bottomed stretches are carpeted with riffle larvae (chironomids), while the fast-water portions are home to an array of stonefly species, including huge black 'salmonflies', golden stones, small green stones and an assortment in grey and brown. Stoneflies are among the first insects to hatch in the spring and, unlike many area streams, the Columbia is open to angling all year, making it possible to fish all the best

to be hold-over Arrow Lake rainbows. Large fish run to about seven pounds; more typical fish weigh about two pounds. In addition to these residents there is a migration of rainbow trout from the U.S. each year, fish which come upriver to spawn and remain through June to

Cicada

stonefly hatches. Perhaps the only positive result of the dam complex is the fact the dams filter enough glacial silt to allow trout to see the flies, both naturals and imitations.

Mayfly variety on the Columbia rates among the greatest in the province. Species include pale morning duns, western green drakes, grey drakes, mahogany duns and blue-winged olives. There is even a small hatch of huge Hexagenia mayflies, silt-loving insects which hatch during early summer evenings in the slow water upstream from Castlegar. Most of the larger mayflies will have completed their mating cycle by mid-July, but the blue-winged olives continue well into October.

Caddis hatch in blizzard numbers in the spring, with smaller hatches continuing

horsepower motors to stem the river's swift currents are required to reach the best water. It is imperative to stay well clear of any rapids and to ensure the boat is of stable design. High-volume currents sheer over each other and easily flip unstable craft. There is a cement launch ramp on the east side of the river just upstream from Castlegar, and another at Trail. There is also public access at Genelle, halfway between Castlegar and Trail, which necessitates a drive over river gravel that may be hard on trailered boats at low water. Canoeing this section of the Columbia without intimate knowledge of the rough sections is foolhardy. The same can be said for the crazy souls

Foam Body Cicada
Hook: Mustad 94840, #8
Body: Closed-cell foam trimmed, shaped & colored w/blk. Pantone pen; covered w/Soft Body glue
Thread: Blk. nyl.
Legs: Rubber Super Floss, banded yel. & blk.
Wing: Zing Wing or section of clear plastic string mat.

throughout the summer. Most of the trout action occurs in the evening when the majority of caddis are on the wing. Caddis are best imitated with #10 to #14 deerhair patterns, greased to float well. Good color combinations include brown body and wing, ginger body/grey wing, olive body/brown wing, orange body/grey wing and the always reliable *Royal Wulff*.

Late summer produces hoards of grasshoppers which the valley's strong winds dump in the river, a terrestrial treat trout rarely decline. A green-and-yellow-bodied deerhair caddis makes a reliable imitation.

Unique to the Columbia is an April/May hatch of cicadas. These shiny terrestrials are similar to crickets and may be effectively imitated by a *Madam X* dressed with rubber legs and a black or dark peacock sparkle yarn body.

Boats at least 14 feet long and sporting 15

Ian Forbes: Chunky terrestrial cicadas hatch along the Columbia River in April after the first two or three days of hot spring weather. The hatch only lasts for a few weeks, but when prevalent winds blow the bugs onto the river, trout will seldom pass them up. The cicadas get stuck in the river's big back eddies where the trout pick them off. The cicada flight signals the start of the Columbia's dry fly season.

who drift the Columbia's eddies in their float tubes; pontoon boats are more stable and useful, but a downstream pickup must be arranged.

Those without boats and solid river navigation skills are well advised to hire a local guide; a number operate from a fly fishing-friendly centre in Castlegar. The Columbia River from Castlegar to the U.S. border may well rank as one of the finest trout rivers in Canada, but it is no place for the ill-prepared. ⌁

Westslope Cutthroat

Like all trout, westslope cutthroat can be finicky fish, but even in such blue-ribbon streams as the Elk and St. Marys, where the dry fly rules and delicate presentations are 'de rigueur', the westslope remains true to the cutthroat mantra. Seldom are they selective and rarely are they shy. Mind, these are pampered versions of the cutthroat strain and the streams they inhabit regularly provide hatches intense enough to trigger selective feeding. As the season progresses, the fish can become shy by cutthroat standards, increasing numbers having felt the sting of steel.

For all that, westslopes tend to retain the cutthroat's free-booting feeding style and the Elk and St. Marys rivers, beyond doubt two of the Rockies' premiere trout streams, rate among the finest of waters in which to find them. These rivers offer free-rising westslope cutthroat and whitefish as well as large, predatory bull trout and relatively easy access, all set against a towering mountain backdrop. No angler can rightly ask for more.

The Elk River starts high in the Rockies adjacent to Peter Lougheed Park in Alberta. It flows southward and slightly west until it joins the Kootenay River near the village of Elko. Managed to provide a variety of angling opportunities, the river is divided into sections (centred on bridge crossings) with different regulations and restrictions for each section. Roads parallel the river and come close enough in a few places to allow anglers to stroll through semi-open forest to the river bank.

Much of the upper river can be drifted in small rafts and pontoon boats, although there are many sweepers, brush piles and small jams, some of which will have to be portaged. Downstream from Elkford to the Line Creek

bridge, the river is marked by slow sections separated by beaver dams. With care, the section from Line Creek to Sparwood can be drifted, but the river is faster, more confined and the sweepers are dangerous, especially during high water. Fording in waders is difficult due to deep, fast water. Downstream from Sparwood, the Elk is suitable for all types of craft and there are several egress points, the obvious ones being the bridge crossings at Hosmer, Fernie, Morrissey and Elko. Distances between crossings average about six miles, and each section provides a full angling day. Dangerous canyon water rules out the section below Elko.

Walking and wading are possible in many sections and by late summer or early autumn the Elk can be forded by those experienced in the intricacies of the craft. Hikes between fords can be long and wading staffs will be required for the faster runs; the bottom is slippery enough to require felt soles.

Mission bridge the river becomes more braided, with many gravel bars.

In a full day of fishing it is not unusual to catch 20 or 30 cutthroat from these mountain treasures. Trout in both streams will range between 10 and 16 inches, with always a possibility of one or more that will go better than 20 inches.

Most often a variety of deerhair caddis patterns tied on #14 to #8 hooks is all that is required. Body colors, in order of preference, are green, yellow, brown, black, orange and grey. These deerhair patterns have the advantage of doubling as imitations for adult caddis, stoneflies and hoppers.

Mayfly imitations should be size 12, 14 and 16. A size 14 *Adams* is a good general mayfly pattern, and in a variety of body colours – grey, tan, olive and brown – will cover most species. All mayfly imitations, including emergers, must drift drag free.

Mayfly emergers may be required for selective trout. A tan-olive-brown sparkle-dubbed pattern drifted in the surface film will fool most of

Pale Evening Emerger
Hook: Mustad 94840, #16
Tail: Wood duck flank feather
Body: Moose mane, nat. gry., dyed pale olv.
Thorax: Pale olv./tan sparkle dubbing
Legs: Wood duck flank feather
Wing: Zing Wing or section myl. string mat.

> **Peter Morrison:** Commercially tied flies tend to be heavily dressed to suit the needs of a variety of anglers and angling situations. Altering either commercial or home-tied flies to suit specific on-the-water needs is simple and effective. Quickly trimmed, a full-dressed dry mosquito pattern becomes an excellent emerging chironomid imitation. Down-size any fly simply by trimming its outside dimensions to suit an immediate need. To instantly turn a *Doc Spratley* into a simple nymph, trim the pheasant rump over-wing to a short stub, thus imitating the wing case of a newly emerging nymph. The possibilities are endless. Required are a quality pair of tying scissors, a little imagination and a sense of fun.

The St. Marys River begins high in the Purcell Mountains west of Cranbrook. It flows eastward until it empties into the Kootenay River near Fort Steele. Upstream of St. Marys Lake, the stream is small and intimate and in its crystalline water, the cutthroat show clearly, suspended over golden sand.

Except for a short canyon stretch above Mark Creek, most of the St. Marys is navigable by raft. Vehicle access is limited, but the country is relatively open and hiking is easy. Below Marysville the river loses velocity and consists of a series of runs and pools with only a few rock gardens and gentle rapids that require tricky manoeuvring; none are dangerous. Only during low water is it possible to wade across the river. Downstream from the St. Eugene's

these fish, so it makes sense to carry a few of these nymphs, both weighted

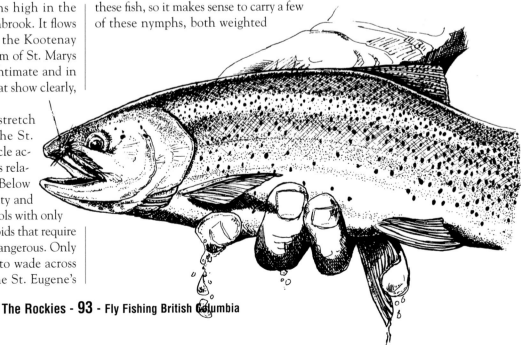

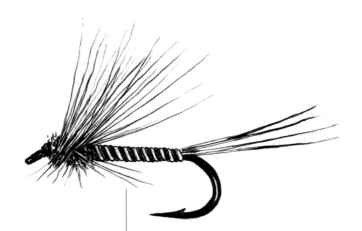

Pale Evening Dun

Hook: Mustad 94840, #16
Tail: Moose mane
Body: Moose mane, nat. gry., dyed pale olv.
Wing/Hackle: Sandy dun pulled to hook's top w/thorax dubbing under
Thorax: Pale olv./tan dubbing

and unweighted. A flash-back bead-head Hare's Ear, in size 14 (Mustad 9671), is an excellent weighted pattern.

On those occasions when the trout are selectively feeding on small flies, try a size 16 or 18 pheasant tail emerger or a glass bead head chironomid. These flies can be suspended under a tiny piece of foam only an inch from the fly.

When golden stoneflies are hatching, try a size 8 weighted nymph with an olive-brown back and creamy yellow belly. Stonefly nymphs crawl to shore to hatch and the adults return to the river to deposit their eggs. Note well: It is the ovipositing adults that bring the largest trout to the surface. There are also huge black and orange stoneflies that hatch in the spring.

Mike Labach: For maximum action on Kootenay trout streams, it is better to cover a lot of water than stay at one pool. We drift the St. Marys and the Elk rivers in rafts and pontoon boats and concentrate on the tiny pockets other anglers might have missed. Every obvious pool has a few trout, but they get pounded by a steady stream of drifting anglers. Try getting your fly into tight places close to the bank. Anywhere a log, root, branch or rock slows the current slightly will hold a trout. Use a bounce cast to push a dry fly under an overhanging branch. If trout are reluctant to rise in the main body of a pool, try the shallow, broken water at the very head of a run. Trout will hold in pockets less than knee deep if there is overhead cover or if the surface is turbulent enough.

Commonly called 'salmonflies', they are best imitated with #4 and 6 long-shank hooks.

From late fall through to early spring, bull trout of more than 10 pounds are caught in the Kootenay River and tributaries: the St. Marys, the Elk, the Bull, the Skookumchuck and others. A few of these char hold over in the rivers through the summer. Bull trout feed primarily on whitefish and kokanee, but will take any fish smaller than themselves. They migrate up from the Kootenay River on their spawning run and readily take a fly at this time, both egg patterns and minnow imitations. Most #2 streamer/bucktails will work, notably the weighted patterns which will sink into the deep holes that bull trout prefer. Note the varying closures and catch regulations.

Look for westslope cutthroat in slightly

Mike Ramsay: Limited backcast area on streams can be extremely frustrating. More often than not, when you finally spot a nice rainbow feeding, it is impossible to present the fly due to limited backcast room. To get around this problem I build my long trout rods using a reel seat with a fighting butt adapter. When faced with limited backcast area, I simply screw in a five- to six-inch fighting butt, effectively converting my rod into a two-handed spey rod. Using a long stiff blank such as the Sage RPL+ 4100, you can easily cast 50 to 60 feet with 10 feet of backcast area. When space permits single-handed casting, I unscrew the fighting butt and keep it in my breast pocket.

slower water than that preferred by rainbow trout. They stay close to shore along outside bends in the river and prefer to hold near boulders or tree roots. Delicate sipping rises seen in tailouts usually indicate the presence of Rocky Mountain whitefish. All Kootenay rivers have great schools of these fish, and they can be surprisingly selective to small flies.

The best dry fly fishing on the St. Marys and Elk is after spring runoff, which normally lasts from late May to June, but sometimes continues well into July. When the rivers warm to about 50 degrees, aquatic insects start to hatch and trout go on the feed. Mid-summer can be scorching hot and the heat will impact the fishing somewhat. Late summer and early fall when the rivers are low and clear is prime time for the dry fly. ✦

Selected Waters

Beaver Ponds

Few anglers know beaver ponds, and most ponds do not show up on maps. Sleuthing is required to seek them out, but ponds offer distinctive, stand-on-your-own-two-feet action for wild trout. That is so even when rivers are in spate or otherwise unproductive. And you'll seldom have company.

Finding them is not difficult. Just driving the backroads, you'll see ponds. Some are right beside highways. Or a creek – never mind how

there only when a hatch or fall make surface feeding worth their while. Keep in mind, too, that trout from downstream rivers often flee summer heat by moving into cooler feeder streams, often ending up in ponds.

Any standard fly or fly technique might prove best, but a sunken fly suspended below a strike indicator and fished dead has special merit. Chironomid larvae/pupae and other sedentary insect forms are standard pond foods and, when trout hold in deep channels separated from

small – may have beaver cuttings nearby. Lacking such clues, any creek that flows through non-precipitous terrain and maintains a relatively constant water volume through the season is worth investigation. Such creeks themselves will likely offer interesting fishing, so this exploration is not at all onerous.

Beaver ponds are, almost all of them, in some stage of a natural siltation process which will eventually transform them to a meadow. A new pond tends to be especially fertile; those near the end of the line are the opposite. The in-between ponds can produce anything from fish-every-cast action for diminutive trout to technically demanding, very slow pursuit of trout that might weigh in the five-pound class.

Small-trout waters dominate, but quite often that is illusory. The eight inchers rising steadily through the day merely represent the younger trout or a strain of early-maturing trout. The larger trout have staked out the prime (usually deeper) bottom-feeding locales and move from

casting positions by weeded shallows, this 'bobber fishing' may be the only effective method.

Dry flies have similar merit. They make it possible to cover any part of the pond and, even when no natural food is on the surface, trout may opportunistically take implausibly large offerings. Pond trout rely mostly on aquatic invertebrates, but terrestrial insects form a substantial part of their diet. A dry fly that suggests it is a beetle, grasshopper, ant or alder worm is therefore a plausible target.

For less obvious reasons, a skated spider, variant or palmer-hackled fly can also work well. Patience, though, is a special virtue on these waters. A pond can seem absolutely barren for much of the day, then mysteriously come alive with feeding trout. Use the waiting time to plot just which log can be teetered onto, which place can be waded to, which place affords backcast room – vital stuff to know when the fishing turns on. ✒

Selected Waters

Small Mountain Streams

While the Elk and St. Marys rivers have definitely been discovered, countless smaller flows in the Rockies are made to measure for those who seek solitude amidst intimate settings. Given the towering mountain backdrops often visible even from the secluded streamsides, angling could easily take a back seat, but there are small mountain gems which hold surprisingly large trout and almost all of them host good numbers of fish in reaches removed from easy road access.

Two Elk River tributaries, Michel Creek and the Wigwam, are superb, crystal-clear streams with well-spaced pools in which trout can be seen delicately rising. The better pools require long hikes to reach, but the rewards are worth the effort. Free-rising westslope cutthroat trout dominate, making floating lines

Ian Forbes: Strike indicators can be made of many materials and serve several functions. Bright wool indicators are used in rivers to keep track of drifting nymphs. The slightest pause of the indicator allows an angler to strike instantly before the trout rejects the fly. Wool indicators are easy to cast and rarely tangle. Small Corkies or foam float indicators allow a weighted fly to be suspended off the bottom, but they make casting difficult. Soft, commercial mold-on indicators are easily attached to leaders, but are not as buoyant as foam or as bright as wool. They do cast better and likely make the best compromise.

Brian Chan: Productive stillwaters experience seasonal changes in water chemistry which affect where and how trout live and feed. Lake turnover is a mixing of the entire water column that changes oxygen, turbidity and nutrient levels throughout the basin. Turnovers occur when lake water temperatures are uniform from top to bottom; a strong wind will initiate the mixing process. The narrow band of oxygenated water formed over the winter is dispersed throughout the water column, resulting in lower levels through the entire lake. Lower oxygen levels in combination with higher levels of hydrogen sulfide, released from the lake bottom, cause the trout to stop feeding for seven to 10 days, or until water chemistry conditions improve. The telltale sign of a lake in turnover is very murky or dirty water and no signs of fish activity.

Unless expertly done, trolling will rarely fool these fish – the largest certainly are wise to continuously moving flies – and anglers who chase rises will more often spook than entice fish to take. More success will be had by letting the fish come to the angler, especially if the anchor is carefully – ultra-cautiously – set on the fringes of an area where fish are concentrated. Stationary craft will not alarm the fish, but too much casting and short, relatively heavy leaders will. This is a game of finesse.

There are definite 'honey holes' where small schools of fish are congregated and working a specific beat. It is possible to antic-

Ron Newman: During spring turnover and as lakes begin to clear, fish often locate in shallow water next to those shorelines with the most wave action. The breaking waves add enough oxygen to reduce stress in the fish and initiate feeding activity. The fish congregate on these shorelines in small to medium-sized schools. Given sufficient 'wave-action oxygen', the fish will begin to feed, providing a great day of fishing during the otherwise slow spring turnover period.

Ian Forbes: Changing to midge-size (#20) hooks may solve a lot of problems in hard-fished lakes. Midge patterns require no more than two or three materials and only five colors: black, olive, brown, grey and tan. Bodies are a simple base of hologram mylar tinsel overwrapped with the appropriate color Superfloss. Allow a thin rib of tinsel to show through. The thorax is one turn of either dubbing, hackle or CDC (Cul de Canard). The fly is fished suspended off the bottom with a bit of foam on the leader, or allowed to settle gently on the marl in front of a feeding trout.

ipate the travel path of feeding fish and set a trap. Once a fly has caught a few fish it should be changed, as the fish quickly become indifferent to the same fly continuously chugging by. After a brief rest, the successful pattern can be tried again.

The fish will feed selectively on Callibaetis mayflies, and on these occasions a #14 *Blue Dun* or *Adams* can be cast and left at rest on the surface awaiting the trouts' return. Any slack in the line should be straightened while waiting, but only a subtle twitch will be needed to entice a nearby fish.

More often, flies need to be sunk within a few inches of bottom. This can be done in two ways: a weighted fly off a long leader and strike indicator connected to a floating line, or a sinking line lying on the bottom. A bit of foam on the leader will keep a sunken nymph from settling too deep in the marl mud. Any of the clear monofilament slow-sinking lines are suitable for this work as they blend into the background and trout are less wary of them.

Rainbows in these lakes average 16 to 22 inches, with a few larger fish; Whitetail Lake also holds eastern brook trout. The lakes can be crowded throughout the fishing season. Both Whiteswan and Premier are in provincial parks and Premier has the advantage of several nearby hike-in lakes ideal for tubers. Nine Bay and Mitten are two lakes south of Golden with similar trout and conditions. ☚

Selected Waters

Largemouth Bass

Largemouth bass have been unofficially introduced (or they migrated on their own) to only a few Kootenay lakes, which is a good thing. Bass are potentially lethal to native salmonids, so it is fortunate that the lakes they inhabit lack the stuff for natural salmonid success. They do complicate stocked trout management, but bass provide high-summer fishing when trout are dour. At Duck Lake bass provide remarkably good fishing in water even squawfish and chubs avoid for the hot part of the year.

For the fly fisher, these bass are an especially available target – a simple matter of their being forced to stay in shallow water. At Duck Lake there isn't anything but shallow water. At the other lakes, the deeper water either remains too cold or is inhabited by rugged native squawfish or stocked trout and char, which grow large enough to intimidate bass. Hence, anglers need only place flies in front of bass whose location is no mystery: shoreline regions with good cover and weedy shoals. A thriving raptor and fish-eating waterfowl population makes short shrift of bass who do not hide well.

At Duck Lake there is a variation on this basic drill. Bass are best located in the deepest spots of this shallow lake, which still leaves a lot of plausible water. And since Duck Lake has so many bass, finding them is no real problem. Poppers, deerhair bugs and the many variations on those themes work well, particularly in early morning and late evening. Wet flies are more consistent and generally produce right through the day.

Fishing amidst weeds and snags is necessary, so sunken flies should be weedless. Several techniques can be employed to produce weedless flies, but one of the best and easiest is to start tying a fly by first attaching a length of stout monofilament and allowing it to extend back like a tail. Tie the fly, then form a loop with the mono which runs under the body to the head and which barely surrounds the hook point.

Deerhair Popper
Hook: Wright McGill popper hook, #2
Tail: 2 dyed yel. & 2 grn. griz. saddle hackle
Hackle: Dyed yel. saddle hackle
Popper Head: Spun, packed & trimmed dyed deerhair
Eyes: Tiny doll eyes
Glue: Soft Body glue/popper head

Such a fly will crawl through the densest weeds, bounce off snags, and still hook bass well.

Darkly hued *Zonker*-style flies seem especially effective, but any large fly can do the trick. It is certainly possible to take bass on #6 to #10 offerings, but more and larger bass will be enticed

Bug Eye Weedless Leech
Hook: Eagle Claw D1197N, #1-2, or Mustad 9671, #2-2/0
Body: Silv. tinsel
Rib: Fine copper wire
Wing/Tail: Thin strip rabbit hide w/fur attached; nat. or dyed blk., maroon, yel.
Eyes: Lead dumb-bell
Weed Guard: 30-lb.-test mono.

by the #2/0s and larger. A three-inch-long *Zonker* is seldom too small, and larger offerings may up the odds on bass over three pounds.

Sinking lines are seldom required and a level #8 floater works admirably in casting large, wind-resistant flies. A six-foot leader is fine; it need not be tapered but should be knotless, for knots will pick up weed and algae. Any retrieve might prove deadly, but very fast and very slow seem the most reliable methods. Almost imperceptible movement regularly does the job, but a fly raced just below the surface with a steady rod lift can trigger strikes from bass that have ignored everything else.

Good largemouth bass lakes include Duck Lake, Baynes Lake, Hiawatha Lake (pond), Jim Smith Lake and Wasa Lake. ◄

Selected Waters

Gerrard Rainbows

I mmense Kootenay Lake remains home to the world's largest strain of rainbow trout despite the often disastrous environmental changes wrought by man. Reliable numbers of record-class Gerrard trout are caught each year in a managed fishery which has established a steady spawning run of about

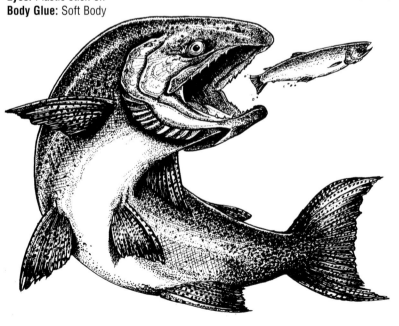

Tube Fly Kokanee
Tube: Plastic Q-Tip w/fuzz removed
Under-Body: Packing foam w/527 glue
Hook Lock: Shrink tube
Thread: Wht. or mono.
Body: Pearl. myl. tube
Wing/Tail: Angel Hair, bait-fish color
Eyes: Plastic stick-on
Body Glue: Soft Body

1,000 fish annually to the Lardeau River redds. Gerrards average 20 pounds and as all anglers well know, very few such trophies come easily. To lure them to the cast fly is to increase the handicap manyfold – anglers must possess a saint-like patience and be willing to suffer long, cold days. The largest fish traditionally are taken between late October and April.

During the warmer months, fly fishers do well on the lake's west arm between Balfour and Nelson. Not unlike a slow-moving river, the west arm is relatively shallow and trout consequently

cruise closer to the surface. Mid-channel riffles marking shoals, such as those found near the channel marker east of Balfour, are good spots to anchor and cast to feeding trout. June offers reliable caddis hatches which continue sporadically during warm summer evenings. Trout cruise the edge of the many shoals extending along the west arm's shore and feed at or near the surface during evenings, early mornings and throughout the fall-to-spring period.

Most Gerrards, however, are caught near Kaslo and those portions of the north arm open to angling. Kootenay Lake's narrow shoreline shoals drop steeply to more than 400 feet. Like chinook salmon following herring, the lake's huge rainbows follow schools of kokanee which, in turn, are keyed to the diurnal vertical migration of mysid shrimp (introduced) and zooplankton.

Trolling lures or large bucktail flies is the local method of choice, but a cast fly will take fish, given the requisite persistence. Trolling one fly on a long line behind the boat – keeping generally to the 15- to 20-foot depth range – is a pleasant way to cruise while scanning for surface sign. A second rod loaded with, for instance, a shooting head coupled to monofilament running line (kept coiled in a plastic tub) allows for quick, accurate distance casts the instant fish are seen – either on the sounder, cruising the shoals or breaking water in chase of kokanee. Flies used are similar to saltwater salmon patterns.

Calm mornings and evenings are key times to spot the Gerrards as they chase kokanee to the surface. Watching for such disturbances with binoculars and then running the boat to within casting distance before quickly launching a fly can be the stuff of high drama. It makes sense for one angler to guide the boat and watch any trolled lines while a second scans with polarized glasses.

Even when feeding trout are found and approached as quickly as wariness allows, as few as one cast in 10 might be rewarded, so this is definitely a game for the true devotee. ➤

Rocky Mountain Journal

It was still early season in the East Kootenays — May 3 — and I was following up on a lead to a new lake. Having just moved to Cranbrook the previous fall, I did that a lot during the past year. The regulations looked good for this lake — a winter-fishing ban and two-fish limit — and its elevation was low enough to guarantee it had been ice-free long enough to have completed spring turnover. I had a reliable report, too, of fast action for two- to three-pound rainbows the previous fall, with a less reliable report of a seven-pounder taken a few years earlier.

The lake turned out to be typical of Kootenay trout lakes. It was less than a mile long, but had some pleasantly mysterious deep water dropping down — abruptly in some areas, gradually in others — from extensive shoals. Its water was clear but had that bit of clouding which usually means good fertility. Only one other angler was out — a white-haired fly fisher anchored well up on a large shoal.

Several parties were camped at the lake, but they appeared uninterested in fishing. Nice. And there seemed to be no chironomids on the lake's surface. That pleased me.

The lake I'd been fishing for the past month and a half always had chironomids, and only chironomids — great clouds of them in the air, solid masses of them emerging at the surface, and hordes of them milling about on the bottom with a zillion or so shrimp. I'd sort of over-dosed on that.

I'd been out on that other lake the late March day its ice melted. This after three earlier days when it hadn't. I was pretty keen to get out. The ice-out fishing should have been spectacular but, handicapped by a leaking rubber boat and not really under-standing this lake's grossly overfed rainbow trout, I caught only two fish. Both went better than two pounds, though, so that should have been enough — but it wasn't. There were these two other anglers who must have released 50 trout between them, and some of those trout were in the five-pound class. I didn't know how they'd done it.

One man was working the bottom in maybe 10 feet of water with what was likely a shrimp imitation, retrieving with very fast two-inch strips. The other was 'bobber fishing' with what I presumed was a chironomid pupa or larva imitation suspended about 10 feet below a strike indicator. Neither of those techniques worked for me — both of my trout came to a *Zonker/Muddler* variation I favor — and I decided trout were just concentrated in the area these guys had staked out.

Maybe they were. I'll never know.

At any rate, the lake became something of an obsession. I was not alone about this. Each day a few more fly fishers would be out and an armada of rowboats, bellyboats and canoes began appearing when the turnover ended and the lake began to boil with rising trout.

Chironomids were the insects drawing those rises and they came off in droves, right through most days, but peaking in early evening. I've seldom seen such consistent hatches, but I've also not seen such inconsistent fishing. The fly fishers were a mostly savvy crew who knew their chironomid lore well, but I never saw more than a very few faring well, and the "high rod" of one evening seldom held that position on the next day. Sometimes no one caught anything. It was all quite wonderful — both the pondering on bad days and the glow when things worked well — but one day I realized that I did not want to tie another chironomid imitation or try even one more variation on chironomid technique. I also wanted to fish

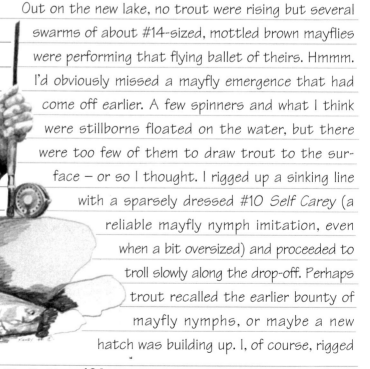

without having to watch and be watched by other anglers. I'd overdosed, simple as that.

Out on the new lake, no trout were rising but several swarms of about #14-sized, mottled brown mayflies were performing that flying ballet of theirs. Hmmm. I'd obviously missed a mayfly emergence that had come off earlier. A few spinners and what I think were stillborns floated on the water, but there were too few of them to draw trout to the surface — or so I thought. I rigged up a sinking line with a sparsely dressed #10 *Self Carey* (a reliable mayfly nymph imitation, even when a bit oversized) and proceeded to troll slowly along the drop-off. Perhaps trout recalled the earlier bounty of mayfly nymphs, or maybe a new hatch was building up. I, of course, rigged up a floating line on another rod and affixed a #14 *Tom Thumb* to it – just in case mayfly duns began appearing.

Nothing struck the trolled *Carey* in the next hour, so I anchored at the edge of a shoal and cast the fly well out into the lake. I started a hand-twist retrieve after counting to 10. Nothing. So I counted to 15 the next time. Twenty proved the magic number. At that depth, trout took on every other cast and, while most were under 10 inches long, several were plumply proportioned 14- to 16-inchers – which is the size I expected. The two- to three-pounders of fall are the same fish as the one-pounders of spring. Trout grow fast hereabouts.

In the interests of science, I changed to a #8 *Spratley*, but it was ignored. So was a #16 *Hare's Ear Nymph*. These trout were onto mayflies all right. On going back to the *Carey* I was back in business.

After releasing a half dozen more trout I'd had enough and pulled up anchor and just rowed around the lake, exploring. Anchored at a similar drop-off, fishing was the same, but here trout began rising uplake from me – all around a tangle of logs. I pulled up anchor and drifted to about 50 feet from the action. I think my first cast was on target, well ahead of a trout that had betrayed his course by rising twice as he moved. The *Tom Thumb* was ignored though, and the cause for that was no great mystery. These fish were coming up for quite sodden, stillborn and spent mayflies that had become concentrated in this area by water current. An emerger pattern featuring no tail, a dubbed brown body, sparse hackle and deerhair wing hung in the film just right, and the trout took it with confidence until they had cleaned off all the surface bounty and moved on.

I hit another little pocket of risers further down the lake and then rowed up on to the big shoal where the other angler had fished. He'd stayed there until leaving a couple of hours earlier and the reason for that was soon obvious. A 100-foot circle of deeper, heavily weeded water had formed there and a school of trout were swimming in it. All were twice the size of any trout I'd taken, but they were darkly hued. The one that struck on my first cast with a *Carey* was 19 inches long but red-sided and lethargic, obviously just recovering from spawning. The others were, I'm sure, the same, so I left them alone and rowed in – planning to return soon and definitely in the fall when the surviving spawners would be recovered and the 14- to 16-inchers would have at least doubled their weight.

I didn't though – a matter of discovering other lakes, several splendid ponds, some river and creek fishing, and even the best bass fishing I know of. Maybe next year. ⌑

— Ron Nelson

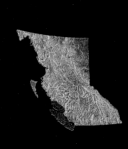

Vancouver

Vancouver Island is as if made for fly fishing. The incredible variety of species available alone places the Island among a select handful of places worldwide. Four species of Pacific salmon are available in two distinct settings – the moving waters of their home streams and at sea in ocean feeding grounds. Two strains of steelhead trout – the winter and summer runs – may be taken on the fly, along with resident rainbow, cutthroat and brown trout. Eastern brook and Dolly Varden char round out the cold-water species, but there is also good fly fishing for trophy smallmouth bass. To this exalted list can be added an ever-growing number of those saltwater species which inhabit rocky headlands, estuaries, lagoons and even the surf itself.

This makes fly fishing a year-round sport on the Island. The winter months usually are reserved for steelhead fishing, although most east coast Island streams now have a December-through-June closure. Sadly, steelhead in many of these streams are facing extinction due to a number of factors, poor ocean survival chief among them. All Island streams have seen a

Island

drastic decline in steelhead numbers, but a few continue to produce sufficient numbers to allow angling.

The Cowichan is one of the few east coast streams with a viable steelhead fishery and the upper river is reserved exclusively for fly fishing. With the exception of Skutz Falls and Marie Canyon, the entire river can be drifted, making the Cowichan a busy river during peak season. Cowichan steelhead smolts appear to survive at sea while the smolts of other east coast rivers do not. Fortunately, ocean survival rates for steelhead from west coast rivers have been far higher.

The Stamp River near Port Alberni and the Gold River across the Island from Campbell River are the two premier winter steelhead streams on the Island. They produce the most fish and have the greatest concentrations of anglers. In steelhead season, both rivers are crowded. With the exception of Stamp Falls Canyon, the entire Stamp River can be drifted, and guides work the lower river daily. In contrast, the Gold is suitable only for kayaks. Steep canyons and dangerous rapids make even rafting hazardous. Winter steelheading on both rivers starts in December and continues into

Foam Black Ant

Hook: Mustad shrt. shank 94838, #10–14
Thread: Blk. nyl.
Body: Closed-cell foam cut w/leather punch, trimmed & colored w/blk. Pantone & lacquered
Hackle: 2 turns of blk.
Wing: None or Zing Wing

Wool Head Sculpin

Hook: Mustad 9671, 2X, #4
Tail: Sandy brn. marabou
Under-Body Head: Flattened lead wire
Under-Body Back 1/3: Packing foam
Body: Sandy brn. dubbing w/marabou fibre tied on top
Fins: Barred body feather from grouse or partridge
Head: Spun wool dubbing chen. trimmed to wedge shape – flat on top & bottom, wide at sides; make dubbing chen. w/different wool color – tan, brn.
Eyes: None or glued-on baby doll

Note: Fly fishes hook point up.

March. By April, most of the steelhead are kelts or are still spawning.

Early spring is the time for steelheading the small streams of the west coast. There are literally hundreds of streams where late-running winter steelhead arrive in March and April. Just about every stream has from a few dozen to a few hundred steelhead that enter during high water. They spawn and leave again within a month. Anglers who shun crowded conditions haunt these tiny streams and use creep and crawl methods to stalk their prey.

Spring is the prime season for the Island trout angler. The season can vary from March on

the lowland lakes of the south to June for the alpine tarns. April is the prime time for the south, while May is the best month for the north. Chironomids, as always, are the first hatch, followed by mayflies, damselflies and dragonflies. There are very few lakes with scuds. Leeches and stickleback minnows fill the void between hatches and are often the mainstay for larger cutthroat.

Well-conditioned rainbow trout to four pounds can be taken in the many fertile farm ponds from Qualicum south to Victoria. These lakes have no spawning streams and are maintained by stocking. Most lakes hold a mix of rainbow and cutthroat trout, but some are stocked exclusively with cutthroat. The north Island has more lakes with only cutthroat trout, and many of these lakes hold only wild stock. Beautifully marked native Dolly Varden char are also found in these waters.

March and April is the time large cutthroat trout gather near their spawning streams in the big lakes. Cutthroat up to 10 pounds are taken in Taylor Arm of Sproat Lake and near the many tributaries of Cowichan, Great Central, Nimpkish, Bonanza, Victoria and Alice lakes. These big cannibals prey on other fish and especially like stickleback minnows. Anglers catch them by trolling minnow patterns, leeches or large dragonfly nymphs.

April and early May is the time to be on the upper Cowichan River. Western March brown mayflies and little brown caddis hatch in great numbers. The resident rainbows, cutthroat and brown trout are there to greet them. The Cowichan is one of the finest trout streams in British Columbia and the fishing can be challenging. Anglers need a variety of patterns and the skills to use them.

By late May the lowland lakes of the south are warming and trout descend to the depths while smallmouth bass move onto their spawning nests. These determined fighters can be found near shoreline structure. Fast-paced bass fishing continues through June, but by mid-summer, evenings are best for productive bass fishing.

June and early July is the season for summer steelhead. Only a few east coast streams have summer runs, but many of the west coast rivers are productive. The Gold and Stamp rivers are both good, but ardent anglers seek the many tiny streams which hold this great gamefish. On the south Island, the San Juan and its tributary, Harris Creek, can be good, as can the Gordon

River, the Nitinat and the Caycuse. There are special restrictions on these rivers.

In the Alberni Canal, the Nahmint River still has a fishable run of summer steelhead, but the numbers in Cous Creek and China Creek are too low for fishing. The Ash, a tributary of the Stamp, is a great little river, and its run is hatchery enhanced. The Heber, a tributary of the Gold, is a delightful little stream that was made famous by Haig-Brown's books.

On the north Island there is the Tahsish, the Zeballos, the Mahatta and the Marble, all west coast streams with fair runs of summer steelhead. The Marble is a special delight as its steelhead come well to the dry fly. Still on the north Island, the Nimpkish and the Tsitika are two east coast rivers with summer steelhead. In the Nimpkish they can be hard to find, and in the Tsitika their numbers are so low that there may be restrictions. This may also be the case for the White River, a tributary of the Salmon River.

Summer is the time to hike in to the alpine lakes of central Vancouver Island. There are several in the Alberni Valley, notably Father and Son, Labour Day and Doran lakes; all have good fishing. For sheer physical beauty it is hard to improve on the lakes of the Forbidden Plateau near Courtenay. Circlet and Moat lakes are set in alpine tundra and surrounded by high mountains. Rainbow trout can be seen rising through the gin-clear water to take a fly.

Summer is also the season to sample the shoreline saltwater fishery. This is when salmon chase herring and needlefish along the beaches. Coho and sometimes chinook often feed very close to shore and can be taken by wading and casting off the beach, or from a boat and casting towards shore. Noteworthy beaches include Bazan Bay near Victoria, Cherry Point near Duncan, the beaches near Qualicum, and beach areas near the Oyster River and Black Creek. During even-numbered years, all the beaches from the Oyster River north to the Keogh have incredible fly fishing for pink salmon.

The summer fishery in Clayoquot Sound near Tofino is becoming famous for its saltwater fly fishing. While a boat is required, techniques are similar to those used on larger lakes. Boats are anchored in protected waters and flies are cast toward beaches, eelgrass flats and alongside kelp beds. The target species is coho salmon, but chinook, cutthroat trout, rockfish and even sole and flounder are taken on the fly. In August and September the fishing is so good anglers will get arm-weary before the salmon stop biting.

September is also the time to return to the rivers. Cutthroat trout fishing on the Little Qualicum can be excellent. All the estuaries have trout moving in and out with the tide. A few early coho salmon will be mixed in with the trout to provide the odd surprise. Chinook salmon return to the rivers in September and, where it is legal to fish for them, can be enticed with a small tinsel fly. Epic battles result when tyee-sized chinook take the fly.

By October the river fishing for coho is in full swing and continues well into November. Chum salmon also start taking the angler's fly. These big bruisers will grab a minnow fly or tiny egg pattern and put up a terrific tussle. An egg

pattern is also the ticket for catching trout in the fall on the upper Cowichan.

By late November die-hard fly fishers will be trolling big minnow patterns for the trophy-sized cutthroats that have returned to the shallows of the big lakes. This will continue until the fall monsoons end the fishing. Anglers then wait for the start of the steelhead season, normally only weeks away. ❧

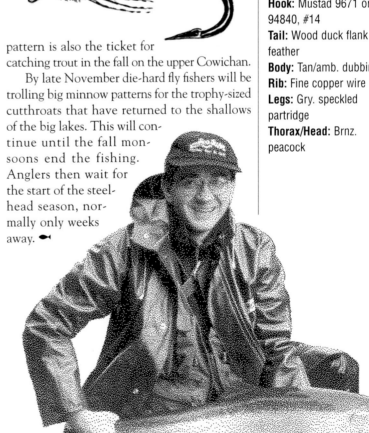

Western March Brown Dun
Hook: Mustad 9671, #14
Tail: Moose mane
Body: Tan/amb. dubbing
Thorax: Orng./brn. dubbing tied under hackle wing
Hackle/Wing: Multi-var. or ging. griz.

Western March Brown Nymph
Hook: Mustad 9671 or 94840, #14
Tail: Wood duck flank feather
Body: Tan/amb. dubbing
Rib: Fine copper wire
Legs: Gry. speckled partridge
Thorax/Head: Brnz. peacock

Steelhead Waters

Vancouver Island still harbors pristine watersheds holding wild populations of steelhead trout which rarely see human visitors – anglers or otherwise. Conversely, many streams have been augmented with hatchery steelhead and are easily reached from the Island's ever-expanding network of highways and logging roads. It is this diversity which gives the Island its unique angling character.

Most Island rivers support runs of winter steelhead which enter fresh water from December through April. Summer-run steelhead inhabit most west coast rivers, but are limited on the east coast to only a few, the Campbell, the White and the Tsitika ranking among the best known. Summer-run fish arrive as early as late June, but the major runs peak between August and October. Sizes for both runs range between four

Ian Forbes: Steelhead are very spooky in low, clear water. Anglers should wear camouflage clothing and approach every pool with caution. Steelhead will hold in surprisingly low water, frequently in the shallow tailouts of pools. Use amber polarized glasses and try to spot the steelhead before planning a fishing strategy. Stay low and make sidearm casts. Don't cast at or over the fish, as the line flash will spook them. Float small #6 or #8 flies in natural buggy colors down to the fish from upstream.

Comet

Hook: TMC 7999, Partridge Wilson, Bartleet, Alec Jackson
Tail: Orng. polar bear & orng. Krystal Flash
Body: Blk. chen. or seal fur
Rib: Silv. tinsel
Hackle: Fl. orng.
Eyes: Brass bead chain
Thread: Red

and 30 pounds, with the average about seven pounds. The waters themselves fall into three distinct categories based on size: rivers, streams and creeks.

Island rivers are those waters best fished with a raft or boat. Boats tend to be used for travel only. When likely-looking pools are encountered during the downstream drift, the boat is beached and wader-clad anglers carefully probe the various nooks and crannies of the holding water. Popular steelhead rivers include the Cowichan, Stamp, Somass, Gold, Salmon, and Nimpkish rivers. It can be difficult to get to the upper reaches of many rivers and may require travel over logging roads with restricted public access at specific times; it is prudent to check locally before embarking.

Streams can be described as those waterways best fished while wading, which takes in the majority of Island steelhead waters. Fly fishing conditions are often ideal; open gravel banks provide ample room for backcasts and crossing from bank to bank is relatively easy at the tailouts of most pools. Some streams, particularly those on the north Island, are deeply colored with tannin leachate from upstream bogs and meadows, making bright flies a must. For the most part, access is via logging roads,

> **Barry M. Thornton:** Hooked steelhead often 'turn tail' and dash downstream. By walking slowly upstream with the rod tip pointed at the fish and your free hand cinching the reel to stop line running out, it is possible to lead the fish back to where it can be played and beached. The trick is to move slowly, allowing the fish to swim up and around boulders, and to not reel in line — if the fish feels vibrations from the reel, it will bolt back downstream. Reel in the slack line as you walk back down to the top of the pool.

but the lower sections of many streams have their own networks of angler/nature trails.

Anglers often fail to recognize the importance of tides to Island steelheading. Steelhead marshal in estuaries prior to ascending their home streams and most often head upriver

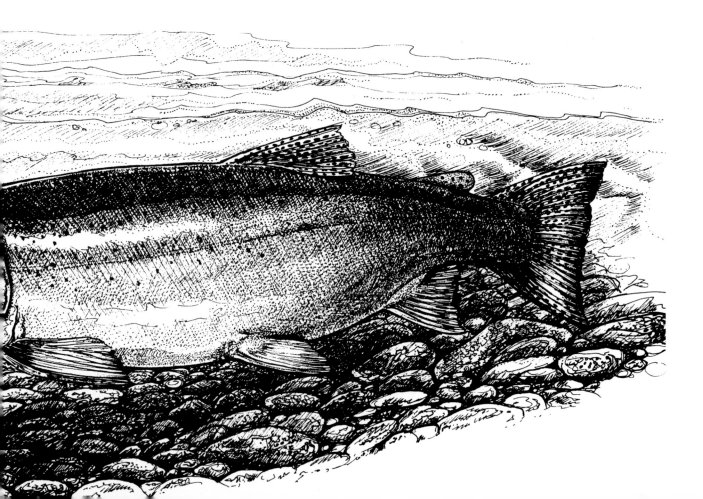

Lady Caroline

Hook: TMC 7999, Partridge Wilson, Alec Jackson, #4–6
Tail: Gold. pheas. breast feather
Body: Mixture of reddish brn. & olv. seal fur
Rib: Flat silv. & fine gold thread
Hackle: Blue heron or blue-eared pheas.
Wing: Brnz. mallard or brn. barred gadwall or widgeon

Klanawa

Hook: TMC 7999, Partridge Wilson, Bartleet Alec Jackson
Tag: Oval silv. tinsel
Butt: Peacock sword
Tail: Gold. pheas. crest
Body: Gold tinsel
Rib: Oval silv. tinsel
Hackle: Nat. blk. hen hackle
Under-Wing: Wht. polar bear
Over-Wing: Orng. polar bear

during high tides or during the first hour of the ebb tide. This re-entry into fresh water can occur at any time of day, but remains tide dictated. Experienced anglers concentrate on the lower portions of streams early in the ebb tide and during the critical few hours following high slack. Fish hooked at these times tend to be chrome bright and often have sea lice still clinging to their skin. Freshly arrived from the salt, they are very active and provide the kind of knee-shaking angling for which steelhead are justly famous. Popular systems include the Quatse, Cluxewe, Keogh, and Nahwitti rivers in the north Island; and the Eve, Quinsam, Oyster, Puntledge, Qualicum, Englishman and Nanaimo rivers on the east coast. Famous West Coast streams include the Marble, Heber, Muchalat, Toquart, and Zeballos rivers. South Island steelhead streams include the Sooke, San Juan, and Gordon rivers.

Island creeks tend to be self-contained, complete watersheds in their own right, with access to salt water. They should not be overlooked simply because of their small size; many are highly productive salmonid producers. Generally heavily overgrown with a dense canopy of overhanging vegetation, creeks can be difficult to fish. On some, the tips of 10-foot rods will reach clear across to catch on the far bank's shrubbery, making roll casts a must. River-bank access trails tend to be overgrown and anglers can expect the usual attendant difficulties; bring the wader patching kit. Popular creeks include Waukwaas, Black, China, Cous and Harris.

Steelhead fly patterns are as varied as steelheaders themselves. Generally, bright pink patterns such as the *Thor* and dark patterns like the *Skunk* are the most effective for winter fish. It almost goes without saying that the only way to get a winter steelhead to strike is to put the fly down immediately in front of the fish, so presentation definitely takes precedence over pattern choice. Successful summer steelhead patterns include the *Thor* and *Skunk*,

Barry M. Thornton: Steelhead often take just as the fly line begins to belly in mid-stream. Attempting to strike in the normal manner will only lift the belly off the water and give the fish slack line. Instead, strike sideways, horizontal to the river, snapping the tip upstream. This retains the full extension of the bellied fly line and gives striking power to set the hook.

but the *Bomber* and the *Steelhead Bee* allow for surface action.

A healthy hatchery program has increased Island steelhead catches during the past two decades and provides a quality steelhead fishery in a few select rivers, the Stamp and the Quatse prime among them. The Somass River and its two tributaries, the Sproat and the Stamp, together account for more than 50 per cent of all steelhead caught on Vancouver Island over the past three seasons. This is strong confirmation the current hatchery program, in conjunction with other watershed enhancement programs, has improved the fisheries in this region of the Island. The fact remains, however, that most Island streams are populated with wild steelhead only.

In recent times the top 10 Vancouver Island steelhead streams have included the Stamp, Somass, Quinsam, Quatse, Nanaimo, Little

Ian Forbes: The rainstorms so common to Vancouver Island draw steelhead upstream. In high, murky water they invariably travel close to shore and will hold in the shallows right next to the bank. Good spots to fish under these conditions are small pockets where tiny feeder creeks enter the main river.

Qualicum, Englishman, Cowichan, Big Qualicum and Gold. It is of interest that the Gold is managed as a non-hatchery catch-and-release stream and usually produces a catch of 5,000 wild steelhead annually. In the past two years there has been a drastic steelhead decline in mid-Island east coast streams. A fisheries management plan has been initiated to address the low number of returning adults to these popular east coast watersheds. ◄

Clayoquot Coho

Catching coho salmon in open ocean waters with a cast fly is not only possible, but also highly effective, as increasing numbers of saltwater fly fishers discover each summer at such west coast destinations as Clayoquot Sound. Leaving Tofino, anglers immediately encounter the shallow, sandy Clayoquot backwaters where ball-ups of prey fish – usually needlefish – are a common sight. The backwaters are typically 15 to 20 feet deep, so coho have little difficulty herding the needlefish schools into tightly massed balls, each prey fish seeking the centre of the swarm. While several hunters slam through the school, raking and crippling their prey, feeding coho remain below, picking off the tumbling casualties. The key to fishing such ball-ups is to approach carefully (cut the motor and drift alongside) and then give the fly sufficient time to sink below the ball before stripping. Feeding birds are the tip-off, but do not be fooled by krill-feeding gulls. Krill patches are much less compressed and the birds consequently will be spread over a far greater area.

Clayoquot Sound's extensive backwaters give way to the open Pacific in a splintered maze of islands. Huge swarms of prey fish congregate among the islands anywhere the tidal current is stemmed. Indentations or small bays within the kelp forests which hug the islands are prime locations, but even the slots between the islands themselves will have slower-flowing streams where both hunter and hunted play their never-ending game. With the flow streaming from right to left, both boats pictured are positioned to fish either the current seams adjacent to the boat or the kelp back eddies astern. Due to the strong flow in these open waters, herring are a more likely choice than needlefish patterns.

Depicted above is a typical Clayoquot kelp bed scene. Both boats are strategically positioned to take advantage of the tidal current, in this case streaming from right to left (note how the kelp is bent by the current). Merely tying to the kelp and casting is not enough, and while there are several other likely locations in the scene, the two anglers pictured have chosen the prime spots. As the current streams past the face of the kelp patch, it curls back in behind to fill any depressions, much the way river water curls in behind boulders or other obstructions to form back eddies. Such eddies mark the prime fishing water, but not all eddies are created equal.

The boat on the far left, while positioned perfectly to fish the pocket, or mini-eddy, just aft of the boat, runs the risk of being jammed against the kelp as the tide/current builds, thus placing the angler in a less favorable casting position (and likely requiring an anchor be set off the stern to hold the boat out). The big back eddy in the centre will absorb much of the building current's force, leaving the angler on the right to fish through the tide without shifting position or the need to set a tide-stemming anchor.

Prey fish such as herring and needlefish use the eddies to escape the current. Coho haunt the current seam, shown in the foreground, and dart in and out of the kelp eddies to feed. The big centre eddy will always hold some feeding coho and drifting schools of prey fish, but the action is scattered, more hit and miss. The mini-eddies will provide the most consistent fishing, but casts should be made across the current and the fly allowed to swing downstream before retrieving along the current seam and up through the eddy immediately aft of the boat. Beware:

Coho regularly follow and take the fly within inches of the surface.

The drawing at the bottom of the page shows the same scene with the tide reversed (flooding). Note how the boats have been repositioned (good anglers, these) to take advantage. As so often when fly fishing, shrewd observation is crucial (keen-eyed anglers will have picked up the seals basking in these drawings).

Submarine reefs and hummocks are ideal locations for fly fishers seeking both chinook and coho salmon. The trick lies in finding them and then setting up so the fly may be properly presented. Aside from using charts and depth sounders, there are surface indicators as well. In this compressed drawing of the submarine reef near Clayoquot's Catface Mountain, the surface of the water on the downstream (left) side is roiled, in contrast to the calmer water upstream. The waves are caused when the tidal current is forced upward by the reef, which also results in a vertical eddy immediately on the downstream side.

Prey fish lurk in this eddy, seeking shelter from strong tidal flows. Typically, the water ranges in depth from 20 feet on the upstream side to 12 feet over the reef or bar and 25 feet on the downstream side. Two possible anchoring positions are shown, but note the boat is tied off at the bow – tying off amidships will almost certainly result in a capsize as the tide builds. Coho hunt behind the school, picking off stragglers swept out of the relative safety of the vertical eddy, so casts should be well out on the downstream side. Since prey fish will be more heavily concentrated in specific locales, expect to shift anchor several times.

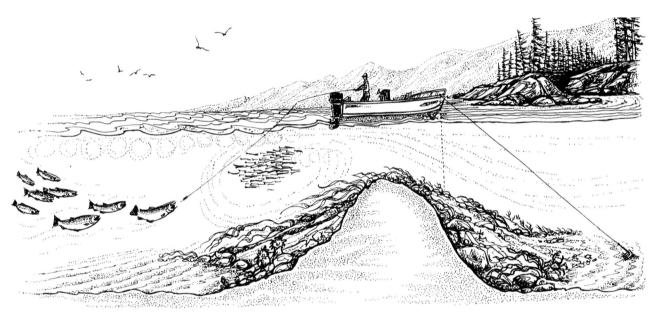

Canny anglers, lured by the sight of coho leaping in shallow-water bays, have discovered needlefish enter shallow, sandy-bottomed bays in the evening to bury themselves in the sand, leaving only a small portion of their heads showing. Coho follow this evening migration and pluck the needlefish from the sand, scooping as they plunder. Constantly leaping coho are attempting to clear their gullets of sand (stomach contents have revealed as many as 30-odd needlefish and an amazing amount of sand). While retrieves are still being pioneered, some Clayoquot fly-fishing guides are retrieving straight up through the water column with good results. Vertical retrieves likely best mimic the up-and-down body attitude of the needlefish in this situation.

Selected Waters

Trout Streams

No two Island trout streams are truly similar. Each is unique. Even sister rivers like the Big and Little Qualicum differ significantly. Although they are about the same size and length, and flow in the same direction to enter the Strait of Georgia only a few miles apart, there the similarity ends. The Big Qualicum is an artifically altered river with a dam-controlled flow. Its pools are designed and built by engineers. The Little Qualicum is a natural stream that relies on nature for its flow, and its pools are formed by floods.

If there is one common thread among Island streams, it lies in the fact that the insect hatches are sporadic and the trout migratory. Only the Cowichan has reliable hatches: the western March brown mayfly and the little brown caddis, among others. This may explain why the Cowichan also holds the most resident trout.

Unless there is an obvious insect hatch, anglers tend to cover the water randomly rather than casting to specific fish. Fly patterns are inclined to be generic. Surprisingly few are required, providing those employed are well presented. Trout will feed selectively during a major hatch; at other times they are opportunistic.

The three most important insects are mayflies, caddisflies and stoneflies. Mayflies on Vancouver Island are usually small, requiring hooks no larger than size 12. The common colors for both nymphs and adults are tan, brown or olive. Island caddis pupae are usually pale olive with a dark grey thorax. The most common sizes are 10, 12 and 14. The adults are commonly a mixture of grey and brown. A deerhair caddis is one of the best searching patterns when no hatch is visible. The same pattern with a yellow body will suffice for the stonefly hatch. The golden stonefly is the most important of that species on the Island. The nymphs crawl along the bottom, and imitations must mimic this behavior. The golden stone has a bright yellow belly and an olive brown back.

As in all fishing, presentation is more important than the pattern being used. Good casting skills and total line control are needed. Distance casting is seldom necessary, but a variety of presentations is required – curve, reach and dump casts are regularly called for.

Best seasons for Island rivers are spring and fall; summer is generally poor because rivers are too low and warm, but estuary areas can be good in late summer for migratory cutthroat trout. The best insect hatches occur in April and May. By June, only the evenings are productive, barring those exceptions which prove the rule. By late fall, trout will be feeding heavily on salmon eggs.

Other trout streams to consider include the Nanaimo, the Stamp, the Marble, the Elk, the Nimpkish and the Muchalat. ✦

Little Brown Caddis
Hook: Mustad 9671, #14
Thread: Match body color
Body: Med. brn. spun fur dubbing
Wing: Brn. dyed deerhair tied sparse & low atop dubbed body
Hackle: Med. brn.
Head: Spun deerhair

Selected Waters

Estuaries

Estuaries are synergy. They are places where the urge to reproduce, the need for sustenance and the pendulum of tidal flow combine to concentrate fish in greater numbers than any one part of this equation would otherwise make possible. Being a successful estuary fly fisher requires sound knowledge of two entities: time of year and tides. Mastery of these two factors, coupled with heightened observation and sightfishing skills, will produce exciting and favorable results.

Pink Hector

Hook:TMC 5262, #8
Thread: Hot pink Monocord
Rib: Silv. oval tinsel or silv. wire
Tail: Pink Krystal Flash
Body: Hot pink chen.
Wing: None
Note: Great for pinks – can be tied weighted for deeper water conditions.

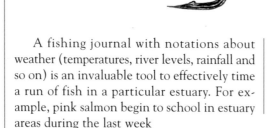

A fishing journal with notations about weather (temperatures, river levels, rainfall and so on) is an invaluable tool to effectively time a run of fish in a particular estuary. For example, pink salmon begin to school in estuary areas during the last week of July, with the run

Sparse Stickle

Hook: TMC 9394 #8, #10
Thread: Blk. Monocord
Rib: Fine copper wire
Tail : None
Body: Silv. Diamond Braid
Wing: Two griz. hackles (tied matuka style)
Note: Great for sea-run cutthroat and pinks.

Dave's White Eye

Hook: TMC 9394, #8,#6
Thread: Blk. Monocord
Rib: None
Body: None
Wing: Peacock sword over wht. polar bear hair
Eye: Holographic, epoxy in place
Note: Dave Wallden's pattern is great for spooky coho.

peaking in the first and second weeks of August. For coho, monitor the beaches from mid-September until the end of October. Sea-run cutthroat trout are available to fly fishers virtually all year. While the various salmon runs will displace them from beach areas, cutthroat will follow the salmon upriver on their spawning run to feed on eggs. While some populations of cutthroat then remain in the river until they begin spawning themselves, others will make a brief return journey to the estuary to feed before re-entering the river to spawn, normally between February and April.

Fishing the correct tide is absolutely crucial in estuaries. There are certainly site-specific variations, but as a rule the most productive parts of the tide change to fish are the middle two hours of the rising and dropping tides. More importantly, the tidal current needs to be moving well (large changes in height in short periods of time are best). When the tide starts to run strongly, it will seem as if a switch has been thrown: fish will show everywhere and their feeding (or predatory) instincts will be on full alert.

At these times, sightfishing skills become paramount, and keen-eyed anglers will be able to target boiling and jumping fish. Locating and then leading a school of fish with quick, precise casts while scanning peripheral areas for the next objective makes for incredibly exciting and demanding angling.

No special gear is required for estuary fishing, but some useful additions might include a stillwater head for your dry line for use during low water levels, some fluorocarbon tippet material, and a half-dozen each of the recommended patterns.

Some of the Island's more productive estuary areas can be found in the Cluxewe and Oyster rivers.

Selected Waters
Island Chironomids

Most small Island lakes are acidic, with the water often stained a weak tea colour. Lakes near dairy farms or communities with septic fields will be high on nutrients but low on oxygen. Yet many of these small lakes, particularly on the south Island where lower annual rainfall allows nutrients to accumulate, are good trout producers. Chironomids are the main food source in these waters, thanks to their ability to thrive in oxygen-poor, silt-bottomed lakes.

evening. In April, the most productive time is between 5:00 p.m. and 7:00 p.m. During the day, the best strategy is fishing the bottom, either with a long weighted leader off a floating line or a fast-sinking line fished straight below the boat. In either case, the fly should remain suspended off the bottom.

As with all chironomid fishing, line and leader must form a straight, direct connection back to the rod – takes are usually very subtle, requiring a tight, straight line to detect.

Chironomids take on the color of their surroundings, making reddish brown the most common hue here. Very few Island lakes have the huge bombers found in the Interior; the most common sizes can be matched with size 14 or 16 hooks. When chironomids hatch in large numbers, Island trout will feed selectively – even freshly stocked fish will feed selectively.

Most chironomid patterns will work if closely matched to the naturals, but thinly dubbed bodies of fur ribbed with tinsel or Super Floss bodies ribbed with wire are standard for Island waters. Patterns are sometimes more effective with the addition of Krystal Flash or glass bead-heads.

More important is where, when and how they are fished. On lower Vancouver Island, chironomids may start hatching in February, given a mild winter. Normally the season starts in mid-March and continues through April. While a rise may occur during the day, the best surface action usually takes place in the

In late winter, trout may be closer to shore where there is more oxygen. This is especially true in years when the lakes freeze over or if the lake is nutrient-rich due to nearby farm runoff. This explains why shorebound anglers regularly outfish trollers during the Island's winter season.

A variety of Vancouver Island lakes fit this description. Elk, Beaver, Prospect and Langford lakes near Victoria have good chironomid fishing. Langford has some very fat rainbows and bass. Further north, Dugan and Fuller lakes both have very nice rainbows that grow fat on chironomids. Tiny Chemainus Lake is almost exclusively a chironomid lake, as are Timberland and Crystal lakes near Nanaimo. ➤

Selected Waters

Smallmouth Bass

It is no longer a secret that southern Vancouver Island boasts a superb smallmouth bass fishery. From Spider Lake near Qualicum to Prospect Lake near Victoria and St. Mary's Lake on Saltspring Island, there are more than a dozen lakes containing bass. In many of these waters, numbers of trophy-sized fish form a significant part of the population, providing an exciting challenge through the summer when trout fishing is at its slowest.

Bass are predacious and pugnacious by nature. They will eat anything smaller than themselves and are curious to boot, regularly sampling likely-looking items. Leeches, tadpoles, small fish, chironomids and other insects all form part of the diet, but impressionistic flies will outperform more imitative patterns. The *Woolly Bugger* is one of the best bass flies ever designed, but even the unlikely orange-bodied *Werner Shrimp* is effective, both on the surface and down deep. Patterns designed to trigger an aggressive response work well, but there are times when the bass will be surly and difficult to entice.

Small to medium-sized bass tend to school for protection. The larger fish, those over three pounds, are more likely to be solitary. True ambush feeders, bass lurk near structure – lily pads, floating mats of vegetation, submerged trees – and rarely roam in search of food, preferring to strike when unsuspecting prey ventures too close. Casting into known structure or cover is far more effective than trolling, and delicate, accurate casts are required – into lanes amidst lily pads, alongside submerged trees, or into small pockets of water behind heavy cover.

Wrestling bass out of such locations is no mean feat. Built for short bursts of speed rather than long runs, bass often take to the air the moment the hook is set, then plunge and twist with the tenacity of a wrestler. Determined fighters, good bass will tire the wrists of most anglers and a full day of good bassing will be long remembered. Patience is required since bass can be slow to launch their attack; it is not unusual to wait a full minute before retrieving after casting to a likely location.

May and June are the spawning months and regulations stipulate all bass caught during this time be released. Males guard the young and they take the job seriously. Fishing then is almost too easy and many anglers question the ethics of fishing during the spawning/guarding period. With proper handling, bass can be caught many times with no ill effect. Grasping them by the lower jaw to remove the hook is accepted practice.

Other lakes in which to seek this introduced species include Long Lake, Quennel Lake, Shawnigan, Glen, Langford, Oliphant, Beaver/Elk and Matheson. Besides St Mary's, Cusheon Lake on Saltspring Island also has good smallmouth bass fishing, and Langford Lake near Victoria holds bass weighing in excess of seven pounds.

Island Journal

Throughout my years of fly fishing, I have shared campfires and dinner tables with many 'well-seasoned' anglers. These monitors of "how great the fishing used to be" frequently made it seem like the time had come to hang up my rod and waders and leave the beaches altogether. No longer. Last season marked the beginning of the return to the glory years on Vancouver Island beaches and suddenly everything changed. The much-revered coho returned in unimaginable numbers and, best of all, this was no accident. While the recent commercial and sport fishing closures produced regrettable hardship for commercial fishers, guides and lodges, the results were unequivocal: never in recent memory have there been so many fish at the estuaries and beaches as there were last fall.

One old-timer I met claimed to have released 170 coho since the first one of the season leapt from the water at his favorite beach. It sounded more to me like a statement of lifetime achievement than a one-season total, but I was about to discover otherwise.

Arriving at first light after a three-hour drive to a Courtenay/Comox-area beach, partner David Wallden and I found the conditions less than ideal. The wind had blown up to the point that casting would be difficult and a light rain contributed to that West Coast feeling. Nevertheless, we geared up with expectant haste and made our way to the beach.

At first there was no visible evidence of fish. The pounding waves had stirred up the normal assortment of 'lettuce' and jetsam, so we had to wade out thigh deep to reach clean water. As the sky started to brighten, we spotted our first fish. They were farther along the beach, off a small point that sloped away from the beach and estuary. Both David and I had tied on chartreuse flies that were weighted to swim with the hook point up, and upon arrival at the point we began to cast them to a large school of coho that was within 20 feet of shore. David immediately hooked a fish that accelerated along the drop-off, breaking him off on some barnacled rocks. It would be the first of many fish that never quite made it into our hands, but was no less exciting for the slightly truncated fight.

By mid-morning the tide had begun to flood and was moving well off the end of our point. The rain had stopped and the sun had come out to reveal a scene so spectacular it made us just stop and stare for a moment. As each jade-colored wave crested and rolled towards shore, schools of coho coursed along its length like electricity through a wire, each fish delineated as if frozen by a camera's flash. Within casting range there were never fewer than 30 or 40 fish. It is a sight I will never forget.

Jolted out of our reverie, we began casting our stillwater lines beyond and slightly ahead of each group of fish, retrieving in short, rapid, six-inch strips. When the strikes came, they were heavily weighted attacks that literally tore the line from our hands, snapping all slack line off the water's surface in an instant. Nearly every fish showed us why coho are spoken of in such reverent tones by fly fishers.

By the end of the next two hours, I had released eight coho, all bright, active fish that had shown me lots of backing and stretched my line perfectly straight. All of the fish had taken the #8 chartreuse fly.

David had enjoyed similar success, but it now became apparent the fish were no longer interested in our offerings, despite good presentations and altered retrieves. Naturally it was at this point that a school of noticeably larger fish caught our attention. They were slightly farther out than the fish we had been hooking, but still within reach. Time was the critical factor now — could we solve the puzzle before the fish moved off?

A brief but intense discussion on fly selection left David still using the first fly, while I changed to a blue version of the same pattern. The results were immediate and bone jarring. On the first cast I hooked a much larger fish than had so far been fooled, and it took such a sharp and prolonged run that it had rapped the reel handle on my thumb no fewer than four times before I could move my hand away. After a protracted battle which culminated in the famous 'coho death roll', I used the waves to surf him closer until I could tail him.

He was a magnificent, solid (and honest), 12-pound buck, unblemished by nets or seal attack and with the beautiful translucent violet stripe above his lateral line, for which coho are so well known.

I hooked several more fish before bottoming out in a second period of inactivity. It didn't take long to arrive at the logical conclusion: the fish had seen enough of my blue fly. I changed once more, this time to a red version in the same pattern. Once again, on the first cast with the new fly I hooked a fish which fought brilliantly, causing my leader to throw off a bow wave as it zipped through the water.

We might have called it quits at that, but the sight of occasional 20–plus-pound fish launching from the troughs of the waves was all the inspiration we needed to stay put, never mind the thrashing we were taking from the ocean. I could tell from the sound of Dave's reel that he too had changed flies and was enjoying the same action I was, but I also knew that our retreat was imminent due to the height of the tide.

Finally, at 2:00 in the afternoon, the tide had risen to the point that the fish were effectively out of casting range. Our stomachs were signalling that lunch was well overdue, so we proceeded to the nearest log to sit down. Our shoulders and wrists were aching from the strain of the morning's fishing, but two bigger smiles had never graced our faces. We had been fishing for eight hours and had, between us, released 36 coho, hooking and losing perhaps that number again. We sat in silence for awhile, each of us remembering our most exceptional fish and realizing that, if for just this one day, we had recaptured something of the historic heyday of Vancouver Island's beach fishing.

David turned to me with a laugh and said, "You know, I don't think I care if I die now."

Amen. ⊷

— Ian Roberts

Chapter 6

Vancouver

Southwestern British Columbia would seem an unlikely candidate for designation as a quality angling mecca. Its mix of skyscrapers, urban sprawl and associated 'development' cloaks the fact another world exists amidst and adjacent to its concrete jungles. Unique in all of urban North America, Vancouver and surrounds legitimately boast the kind of angling more often associated with far-flung destinations. Solid resource management coupled with hatchery and stocking programs ensure reliable – often unbelievable – angling for five species of Pacific salmon, sea-run and resident cutthroat, steelhead, rainbow trout, Dolly Varden and bull char in a diverse range of waters and settings.

In no other North American metropolitan region could an angler start the day casting a fly for summer-run steelhead, probe the shoals of an

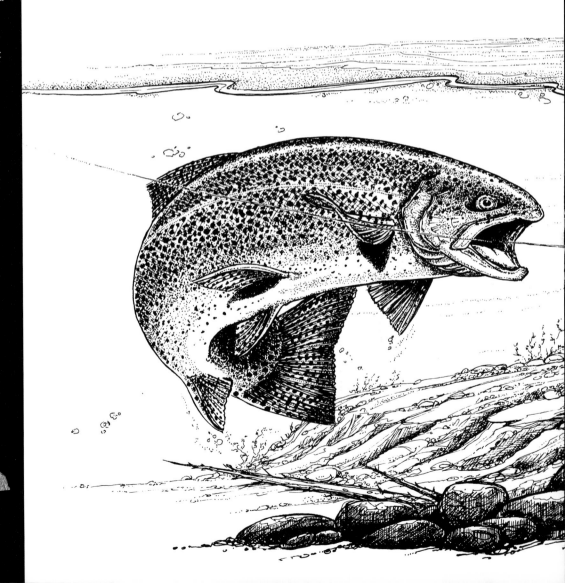

Coast Mountains

alpine tarn through the afternoon, and still be in time for an evening emergence of Ephemerella Grandis on a river only moments from the downtown core.

For all this wealth of opportunity, river angling is the region's forte, thanks in no small measure to the Fraser River, North America's greatest free-flowing producer of Pacific salmon. Salmon and steelhead are present in almost every river, stream and slough connected directly

KCK Red/Orange

(Contributed by Kelly Davison)

Hook: TMC 5263 or similar, #6
Thread: Flymaster Plus 2/0
Tail: Red hackle fibres
Body: Rear half–fluor. red plastic chen., front half–fluor. orng. plastic chen.
Throat: Coachman brn. hackle
Wing: Teal flank feather
Over-Wing: 5 strands pearl. Krystal Flash

or indirectly to tidewater. Many host one or more anadromous species all year long, as well as resident rainbow trout, Dolly Varden and predatory sea-run cutthroat, which constantly prowl between fresh and salt water. On any given day of the year it is possible to fish a stream and tempt one or more species to the fly.

Chinook salmon – both the red and white strains – run throughout the year, coming in as early as March and April on the Campbell and the Fraser. The main runs enter systems such as the Harrison, Capilano and Chilliwack/Vedder in mid- to late summer, bullying their way into the deep pools where a well-presented fly might readily take fish of trophy proportions. Steadily increasing in both size and quantity over recent years, chinook are giving rivers such as the Chilliwack new reputations for gargantuan fish – chinook in the 50-plus-pound class have been taken.

The silvery coho, however, remain the most coveted of salmon for the region's growing fly fishing population. These fish enter all major area waterways from September to December. Anglers approach coho more scientifically than they do other salmon, and a number of patterns, such as the *KCK* and various alternative *Rolled Muddlers*, have been developed as a result. An early run of coho, which enters the Seymour and Capilano rivers in May, is regularly greeted by a legion of anglers.

Sockeye show up in the Fraser in the summer

Barry Brommeland: Moderate climate makes winter fly fishing on our local lakes possible, provided they are ice free. Forget fishing the surface. Fish deep, with high-density lines and leaders as long as 20 feet. This makes for ugly casting, but the fish are consistently deep, more so as water temperature drops. Structure draws in winter trout, and such areas should be carefully explored. Since fish are not aggressive in cold water, they must be tempted at close range. Use a depth sounder to locate fish and then drop the fly right on top of them. Fish very slowly and be patient.

anglers, rapidly became a quarry of fly fishers, thanks both to their vast numbers and their incredible acrobatics following a hookset. River fishing for sockeye is relatively new, its origins dating to 1993, but fly fishers were quick to respond and a host of established patterns and strategies is now in place.

Pink salmon enter the Fraser during odd-numbered years and, like sockeye, arrive in incredible numbers, normally starting in late July. Averaging between four and six pounds and showing a marked preference for shallow water, they are an ideal fish for the fly rod. Ever inventive, growing numbers of fly fishers are learning to take these hard-running fish on specially adapted dry flies fished in much the same manner as when angling for summer steelhead.

Chum salmon enter the rivers at about the same time as coho and take the fly more willingly.

Kelly Davison: There are three important techniques the coho fly fisher should know. Always keep the rod tip low to the water while retrieving. If the rod is held straight out two to three feet above the water, the belly of the line falls, creating a completely different retrieve. Second, always strip in a few feet of line immediately following the cast to straighten the leader. Coho are notorious for picking up the fly as it is sinking. If the leader is not straight and the fish hits the fly, detecting the strike is difficult, and the hookset impossible. Finally, always commence the retrieve slowly, increasing in speed until the fly is within a few feet of the rod tip.

and, once opened to

Second largest of the Pacific salmon, they will tax anglers' gear and stamina to the limit. Not surprisingly, the term 'dog salmon' is falling into disuse as more and more anglers discover the sheer excitement of presenting a fly to large and clearly visible fish which, once hooked, fight in a style reminiscent of the largest steelhead.

Summer steelhead numbers, never great, have declined further in recent years, but for those who have become addicted to tracking these rare prizes, an investment of many hours over long days is small payment for the reward of seeing a dazzling summer-run explode from the water on being pricked by a *Grease Liner*, *G.P.* or *Glo Bug*. The Chehalis, Seymour, Capilano and Silverhope all have small runs which lure a loyal following of dedicated anglers.

Winter steelhead numbers are higher, and while many runs have arrived by January or

February, angling is better in March and April, after water temperatures have moderated sufficiently for the fish to overcome the low metabolic rates of winter. During the coldest months the fish will rarely move more than a foot or two to intercept a fly. Fish typically average between eight and 18 pounds, but rivers such as the Chilliwack produce fish of 20-plus pounds.

Small to medium-sized streams such as the Skagit and Sumallo hold good populations of rainbow trout and provide anglers with a unique opportunity: wild trout only moments off the freeway. Mandatory release regulations have had

an impact on fish sizes; 20-inch fish are increasingly common. Mayflies, stones and caddis are the mainstays on these idyllic trout streams. Dolly Varden and bull trout are available in surprisingly good numbers and sizes – far larger, in fact, than might be expected in such typically nutrient-poor flows. A fertilization program is being tested on several streams (Big Silver Creek, for instance) which may increase aquatic insect populations and fish size and abundance. Preliminary results look promising.

Lakes in the region tend to be oligotrophic, largely due to the flushing action resulting from high annual rainfall, but nutrient loading is in any case poor to begin with. Exceptions are lakes such as Morgan in the Stave Lake watershed and those few waters with reputations for larger trout, Ivy and Mosquito in the Whistler\Pemberton area prime among them. Even marginally productive lakes, it is worth remembering, will hold larger specimens provided populations remain relatively low, as in those waters with limited spawning potential.

Given good populations of prey species such as stickleback or kokanee, lake-resident cutthroat will grow to trophy sizes even in nutrient-poor water. The lakes of the Powell Forest on the north Sunshine Coast produce cutthroat trout of exceptional sizes and angling pressure remains relatively light. Lakes such as Goat, Nanton,

Lois and Powell all hold wild fish which regularly reach double-digit weights.

Closer to Vancouver, the Whistler area provides a mix of low-lying coastal and high-country lakes such as Garibaldi, surrounded by glaciers and full of beautiful trout, some reaching respectable sizes. Branching from the Fraser Valley, the rugged Pitt, Alouette, Stave and Chehalis valleys all hold lakes offering fair to good fishing. Sayers (Cedar) Lake is easily reached and can provide some great moments. The rearing hatchery at the lake's south end is a focal point for escaped fry and broodstock fish, as well as wild stock. Anglers never know if the next cast will produce a fish of 10 inches or 10 pounds – one is as likely as the other. (The bubble zone around the hatchery area exists for the protection of fish and should be respected.)

The Harrison Lake area offers a mix of largely clear, mud-bottomed waters interspersed with swamps and beaver ponds. These are classic chironomid waters, providing by-the-book hatch-matching from March to May. Other important food items include dragonflies, Callibaetis mayflies and Hyalella scuds. On the west side of Harrison Lake, Wolf, Francis and Wood lakes all produce well, while Trout and Moss lakes are good bets on the east side. Fish are on the smallish side (between eight and 14 inches), but several in the low 20s are taken each year.

The Chilliwack and Skagit valleys are known for the kind of alpine lakes anglers dream about. These are waters for those who are willing to put in the effort required to attain solitude within striking distance of the city – which means walking in. The rewards are eager rainbow and cutthroat trout, which will explode on the surface, full of the frenzied energy typical of the short high-country season. Pierce, Lindeman, Greendrop, Flora and Eaton lakes all fish well from the end of June to the start of October. Given the short season, anglers can expect many crossover hatches – the seasonal evolution, which takes six or more months elsewhere, is compressed into three months or less in the alpine. ><>

Kevin Longard: A derivative of Colonel Carey's famous pattern, this soft-hackle-style fly is extremely versatile. In both lake and stream, it is a good emerging sedge imitation. Thickly dubbed and teased, it doubles nicely as a dragonfly nymph. Tied sparse with a thin body, a damselfly nymph pattern is created. The Krystal Flash mimics the glistening air bubbles which sheath caddis pupae, and acts as an enticement when imitating other lifeforms. As a searching pattern or during low activity periods, this fly is hard to beat. A simple strip retrieve often suffices in lakes. In moving water, punctuate a dead drift with short, quick strips.

Olive Krystal Carey
(Contributed by Kevin Longard)
Hook: Mustad 3399 or similar, #6-12
Thread: Unithread 6/0 olv.
Body: Coarse dubbing, olv.
Hackle: Blu. phase pheasant rump
Over-Wing: Olv. Krystal Flash

Ken Ruddick: Dragonflies inhabit the muddy, weedy areas of lakes, and that is exactly where the wise angler will fish nymph patterns. If the fly isn't hanging up occasionally, some of the best water is being missed. When there is an undercut bank along the shoreline, allow the fly to land right against it and sink – even if the water is only a couple of feet deep. Intermittent twitches with the rod tip will cause the dragonfly nymph to rise and fall as it is manoeuvred through shoreline vegetation. When casting along the drop-off, allow the fly to settle to the bottom. Retrieve it in 10-inch intervals, leaving it to resettle in between. As fish cruise along, the disturbance in the mud will attract them. As the nymph sinks back down, the fish will pick it up.

Phil Rowley: Sloughs are slow-running streams rich in aquatic insects, but anglers would do well to approach them as lakes. Heavy vegetation and muddy bottoms provide the right mix for streams such as Dewdney Slough and Hope River to have great chironomid, damselfly and dragonfly populations. The fish respond well to patterns simulating these insects. Callibaetis and March Browns are among the prolific mayflies present; even Hyalella scuds are common inhabitants. Fly fishers who view sloughs as lakes rather than streams will be surprised at the results.

A Gilly's Streamside Notes

One of the many ironic maxims of river fishing dictates the most sought-after species are invariably the most difficult to find, and this is certainly true of the Fraser's coho. These fish can be extremely difficult to locate, sheltering in such strongholds as the logjams above Slesse Park on the Chilliwack River. Except during very high water, anglers will rarely see coho quietly finning their way up along the shallows.

Reliably finding coho means seeking and cataloguing the quiet waters they use as staging areas. These remain constant on a given river, barring any major change to the river's configuration. Look for them during low water when the lies are well defined and the fish are concentrated. Coho also will stack up at river confluences, such as the junction of the Chehalis and the Harrison, during low-water periods. Taking note of these staging areas and applying the knowledge during higher water levels is often the only way to hazard a guess as to where the fish might be positioned. Even backwaters such as Dewdney Slough, which look remarkably homogeneous when seen from the surface, will have preferred coho lies. Low water is the time to find and note them.

In slack current and low water, slow sinking or even floating lines can be used. Under these conditions, coho will give chase, so a variety of aggression-sparking retrieves ought to be worked into an angler's arsenal. Slow-moving clear water such as that found in the mainstem Harrison calls for clear fly lines which are less likely to spook holding fish.

In faster waters, swinging a fly on a bellied, sinking fly line can trigger a chase response from coho. In many instances they will chase downstream as well, which explains those fish hooked in the 'wrong' side of the jaw. The technique also works well in stretches of water with a moderate current, allowing the fly a long, non-stop run. Coho tend to cease chasing as soon as the offering ceases to flee.

Coho flies are diverse both in color and configuration: *Rolled Muddlers* and *Harrison Fiords* are just as likely as bright egg patterns or flowing marabou *Popsicles*. Sizes range from #1 through #8, with smaller patterns preferred as water clarity increases.

Chinook

With increased chinook returns to many southwestern B.C. rivers, pursuing the largest of the Pacific salmon with a fly is becoming increasingly popular. Tyees exceeding 50 pounds are a real

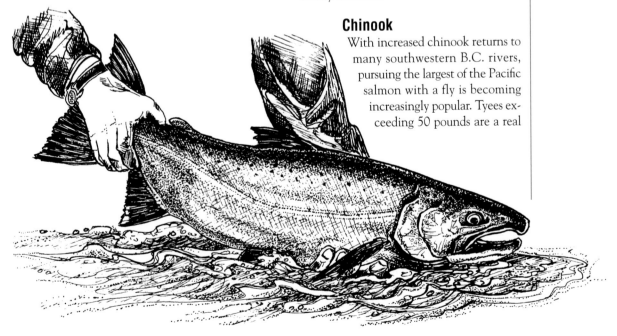

Gloria's Green Skirt

Hook: Eagle Claw 1197, #2-6
Thread: Flymaster Plus 2/0, fluor. red
Abdomen: Chen., fluor. red
Hackle: Chartreuse saddle, webby; tied in halfway up shank
Thorax: Chen., chartreuse

possibility on rivers such as the Chilliwack/Vedder and the Seymour. Heavy gear, coupled with fast-sinking lines and short, strong tippets, is required to reach these fish in the deep lies they prefer. Interchangeable shooting head systems, ranging in length from five to 25 feet in varying densities (all high), are all but essential to master the many current speeds and depths of a given river. Teeny Nymph lines are practical pre-made shooting heads which handle easily and sink like rocks, ranging in density from 130 to 500 grains. Chinook will rarely chase a fly, so deep, slow fly swings or drag-free nymph-type drifts to precise locations are required. The deeper the flow, the more vital line control becomes. Constant upstream and downstream mending keeps a belly out of the line and allows more precise depth control.

Chinook patterns are not restricted to bright colors. Emerald and black flies are fished as commonly as pink and orange. Dark patterns, such as black and purple, are effective most of the time; brighter colors are best early in the day. Patterns integrating both bright and dark colors are often the most successful over the long haul. When the water is up, big weighted *Woolly Buggers* on #2 4X-long streamer hooks are effective, but a *Marabou Egg* fished dead drift through the school can be just as good. Heavy, tough hooks such as Eagle Claw's 1197 stand up well to bottom scouring, will not straighten in the jaws of large fish and will outlast lighter-wire models by a wide margin.

Chum

Chum salmon are not as widely targeted by fly fishers as they might be. Although they color quickly on entering fresh water, chums remain strong and acrobatic. Preferring fast, shallow water and schooling in great numbers, they provide the perfect opportunity for dead drifting a small fly on floating or intermediate sinking lines. Deeper runs require heavy heads and weighted flies, which unfortunately increase the likelihood of foul-hooked fish. Brightly colored flies tied on extra-strong hooks are normally sufficient, but heavy tippets, lots of backing, and beefy rods are mandatory.

The Harrison River, as well as those streams flowing into the west side of Harrison Lake, is home to some of the best chum waters on the south coast – clear, shallow runs and fresh fish, some approaching the 20-pound mark, are the area's hallmarks.

Steelhead

Winter steelhead first nose into area streams in December and continue to trickle in until late April, but March and April are the key fishing months. The Chilliwack/Vedder system is a good bet for winter-run fish, as numbers are higher than elsewhere and the wide, flat runs in areas such as those found near Peach and Lickman

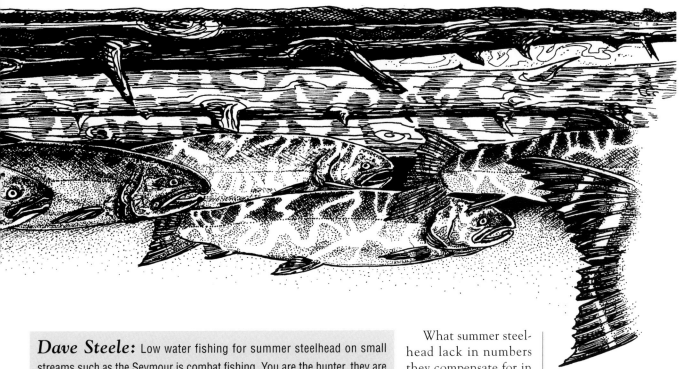

Dave Steele: Low water fishing for summer steelhead on small streams such as the Seymour is combat fishing. You are the hunter, they are the hunted. Sneak up low and slow. Begin fishing as soon as there is a hint of daylight. Once the light is on the water, these easily spooked fish develop lockjaw. Avoid using sinking lines and gaudy flies. Under such vulnerable, gin-clear conditions, even waking flies can put steelhead down. A dead-drifted or slightly twitched dry fly, such as a large *Adams Irresistable* or *Elk Hair Caddis*, works well. Stack mending, so that only the fly and leader drift freely across the fish's path, is also helpful.

What summer steelhead lack in numbers they compensate for in just about every way imaginable. Not only do they run and leap in a manner designed to thrill an angler's heart, they will actively chase a fly, even rising to take dry and waked patterns. Small wonder they are fish of legend.

Small runs interspersed with pockets of slower water make typical summer steelhead habitat, and this is precisely the kind of water found in such streams as the lower Silverhope. Determined anglers must probe every nook and cranny; the fish regularly tuck themselves into impossibly tight cover to avoid detection, even in very shallow water. Dry lines and long leaders are best for summer fish, except in the deepest holes where a fast sinktip with a short leader will take offerings to the bottom. Everything from waking patterns such as *Grease Liners* to bottom-bouncing, weighted stonefly nymphs may be used, but for sheer drama, there is nothing like seeing a summer-run's shadowy shape emerge from the depths behind the waking vee of a fly skating the surface. ✒

roads do not require the heroics involved in tossing heavy shooting heads. Slow sinking and even floating lines are adequate in such water if coupled with weighted egg patterns or other traditional weighted offerings.

The faster runs with large rocks and boulders found in the Slesse Park area are more typical of the region's steelhead water, requiring lines which quickly sink to a variety of depths (read shooting head systems) and allow the fly to probe fast-water slots at optimum depths before swinging clear. Sinktip lines or shooting head systems of between 300 and 500 grains are widely used in canyon water and slow, deep pools such as those found on the Allison. Marabou patterns such as the *Popsicle* are ideal here as the barbules undulate even in slow water, breathing life into the offering.

Dtap
Hook: Eagle Claw 1197, #4-8
Thread: Flymaster Plus 2/0, chartreuse
Body: Fluor. pink chen.
Wing: Marabou, emerald over chartreuse
Over-Wing: Chartreuse Krystal Flash

Fraser Valley
Salmon & Steelhead Guide

RIVER	SPECIES	RUN TIME	PEAK	WILD/HATCHERY
Alouette	coho	Oct-Dec	*	W/H
	steelhead w	Dec-Apr	Feb	W/H
Campbell	chinook	Apr-Oct	*	W/H
	coho	Sep-Nov	*	W/H
	steelhead w	Jan-Apr	*	W/H
Capilano	chinook white	Sep-Nov	*	W/H
	coho	May-Sep	*	W/H
	steelhead w	Dec-Apr	Feb	W/H
	steelhead s	All Year	Jun	W/H
Cheakamus	chinook white	Jul-Aug	*	W/H
	coho	Oct-Dec	*	W/H
	steelhead w	Mar-May	Apr	W
Chehalis	chinook red	Jun-Aug	*	W/H
	coho	Oct-Dec	*	W/H
	steelhead w	Dec-Apr	Feb	W/H
	steelhead s	All Year	Jun	W/H
Chilliwack/	chinook white	Sep-Nov	*	W/H
Vedder	chinook red	Jul-Aug	*	H
	coho	Sep-Nov	*	W/H
	steelhead w	Dec-May	Jan/Apr	W/H
Coquihalla	coho	Oct-Dec	*	W
	steelhead w	Dec-Apr	Feb	W
	steelhead s	Jul-Oct	*	W/H
Coquitlam	coho	Sep-Nov	*	W/H
	steelhead w	Dec-Mar	Feb	W
Dewdney/	coho	Oct-Dec	*	W/H
Nicomen	steelhead w	Dec-Apr	Feb	W
Fraser	chinook white	Jul-Dec	*	W/H
	chinook red	Mar-Sep	*	W/H
	sockeye	Jul-Oct	*	W/H
	coho	Sep-Dec	*	W/H
	pink	Jul-Sep	*	W/H
	chum	Sep-Nov	*	W/H
	steelhead w	Dec-Apr	Feb	W/H
	steelhead s	May-Nov	Oct	W

RIVER	SPECIES	RUN TIME	PEAK	WILD/HATCHERY
Harrison	chinook white	Sep-Dec	*	W/H
	sockeye	Aug-Oct	*	W/H
	coho	Sep-Dec	*	W/H
	pink	Aug-Sep	*	W/H
	chum	Sep-Dec	*	W/H
	steelhead w	Dec-May	Feb	W/H
	steelhead s	May-Nov	Jun	W/H
Inch	coho	Oct-Dec	*	W/H
Indian	coho	Sep-Nov	*	W
	steelhead w	Dec-Mar	*	W
Lillooet	chinook	April-May	*	W
	coho	Oct-Dec	*	W
	steelhead w	Dec-May	*	W
Nicomekl	chinook red	Aug-Sep	*	W/H
	coho	Oct-Nov	*	W/H
	steelhead w	Jan-Mar	*	W/H
Pitt (upper)	coho	Sep-Nov	*	W
	steelhead w	Dec-Apr	Feb	W
Seymour	chinook white	Jul-Sept	*	W/H
	coho	Jun-Oct	*	W/H
	steelhead w	Dec-Apr	Feb	W/H
	steelhead s	All Year	*	W/H
Silverhope	steelhead w	Jan-Apr	Mar	W
	steelhead s	Jun-Oct	Jul	W
Squamish	chinook white	Jul-Aug	*	W/H
	coho	Oct-Dec	*	W/H
	steelhead w	Mar-May	Apr	W
Stave	chinook white	Sep-Nov	*	H
	coho	Sep-Dec	*	W/H
	steelhead w	Dec-Apr	Mar	H
	chum	Sep-Nov	*	W/H
Suicide	coho	Oct-Dec	*	W/H
	steelhead w	Dec-Apr	Mar	W

*Rainfall affects these runs so peaks vary.
Consult regulations carefully; the presence of fish in no way implies a river or section of river is open to angling.
w = winter run
s = summer run

Grease Liner

Hook: Partridge, single low water
Thread: Blk. Monocord
Body: Blk. seal or seal substitute
Wing: Extra-long deer or elk hair, leaving trimmed butt fibres intact for waking

Sea Run Cutthroat

Sea-run cutthroat trout are at once aggressive opportunists and tight-lipped skeptics. Frequently willing to take almost any offering tossed their way, there are also days when these primitive salmonids rate among the most selective of trout.

Hardly surprising then that the sea-run requires a multi-faceted angling skill set tempered by an intuitive understanding of their environment.

Ryan Pohl: There are many reasons why sea-run cutthroat entering Vancouver-area rivers are so nomadic. Still, it is perplexing why a fly fisher can catch 20 fish one day and none the next – even when fishing the same spot. This does not necessarily mean the fish have left. Years of journal entries show a consistent correlation between barometric pressure and cutthroat success. Optimum readings, always coinciding with successful days, range from 100.25 kpa to 101.35 kpa. Going outside these parameters doesn't mean fishless days, but being within this pressure range has always meant more fish on more days.

Mastery of the effects of tides on the behavior of sea-runs is the first prerequisite. After tides, anglers must know the best angling times of year. Skills such as sight fishing and cutthroat sign recognition are also significant, as is the role of weather. Choosing just the right beach or estuary can be a frustrating game, but it's essential since knowing the cutthroat's habitat is the real key to luring the matchless sea-run to the fly.

Tide is the single most important factor to consider when planning to fish for sea-runs. The best part of the tide change to fish depends somewhat on which beach is being fished, but as a rule the most productive times are the middle two hours of both the rising and falling tides. In some instances the last two hours of the drop are best, but it is most important

that the tidal current continues moving well. Hence, large changes in tide height over short periods of time are best. There are no real limitations on high tide levels with regard to cutthroat fishing, but very low tides (three feet or less) are generally fruitless. These tides occur around the summer and winter solstices, as well as at other indeterminable times during the year, so a book of tide tables is essential equipage.

Two times of year are of major importance to the sea run cutthroat angler. First, and of greatest significance, is the early spring. At this time, cutthroat concentrate in the estuaries of rivers with good salmon runs to feed on descending fry. Sea runs are at their most selective at this time so realistic fry patterns (coho, chum, chinook or pink) are required, as are correspondingly aggressive retrieves – the fly's action must mimic the movements of fleeing prey. Also, flies must remain size-matched to the fry as they grow over a period of some weeks. A range of sizes from #8 to #2 usually will suffice.

David Wallden: Some beaches get more pressure than others and the cutthroat get wise to us after we release them a few times. A sure-fire way to trick them is to use a bright attractor fly with a second smaller, more natural fly tied to the bend of the hook and trailing about 24 inches behind on a fine tippet. The sea-run will charge the attractor, refuse it, and then as it turns, take the "dropper" fly. An effective combination is a #6 *Mickey Finn* with a #12 euphausid trailing. Try this technique dead drift in tidal current or when targetting visible fish.

Cutthroat aggressively attack schools of fry, frequently chasing them into mere inches of water. While adhering to the technique of targetting and leading fish, cast a long line and then strip as fast as possible. Clamping the rod under one arm and using both hands to maximize stripping speed excites the cutthroat's instinct to give chase.

The other main time of year is early fall, before the salmon have made their way into the rivers to spawn. Cutthroat gather in estuaries in anticipation of the rich salmon egg harvest they will soon reap. Also, from December through January, cutthroat school in estuaries in preparation for their own spawning run.

The best days to fish for sea-runs are those on which most anglers would question going out at

Ian Roberts: Some beaches have fast-running tides, and areas that hold fish can quickly fill with water, leaving them too deep to fish effectively with a floating line. Instead of wasting valuable time changing spools during the best part of the tide, I carry a clear Stillwater head which I can loop onto my line in seconds. The sinktip puts my fly into the zone faster and helps the fly swim deeper as the tide picks up speed. This technique also works well for pinks and coho in shallow-water situations when a full Stillwater line is not appropriate.

all. An overcast morning on which a fast-rising tide occurs at or around first light, with a breeze creating a minor chop on the water, is ideal. Add a few light, intermittent showers and we have all the ingredients for cut-throat nirvana.

Sight fishing is the skill most wanting in many sea-run cutthroat anglers. Cutthroat are highly visible fish, making them susceptible to a well-placed fly. Knowing they are opportunists, it follows that a fly placed in their window of vision will be struck. Expect to see obvious signs like jumping and rolling fish, but look too for more subtle signs – the keenly observant angler will hook far more fish. Small boils caused by an upwelling of water when a fish takes prey close to the

surface are a sign most anglers miss. Another is a vee wake (often accompanied by leaping feed fish) caused by a cutthroat chasing prey. Any abnormal surface variation usually can be attributed to fish. If a cast is made to each abnormality, success rates will improve dramatically.

Good cutthroat beaches are treated with an elevated degree of secrecy by anglers, largely due to the fact they are uncrowded, difficult to find and hard to decipher. Such beaches are discovered by 'paying one's dues', but with a little common sense and exploration, good beaches will be located readily enough. Look for gently sloping beaches with gravel bottoms. The presence of saltwort at the high tide line is a good indicator, as are swans and other waterfowl. It is rare to find sea-runs farther than a few miles from fresh water, so straying too far from stream areas is generally counter productive.

Historically, nearly every estuary carried pop-

Eric Schulz: During periods of inactivity or when the fish are not obviously staying in one place, fan your casts out in a 180-degree pattern to cover more water. Place some casts parallel to shore and in the trough between waves. A cutty will nail prey it believes is trapped between itself and the shore. Remember, sea-runs are roving fish, so repeatedly casting to the same place is often counter productive. Try to cast with the tidal current or with the wind to keep your line tight and help you detect every strike.

ulations of sea-run cutthroat, but like so much fish habitat everywhere, that of the sea-run has suffered. Fortunately, it is still possible to find good populations in many areas, from the backwaters of the Fraser River north up the Sunshine Coast and including Desolation Sound.

Trophy Cutthroat

Large lake-resident cutthroat trout are an enigma. In British Columbia they are found typically in nutrient-poor coastal lakes with minimal shoal areas and meagre aquatic vegetation. Many would judge such waters incapable of growing trophy-sized fish, but coastal cutthroat often do remarkably well in their acidic environments, regularly attaining lengths of 20 inches and more, often much more.

Most of the lakes holding such fish are remote, requiring either aircraft or seaworthy boats to reach, but the lakes of the Powell Forest near Powell River on the north Sunshine Coast have logging-road access and many of them hold good numbers of these enigmatic fish. Every year knowledgeable anglers catch and release cutthroat trout in the 30-inch range from these waters. The unofficial record was a fly-caught fish (taken on a *McLeod Stickleback*, see Selected Patterns) measuring 36 inches and estimated to weigh about 20 pounds. It too was released.

These figures are quite staggering and many fly fishers will be hard-pressed to give them credence, so it may be prudent to dwell on the matter of coastal cutthroat size for a moment. For a number of years the Powell River Salmon Society ran a small cutthroat hatchery program in which broodstock fish were captured by rod and reel. During a three-day 'broodstock derby' 10 fish were delivered to the holding pens in Powell Lake. The smallest weighed eight pounds, while the largest was a deep-sided trophy weighing 14 pounds. This impressive catch yielded an average weight of almost 10 pounds for each fish, so there is no doubt exceptional trout can and do exist in nutrient-poor coastal waters.

Prey species such as kokanee and stickleback account for the exceptional sizes of the cutthroat found in these and similar coastal lakes, but even so, the presence of 30-inch trout in any number verges on the miraculous given the nature of these aquatic environments. A lake's ability to nurture life can be measured by the amount of total dissolved solids (TDS) present in a given unit of water. The nutrient-rich waters of the southern Interior typically yield counts of between 200 and 300 TDS, while average coastal lakes will yield counts of only 20 to 30 for the same measure of water. Hence, an Interior lake is capable of producing or sustaining about 10 times as much life per volume of water as a typical coastal lake. Large, fast-growing trout are most often found in hard, alkaline waters; small, slow-growing trout are often products of soft, acidic waters. Similarly, nutrient-poor lakes are most often

Muddler Minnow
Hook: Mustad 9672 or similar, #2-10
Thread: Monocord 3/0 #429
Tail: Mottled turkey quill
Body: Gold or silv. Diamond Braid
Under-Wing: Gry. squirrel tail
Wing: Mottled turkey quill
Collar: Deerhair
Head: Deerhair, spun & trimmed to shape

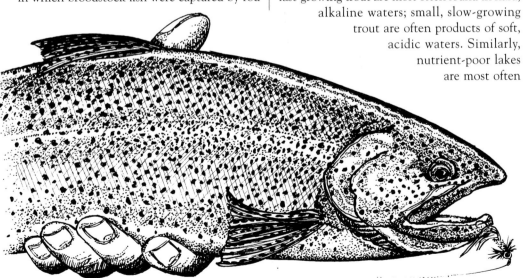

Wool Head Sculpin

Hook: Mustad 9671, 2X, #4
Tail: Sandy brn. marabou
Under-Body Head:
Flattened lead wire
Under-Body Back 1/3:
Packing foam
Body: Sandy brn. dubbing w/marabou fibre tied on top
Fins: Barred body feather from grouse or partridge
Head: Spun wool dubbing chen. trimmed to wedge shape – flat on top & bottom, wide at sides; make dubbing chen. w/different wool color – tan, brn.
Eyes: None or glued-on baby doll
Note: Fly fishes hook point up.

acidic while nutrient-rich waters are most often alkaline. It comes as no surprise then that alkaline waters produce exceptional fishing while acidic waters most often yield poor angling, and most coastal lakes are acidic. Common pH values in coastal lakes might range between 6.0 and 6.5; in rich Kamloops trout waters common pH values range between 8.4 and 8.6. It follows, then, that a typical coastal lake might be 100 times more acidic and less alkaline than a typical Kamloops trout lake.

Scale samples taken from Powell Lake cutthroat indicate low growth rates until the fish attain a length of about 17 inches, normally in their sixth or seventh year of life. At that point they suddenly leap forward, growing by as much as five inches in a single year. A cutthroat in its 10th year might reasonably measure 32 inches. Not only do they grow longer, they grow deeper as well. Anglers confronted with such trophy cutthroat for the first time most often liken them to coho salmon. Decidedly, these are not the long, skinny fish typically associated with nutrient-poor water.

Catch-and-release ethics likely go a long way towards explaining their continued existence in waters with road access, a reflection of the burgeoning interest in fly fishing. Fly fishers release more fish, so while angling pressure on Powell Forest lakes has increased during the last 10 years judging by the number of anglers on the water, the number of fish killed has dropped. Whatever the reasons, good numbers of these trophy cutthroat can be found in such lakes as Lois, Nanton, Ireland, Dodd, Inland and Khartoum, all of which are well-suited to fishing with a fly, even if the strategies employed often differ radically from those used in the Interior.

Insect hatches, while still important, play a far lesser role on these coastal lakes, as does the floating line and long leader technique which serves so admirably in the southern Interior. Full-sinking lines are used far more often and many anglers favor fast-sinking, high-density lines over the more moderate sinkers. Type IV and V lines are quite standard and leaders as short as four or six feet are regularly used to probe the steep shorelines typical of coastal stillwaters. The lake fishing seasons are also entirely out of kilter with the rest of the province. Winter, in fact, can be a prime period, accounting for many of the larger fish, and often the very largest. Only rarely does ice form on these lakes and seldom does it remain for any extended period.

The slowest months are December and January when water temperatures are at their lowest. By February, the fish again become active,

apparently having adjusted to the colder temperatures. Infrequently, but often enough to merit mention, chironomids hatch at this time in sufficient numbers to draw notice from the fish. Imitations tied on #18 hooks can be fished on floating lines, as can blue-winged olive mayflies which hatch in inflowing streams and often drift out onto the surface of the lakes. More typical offerings are the old cutthroat standbys, the leeches, sculpins and sticklebacks fished deep in 30 to 60 feet of water on full-sinking lines. Bloodworms fished at the same depths also produce at this time. Imitations are fished vertically on sinking lines by stripping and casting only as much line as is needed to suspend the fly just off bottom. After casting, the line is allowed to sink until it hangs vertically from the rod tip, at which point the fly is 'jigged' upwards with a series of slow hand twists for several feet before being allowed to settle back down.

In most instances, strikes are very subtle, indicated by the merest hint of resistance. This is especially true when fishing stickleback, sculpin or leech imitations. Fish bump these offerings before turning back to take the fly. The key is to stop the retrieve the moment the first light bump is felt, giving the fish time to make its turn.

The fish stay deep through much of March, prowling the shoals only towards the end of the month and only if temperatures moderate. Stickleback and sculpins remain the best bets, with sculpins favored. Stickleback are spring spawners and while there will be large balls of them scattered in the lakes during April and May, the greatest number become available in late summer and fall after the fry have matured sufficiently to be noticed.

Insect hatches peak in April and May, with chironomids dominating over lesser hatches of grey drakes and small Callibaetis. Lakes holding smaller fish – Lewis, Spring and Little Horseshoe among others – will offer fast action for 12- to 14-inch fish, but the large, predatory cutthroat will stay with their almost unvarying diet of sculpins and sticklebacks. The fish will be in shallower water, so shoals can be probed with some measure of confidence, but the deeper water just off the drop-offs tends to produce more fish than the shoals themselves.

Similar fishing continues through June, then drops off markedly through July and August, not picking up until the glory days of fall. This is when the kokanee spawn, the sticklebacks are at their peak and the cutthroat themselves are in prime condition. Large trout readily take kokanee as long as 14 inches, proving beyond doubt the cutthroat is a truly voracious predator, but even during the height of kokanee activity, with hundreds staging near inflowing creeks, the cutthroat rarely refuses a stickleback imitation. ✦

Selected Waters

Alpine Lakes

Bodiless Caddis
Hook: Mustad 94833, TMC
101 or similar, #8-16
Thread: Black Monocord
Body: None, except single
strand coat of Monocord
Wing and Head: Medium
deerhair, tied on elk hair
caddis style
*Note: True medium deerhair
should flare to about a 45-
degree angle from the hook
shank.*

Stunning alpine vistas notwithstanding, life as lived in the high lakes of the Coast Mountains is far from poetic. These mountain treasures are home to aggressive, opportunistic trout that wrest a hard-won existence from strikingly clear, but virtually sterile waters. Oligotrophic as a result of being flushed by nutrient-poor surface runoff, and with only three to five ice-free months each year, Vancouver-area alpine lakes produce a special breed of trout – fish that will never know what it means to feed selectively.

While match-the-hatch skills are rarely, if ever, required in the alpine, angling remains both challenging and demanding. More successfully fished by method and observation than by fly choice, alpine trout haunt the meagre shorelines of their sky-high waters. In most instances, the littoral zone is minimized due to the steep terrain common in the North Cascades. Beyond the lim-

ited shoal areas, food forms are virtually non-existent, so most angling occurs within a fly line's length of the shore. Hence, sight fishing along the shore is the most effective method.

Blindly casting to the shallows is not adequate. These trout may be risk-takers, both in what they feed on and where they feed, but they are not foolish. They are masters at using the limited structure of the alpine shoals, both for defence (cover) and as hunting grounds. Structure in alpine lakes takes the form of boulders, overhanging flora, drowned logs, even shadowed areas.

This is where the trout and their prey will be found. Creeks which enter or exit and have sufficient cover are prime habitat – it is here that terrestrial and spent insects are carried in or funnelled out of the lake.

Kevin Longard: Fish looking to the surface from a lake or stream are limited to a window of vision. The angle of this window is 97.12 degrees from the fish's position to the water's surface. This is somewhat enhanced by light refraction, which allows fish to see items floating on the meniscus before it actually enters the 'vision' cone. As the fish ventures deeper, the angle does not change but the size of the cone will. Trout near the top will see much less surface area, fish down deep will see more. When lead-casting to stillwater fish, attempt to get within the edge of this cone, but not so close as to spook the quarry. Thus, the fly will be seen, but not as a threat. In running water, simply allow the fly to drift into the fish's window.

Reach casts and roll casts become commonplace, as does stealthily creeping along lake margins while tempting the trout to take. General purpose nymphs such as the *Carey*, *Spratley* or *Soft Hackle* are adequate here. Strike indicators are useful for this style of fishing, but when conditions are perfect for sight fishing – the water calm and the sun bright – the indicator can be dispensed with.

For surface-feeding alpine trout, the *Bodiless Caddis* is an effective pattern. It has a nondescript wing formation, allowing it to imitate both up- and down-wing naturals. Tying it with deerhair flares the wing higher and provides better floating capabilities. This pattern also ties and dries very quickly.

Alpine lakes come in a variety of guises. Some, such as the Slollicum lakes, become overpopulated due to lack of harvest and good spawning habitat. A very few lakes have minimal spawning areas, which sets the stage for low numbers of larger fish, even in water that is minimally productive. Garibaldi Lake in the Whistler area and select lakes in the Pemberton and Skagit areas potentially offer fish upwards of 20 inches

The happy medium is those lakes with good populations and fish in the respectable nine- to 15-inch bracket. Flora and Greendrop lakes in the Chilliwack River Valley and Thunder Lake in Manning Park are good examples. ➤

Dollies & Bulls

Dolly Dredger

(Contributed by Kevin Longard)

Hook: Mustad 79580 or similar, #1-4
Thread: Flymaster Plus 2/0 fluor. red
Body: #10 flat silv. tinsel
Rib: Med. oval tinsel, silv.
Wing: Krystal Flash, silv., gold or olv.
Eyes: Large, plated lead eyes

Dolly Varden and bull trout have gained an undeserved reputation as coarse, bottom-feeding fish. In truth, these aggressive char combine legendary beauty with doggedly determined fighting abilities. In the streams of the Coast Mountains, both fish are much more common and accessible to the fly fisher than many realize. Such well-known waters as the Skagit, Squamish, Silverhope, Lillooet and the upper Stave and Pitt rivers hold good numbers of both species. They are good-sized fish as well, commonly attaining weights of several pounds.

Dollies and bull trout are close relatives and their habits and general appearances are similar, but to the trained eye they differ markedly: the bull trout is stockier with a flatter, blunter nose and is generally larger than the Dolly Varden.

Char spawn in the fall, moving up and out of the lakes or the ocean to join their resident counterparts in rivers and streams. The combination of both residents and visitors means good populations of fish are available from September to January. They do not cease feeding during spawning, and their propensity to attack anything within striking distance, particularly small fish, is well known by those who regularly pursue them.

Both are very specific in the river areas they inhabit, particularly the bull trout, which commonly stage in concentrated numbers, resembling cordwood lined up parallel to the current. Generally, these two species prefer deep, slower areas, or the tailouts of those waters. On occasion, when spawning fish are moving up, they make themselves surprisingly vulnerable, holding in open, medium-fast, shallow water. Lone fish will often tuck themselves in the deepest of water under logjams, leaving the angler an interesting problem.

Once found, these char are quite easy to catch, provided some specific steps are followed. A type IV or faster sinking line, or sinktip line, is essential for all waters more than a few feet deep. In shallower water a floating line will suffice, provided a weighted fly is used. Fast-sinking tackle and techniques such as downstream mending or upstream casts are essential. Patterns must not only sink deep, but must remain in the depths while quick, erratic movement is imparted to the fly.

These simulations of distress are the single most important technique needed to trigger the feeding response in Dollies and bull trout. They love to chase, and any forage fish pattern that is sunk deep with a 45-degree downstream swing in front of staging fish will elicit a take under most circumstances.

For char, the general rule is, the bigger the forage fish pattern, the better. Long hooks with small gapes are preferred. In this region, all river-dwelling char are wild fish and must be released. Hook gapes larger than about half an inch increase mortality rates significantly, often penetrating to the skull area. Fry patterns must be in-your-face flashy, both in material and undulation. Silver or gold flash with brown, olive, chartreuse or grey are appealing combinations — olive being a favorite. ◄

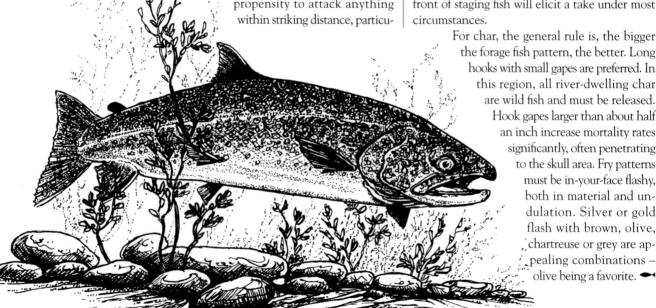

Selected Waters

Small Streams

Small streams do not always mean small fish. This hidden world can house everything, from the small resident rainbows typical of generally sterile coastal water to big sea-run cutthroat, which are measured in pounds, not inches. Add to this the fact these fish regularly sip small dry flies, and the recipe for quality angling in secluded settings is complete. Not knowing what will rise to the fly sweetens the mystique. In either case, whether large or small, these fish will be in optimum condition and anglers had best be prepared for what follows once the hook is set.

The best rule of thumb for dry fly success on these waters is to eat lunch first, fish later. Too many anglers cast their *Tom Thumbs* or *Elk Hair Caddis* patterns all morning with no success and conclude that there are few or no fish. And yet

tiny pocket waters under overhanging flora. Use drag-free drifts where possible, but these opportunists will chase down a skating pattern as well. Cover each seam, pocket, run, glide and pool thoroughly. Fish in small streams will spread out and are less predictable in their lies. Careless anglers will regularly spook those fish, which hold within feet of the shore.

Small stoneflies such as the little greens and yellows (Chloroperlidae) are in evidence throughout the summer. Myriad species of small caddisflies commonly flit above the current, and of course mayflies (pmds, western green drakes and Epeorus) are all common. This divides dry fly selection into two basic categories: upwing and downwing. Beyond that it is simply a matter of

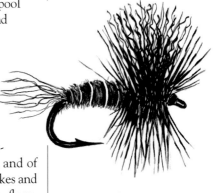

Western Green Drake

Hook: Mustad 94840 or similar, #10-16
Thread: Unithread 6/0 or 8/0 olv.
Tail: Calftail, blk.
Body: Fine olv. dubbing
Rib: 1 strand yel. floss
Wing: Divided calftail, blk.
Hackle: Griz., dyed olv.

that very afternoon, a fish a cast may be the norm.

It is vital to hunt as well as fish. Stay low, remembering that because of light refraction, fish can see the angler more easily than the reverse. Sneak up low, with the lightest equipment possible. Short two- to three-weight rods are best, coupled with double-tapered fly lines for gentle presentations. Backcast space will be limited, so be prepared to use roll and steeple casts constantly; often the clumsy 'bow and arrow' cast will be the only way to tuck flies into the

matching size and color. Carry downwing patterns in light green, yellow and medium olive. Mayfly patterns in olive and black will normally suffice, but cream or pale yellow will sometimes come in handy. If naturals are not in evidence on the water, shake the streamside bushes where emerged adults often hide.

Streams such as Tamihi in the Chilliwack Valley, Slollicum Creek, which feeds Harrison Lake, or Lynn Creek in North Vancouver are all typical examples.

Selected Waters

Fraser Sockeye

In the summer of 1993 a historical opening took place on the Fraser River. Sockeye bound for their home streams, some hundreds of miles away, were opened as a sport fishery on the Fraser's mainstem. Many anglers used drift rods to bounce green yarn through 'walk across' schools of fish. Others used fly rods.

Sockeye enter the Fraser in early July, as the spring freshet is receding, and continue into November. They move quickly upstream, covering upwards of 20 miles a day and taking the most direct routes with the least amount of current resistance. Due to the Fraser's turbid water, the fish feel secure in near-shore areas with moderated current speeds. To find preferred sockeye water, throw a stick into the river and walk beside it. If the stick floats just slightly faster than walking speed, the current speed is right.

Reading a large river such as the Fraser means breaking it down into smaller pieces by defining deadwater areas, eddies, flat runs, riffles and seams. The key to taking sockeye on the fly rests on intercepting their migration while the fish are in an aggressive mode. Areas where the fish stack up, such as current seams and riffles at the top of a run, have the greatest potential. Look for them on the inside of bends or on the downstream sides of gravel bars. Fish migrating upstream travel through the run and congregate at the top where the current is generally faster. Shallow water runs (less than six feet deep) also have good potential. The warmer the water, the deeper and faster the preferred areas will be. Fishing in two to four feet of water in early morning and evening is generally productive; however, during the high light/temperature hours, fish 50 per cent deeper.

Short five- to seven-foot leaders with 10- to 12-pound tippets cover most situations. Long leaders allow non-weighted flies to boil to the surface, even though the fly line is well down. High-density sinktip lines with 13- to 24-foot heads are regularly used except in the shallowest situations. Seven- through nine-weight rods are standard, with eight-weights optimum for general application.

Cast the fly directly across the current, allowing the head to sink while executing quick downstream mends. Follow the line with the rod tip as the fly fishes down and swings shorewards directly downstream. Any hesitation should be answered with a hookset. If the fly is not ticking bottom, cast further upstream (to about 15 degrees) and feed more line out between downstream mends.

Fly selection generally revolves around various shades of green – from chartreuse to forest. Flies as small as #8 are commonly used; however larger, more pulsating patterns perform better as water clarity decreases. Effective sockeye flies combine elements of sparkle and 'life'.

Sockeye Bunny
*(Contributed by
Ron Tarnawski)*
Hook: Eagle Claw 1197,
#2-6
Thread: Flymaster Plus 2/0,
fluor. red or fluor. pink
Tail: Pearl Flashabou
Body: Cross-cut rabbit
strip, chartreuse or fluor.
grn., tied in 1/3 forward on
hook shank.

Selected Waters

Pink Salmon

In each odd-numbered year, southwestern B.C. is inundated with pink salmon intent on entering fresh water and dispersing their seed throughout the vast Fraser River system. Pink salmon take the fly surprisingly well in fresh water, probably due to the imprinting which takes place during their youth.

Pinks are not difficult to find in fresh water as they generally prefer very shallow, glassy runs with moderate current speeds. They also crowd into tight schools, resembling dark pulsating bands which may be detected even in the murky waters of the Fraser.

By the first of August, the inaugural run of pinks is in the Fraser. Those that are mainstem spawners remain, while others continue up into streams such as the Harrison and Vedder. The run continues until about September 30, after which the fish are no longer fresh. Pinks deteriorate quickly on entering fresh water, so for hard-running, bright fish concentrate on the early runs and choose locations as close to salt water as possible. The fish are also quicker to respond to a fly during these early days.

Six- to seven-weight fly rods are adequate for pinks, but large, humpbacked males will be difficult to turn in the current, so going too light is not recommended. Longer rods are useful for the frequent mending required to manipulate the fly into position. Floating lines or slow sinkers are standard on the Fraser. Combined with lightly weighted fly patterns, such set-ups provide the most hassle-free angling.

There are two basic techniques. The most common calls for a drag-free, shallow-water drift, with or without a strike indicator, where the fly is allowed to bump seductively along. As when fishing nymphs, the slightest hesitation during a drift should be met with a hookset. Black rabbit strip tied onto a short-shank hook and fronted with a ball of cerise chenille is deadly with this technique.

Less well known, but gaining steadily in popularity, is the dry fly technique for pinks. The traditional drag-free dry drift has proven only marginally successful, but a downstream skated or waking fly will draw fish in shallow water (less than three feet) to the surface.

The fly of choice is the Pollywog. This fly gained notoriety for taking coho salmon on estuaries and rivers in Alaska. The pattern is designed to float and skate across the surface, creating a disturbance which may trigger a response. The take is very subtle, visible only as a slight bulge in the meniscus. Wait until the weight of the fish is perceived on the line before lifting the rod. Then hang on and tell yourself how good life is.

Pink Pollywog

Hook: Diiachi 2050, #5 or #7
Thread: Flymaster plus, #501
Tail: Pink marabou with three to four strands of pink Krystal Flash, tied long
Body: Pink deer belly hair – spun, trimmed flat & triangular (point toward back)

Coast Mountain Journal

The young man arrived from the East Coast in the mid-1970s. Immersed in the pressures of a budding career, mortgage, marriage and raising a family, he sought brief moments of solace in the wilderness sanctuaries of rivers and lakes nearby.

In winter he stopped at the Maplewood Pool of the Seymour River on his way home, pulling boot-foot waders over his city-slicker clothes to cast a fly at last light. Occasionally he intercepted a bright winter steelhead. Almost the last of a wild strain, they got a boost just in time from the student-run enhancement facility at the foot of the Seymour dam, founded by Dr. Chuck Chestnut, then of BCIT.

On weekends he would wander, with his English setters and daughter in tow, past the "Angler Access Only" gate guarded by a GVRD warden, into a near-deserted world of old-growth cedars, second-growth Douglas fir and towering alders.

When there was only an hour to spare before dinner, he would prowl the estuaries of the Capilano River, McCartney Creek and smaller North Shore beaches, drawing bemused looks from passersby as he flung a fly, a seemingly futile effort, into the vast expanse of the Pacific. But there were lovely, jewel-like cutthroat to be caught for most of the year, and occasionally coho and even the rare chinook would peel off a hundred yards of backing in a burst of unstoppable energy.

More time and the camaraderie of fishing clubs allowed more ambitious outings to the Vedder which, with the advent of the Salmonid Enhancement Program, was bursting with fish and thus, not coincidentally, with anglers. For solitude he sought out the wild steelhead, Dolly Varden and coho of the Squamish, a system encircled by towering mountains populated by goats and grizzlies, less than an hour from North Vancouver.

When, as increasingly occurred, the Squamish ran turbid from glacial melt, a phenomenon made worse by horrendous logging practices in the 1980s, he would fish the Cheakamus near Fergie's Lodge or hike up the Mamquam that had a run of steelhead peaking in May.

For a pleasant, Class 1 canoe ride in the fall, he would drift down the Harrison River, stopping at likely-looking riffles to try for sunburst-yellow harvest cutthroat and poling around in the side channels for coho, which his newly converted bait-fisher comrade was amazed would take a fly. They hooked 13 on the first day. It was like travelling a benign, fecund, moving sea.

During the soft, grey days of winter he would ply the sloughs of the Fraser — Popkum, Mariah, Nicomen, Desroches — for orange-finned cutts that could be shamelessly eager or frustratingly coy when he proffered a *Cutthroat Candy* dry fly or a *Professor* in the surface film.

With the Interior still in winter's icy grip, he would venture out in the early West Coast spring to the secret little lakes of Abbotsford, Squamish, Whistler and Pemberton. They were teeming with chironomid hatches fed upon by startlingly large — for coastal lakes, that is — rainbow of two to four pounds.

A little later he would venture up to Norton Lake off the Indian River, into which a trapper had hauled rainbow fry in a packsack filled with water years before. They had grown to five, even 10 pounds. One spring he arrived to find the forest scalped to the shoreline, with the water almost inaccessible for the trees and stumps ploughed into it. There were other signs of human despoilers — fish-heads of what were once great trout, scattered by the dozens around the shore. He never went back, though he often wondered how the lake was recovering. He did return, however, to the Indian to catch and release pink salmon by the dozens in the fall of the years of great runs, one of nature's dramatic and comforting displays of riches.

The now-veteran West Coast fisherman was overwhelmed by the opulence of the natural fisheries within an hour's drive of virtually anywhere in the Lower Mainland, and perhaps foolheartedly he vowed that he would fish nowhere else until he had exhausted its major waterways.

I am that angler and I never made it. Within a few years I was seduced by the charms of Vancouver Island, the North and the Interior.

More poignantly, 24 years later, as a middle-aged, though now hopefully wiser, Vancouver chauvinist, I realize I never will. I have yet to fish Crescent Beach for its famed cutthroat and coho. I have never wet a line in the little Campbell for its restored salmon and steelhead runs. Nor in the Alouette which now, thanks to the efforts of the Steelhead Society of B.C. and other conservationists and their lawyers, benefits from more water that BC Hydro is forced to release, and hence from more fish. The Chehalis has both winter and summer runs that I haven't fished, and there are rumors that steelhead and cutthroat have returned to both the Lynn in North Vancouver and the Brunette in Burnaby. Only three years ago did I finally fish the hidden paradise of the Upper Pitt, which lodge owners Danny and Lee Gerak are doing their best to protect from the loggers and poachers — a wilderness jewel only an hour and a half from downtown Vancouver.

Simply put, the Lower Mainland, even with its burgeoning population now exceeding two million, is perhaps the ultimate destination for freshwater fishing in British Columbia. Thanks to the blessing of its great rivers, its mountains and valleys and the benevolent, tempering influence of

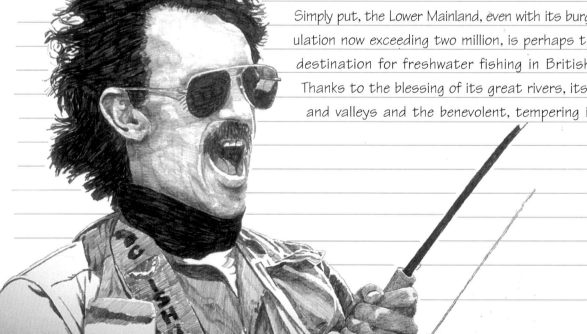

the Pacific, even after suffering the mixed blandishments of mankind for over a century, there is something for the angler to pursue in relative comfort, less than an hour from his or her home in every month — in fact, every day.

That is a statement calculated to evoke howls of indignant protest from parts of the province I love dearly and visit every year — Vancouver Island (fall, winter and spring), Thompson-Nicola (my second home and closest to my heart), as well as the Chilcotin and Skeena (in our summer and fall), the greatest places to fish in the world, but in season. There is no high season for the Lower Mainland. It is a destination for all seasons.

As I write this it is spring and the eagles are calling in their oddly frail way from the great cedars that dwarf my house at Hole-in-the-Wall just outside of Horseshoe Bay. Trollers patrol the waters outside my study window for mighty chinook. There is a flurry of activity on the water. Herring are spawning and I may go out and, bizarrely enough, take a cod or two right near the surface as they pursue the spawning fish; the only time of the year I can actually take cod on the fly. But then again, my friend David Goodman, visiting from Washington, D.C., and I hooked a couple of fine steelhead yesterday on the Squamish and I ran into a fellow who took two on the Seymour. What to do? Oh what a delicious dilemma to be suffering in the last year of the millennium.

— Ehor Boyanowsky

Chapter
7

Selected
Menu

Selected Menu

Scuds

Scud populations in the shallow, productive lakes of south-central British Columbia can be likened to an infestation. Their key role in the food chain is well known to stillwater anglers versed in the lore. Each piggy-backed pair of mating scuds might produce as many as 20,000 offspring in a season, providing trout with a staple food source and growth rates as high as two pounds annually.

Chameleons of the underwater jungle, scuds are capable of a wide range of coloration and match their color to that of the local environment. In the clear marl lakes, scuds vary from light olive to tan; in the rich algae-type lakes, dark olive colors predominate. Pregnant scuds are identified by a distinct orange brood pouch, or marsupium, located in the middle of their bodies. Trout key on the orange spot, so suitable patterns should be carried in an array of color schemes. As scuds mature, they lose their ability to camouflage. These tattered seniors are identified by their yellowish hue and are a common sight in the fall. This is when the golden olive to yellow patterns come into their own. A well-stocked fly box must mirror the full range of color diversity.

Always useful for probing weedbeds, scud patterns are most productive during early spring and late fall. In the early spring weed growth is low and few other food sources are available. In the late fall similar conditions exist. Fish rolling at the surface in the shallows during these times are almost certain to be scud-feeding trout. Color-matched patterns retrieved in a random and erratic manner on either a floating or intermediate line can be pure magic under these conditions.

Smaller-sized patterns often fool trout in the fall when they consume vast quantities of the tiny Hyalella scuds, but it would be a mistake to limit the use of scud patterns strictly to early spring and fall. There are prime scud times each day as well. Scuds are most active during low light conditions, making appropriate patterns a prime choice on the shoals during early morning or evening. On overcast days, scud patterns can produce all day long.

Anglers who have found scud patterns less effective than their billing suggests often fail to recognize the key importance of color – matching the hatch – and the daily and seasonal cycles that influence scud behavior. Neither factor is lost on the trout. ⚬

Pearl Shrimp

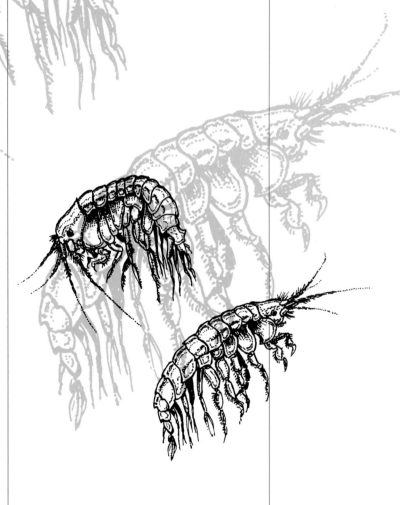

Selected Menu

Callibaetis Nymphs

Lac des Roches Nymph

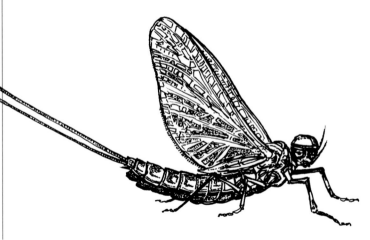

A warm breeze, rippled water and overcast skies make the perfect combination for fishing a Callibaetis mayfly emergence. Cruising confidently under the protection of wind-textured water, trout avidly root out pre-emergent Callibaetis nymphs. The nymphs become active as they near maturity, rising and falling above the Chara beds in an undulating dance as if by design to drive trout mad. Absorbing air and gases from the surrounding water, pre-emergent nymphs take on an enticing sparkle, breaking up their usual mottled tan to acquire olive color schemes.

Opportunistic trout key on the sparkle, taking the suddenly vulnerable nymphs with abandon. Nymph patterns with this hint of flash will make for memorable days, but the best patterns are as skinny and anorexic looking as a chironomid imitation; more robust patterns do not fare nearly as well, especially as the hatch progresses and the trout become increasingly selective.

Fishing nymph patterns in Callibaetis-rich lakes – most often marked by clear water, Chara beds and marl shoals – can be highly effective even if mayflies are rarely the dominant food source in stillwaters. Where they occur in sufficient numbers, Callibaetis nymphs spark interest from trout, and most anglers now recognize the characteristic arched posture, fluttering abdominal gills and darting, minnow-like motion of these dainty nymphs.

Hatching nymphs begin their daily warm-up activities with clockwork regularity and the trout quickly learn the prime times to saunter from deep water to the shoals. Anglers can intercept shoal-bound trout by casting beyond the drop-off and retrieving back to the shoal. Floating lines and long leaders allow suitable patterns to be wind-drifted onto the shoals. As the hatch intensifies, cavalier trout spread out in loose schools to patrol the shoals. Intermediate sinking lines allow an angled retrieve back to the angler, nicely duplicating the emergent swim of the nymph.

Whatever the approach, use a slow hand-twist retrieve, coupled with frequent pauses, to imitate the flutter-rest swimming motion of the nymph. Diving swallows and nighthawks allow anglers to locate feeding fish with a minimum of effort. Always, the hatch will be most intense in specific locations, so it pays to keep a constant watch for unusual or concentrated activity.

On the premiere Callibaetis waters of the south-central Interior, mayflies hatch from mid-May through August. With each successive hatch, Callibaetis nymphs and duns decrease in size due to the reduced growth span between generations. The #12 nymphs of the spring become #14 or #16 by mid-summer, and tiny patterns work wonders in the fall. Hatches occur with startling regularity each year, beginning the same time each season, depending on conditions. Callibaetis hatches are cyclical in nature, some years offering blanket hatches of epic proportions while other years see only sporadic activity. ❧

Selected Menu

Sedge Pupae

Even devoted nymph fishers forsake sunken presentations when confronted with British Columbia's justly famous travelling sedge hatch. The heart-stopping, swirling rises of trout to these large, moth-like insects make the dry fly all but irresistible, but to wring the most out of these often intense hatches, anglers must be proficient in the intricacies of imitating the emerging pupae.

Metamorphosing in the security of their weedy larval homes, the pupae cut their way free to begin an arduous journey to the surface. Like chironomids, large caddisfly pupae are poor swimmers. Using their large, feather-like hind legs the pupae scull trundlingly upwards, often settling again and taking as long as four days to complete the journey to the surface. During this staging process a floating line, a heavily weighted pattern and a 15-foot or longer leader will work wonders. On breezy days, let the pattern drift and bob with the wind as trout love to cruise under the security of rippled water. Trout gently inhale pupal imitations, so the only indication of a take may be a straightening of the line.

As the hatch progresses, the pupae become more active, often streaking skyward using broad rowing strokes. This is the time for a bold strip-pause retrieve, combining foot-long strips with brief pauses. Anglers can anticipate confident takes following the pause just as the fly begins to sink. Intermediate lines are ideal under these conditions.

Pupae scull along just beneath the surface immediately prior to emerging, making buoyant sedge emerger patterns ideal at this stage. Some sedge species emerge in near-shore shallows (or even completely out of the water) and the sub-surface shoreward migration can cover quite a distance. Once ready to emerge, the pupae hang motionless in the surface film, allowing cruising trout to leisurely sip their hapless prey. This results in a series of predictable riseforms, allowing anglers to cast greased pupal patterns ahead of anticipated rises. Even if a fish is seen taking adults, an emerger cast into the ring of the rise is rarely refused.

Pupae of the large travelling sedge are typically dark to medium olive in color with a prominent yellow to lime green banding along the abdomen. Except for the dangling hind legs, the remaining legs are carried tucked neatly underneath the thorax. Prominent wing pads trail along each side of the body, a feature imitations should incorporate. Ragged, scruffy patterns with a little shimmer and soft hackle for subtle animation work best. ✦

Hollywood Caddis

Selected Menu

Dragonfly Nymphs

Butler's Bug

Floating Carey

In the stillwater jungle, the dragonfly nymph seldom plays second fiddle. These fierce underwater predators are a confirmed stillwater staple which, depending on the species, can remain as nymphs for up to four years before transforming to the winged adult stage. The weed-dwelling darners attain lengths of more than two inches at maturity, while the squat, spider-like crawlers reach lengths as long as 1.5 inches.

Anglers will find the largest nymphs in the spring, as these mature nymphs will emerge into adults during the coming months. Their rotund shape makes them a great early-season choice as the large body is difficult to hide and many fall victim to hungry early-season trout. During the fall months, dragonfly nymph patterns are an excellent choice as trout feed ravenously in anticipation of winter. The #6 and larger patterns of the spring are replaced with smaller #8 and #10 imitations. Dragons grow through a series of moults called instars, and freshly moulted nymphs are a distinct bright green color. These 'neon nymphs' are shy and reclusive, perhaps because they are preferred by the trout. Many anglers carry a selection of bright green dragonfly nymph patterns for just this reason.

The larger climbing nymphs of the family Aeshnidae favor the rich algae-type lakes, whereas the sprawling Libellulidae nymphs occur in large populations in the clear marl lakes. Creeping a buoyant sprawler pattern over dense beds of Chara is a great searching method. Both families are capable of absorbing water through their abdomens, creating a natural jet-propulsion system when the water is expelled. The aggressive darner nymphs put this skill to good use, while the sedentary sprawlers prefer to crawl from one ambush position to the next.

Retrieves for darner imitations should incorporate a few quick strips, especially when traversing barren patches between weed beds. Sensing their vulnerability, the nymphs attempt to avoid cruising trout by darting for cover.

Dragonfly nymph patterns are ideal when casting to visible fish. Cast the pattern well ahead of the anticipated travel path and allow it to sink to bottom. As the fish nears, pop the rod tip or give one quick strip to draw attention. Exercise patience and wait for the trout to make its move – often a fish will appear to pass by, only to turn and pounce at the last moment, like a dog stealing table scraps.

For the reclusive sprawler, a slow, methodical hand-twist retrieve on a full sinking line works best. Working sprawler patterns up the lip of a drop-off is a great method when prospecting new lakes. Takes are soft, opposite of the vicious strikes typical when fishing darner patterns. ◄•

Selected Menu

Leeches

Growing to lengths in excess of eight inches, leeches are popular on the menus of most trout, but it is the smaller specimens which receive the most attention. Trout favor leeches in the three-inch range and smaller, sometimes much smaller. Experimenting anglers have found leech patterns tied on #10 and smaller hooks to be highly successful, especially in near-shore shallows during the late fall.

Evidence has also shown trout often take leeches following intense feeding on chironomid pupa, apparently as a natural cork used to stopper down the vast numbers of pupae consumed. Nightfall, however, is prime time for leech patterns. Primarily nocturnal, leeches go on the prowl under cover of darkness, and while dusk is a key time, fishing large, 'noisy' patterns well into the night is a serious option, particularly during the heat of the so-called summer doldrums.

A stillwater staple with year-round appeal, leeches are most often used in early spring and late fall. Trout are then concentrated in the shallows, often in areas with barely enough water to cover their backs. Small patterns presented on a floating line and 15-foot leader can be very effective in these situations. Strike indicators can be used to suspend leech patterns at precise depths, allowing the fly to be properly presented in even the shallowest water.

Leeches make the ultimate 'chuck it and chance it' pattern, thanks to their active swimming habits. Trout seldom refuse a leech undulating in open water. When the fish are active, a slow 12-inch or steady four-inch pull retrieve is effective, particularly with the more gaudy patterns designed to draw trout from a distance.

Bead-head patterns add an enticing jigging action to the fly, but when trout become fickle, somber patterns crept along bottom with a slow, methodical hand-twist retrieve seem to work best. The horizontal presentation afforded by slow-sinking, intermediate and stillwater fly lines makes these lines mandatory for serious leech fishing.

The majority of popular patterns lean towards dark colors, mainly black or maroon. These color schemes offer a great silhouette and are the patterns of choice for low light or evening fishing, but leeches come in a myriad of colors, including brown, olive and green. On bright days the earth tones of a brown, or the camouflaged mixture of a green and olive leech, can make all the difference. ✦

Glenn's Leech

Selected Menu

Stonefly Nymphs

Lohr's Rubber Leg Stone

Stoneflies are to rivers what leeches, scuds and dragonflies are to stillwaters. They are the number-one staple food item of choice for river trout in British Columbia. At the top of the cobble tumbler's list, stonefly nymphs will double the catches of anglers prepared to put the dry fly aside long enough to learn the intricacies of fishing sunken stonefly imitations.

Depending on the species, stoneflies can remain as nymphs for up to four years, which means trout regularly see tumbling stonefly nymphs. Requiring constant moving water in order for their rudimentary gill systems to function, stonefly nymphs are found in the rough-and-tumble sections of rivers, and never in lakes.

Rummaging about the loose rocks and boulders along the stream floor, stonefly nymphs are often swept adrift. Feeble swimmers, they barely have enough co-ordination to right themselves. Stoneflies also disperse themselves through a phenomenon known as behavioral drift, which basically consists of letting go and drifting downstream to other suitable locations. Bouncing heavily weighted nymphs along the bottom is consequently a great way to scour riffles for trout.

Prior to emerging on shore, the nymphs mass in the shallows and trout follow them tight to shore, picking off the nymphs as they labor along the bottom. Emergence often takes place during the spring freshet, making stonefly nymphs a prime pattern at this time.

Successful stonefly presentations most often call for floating lines and leaders nine to 12 feet long. Strike indicators, positioned so the leader below is about twice as long as the depth being fished, are a necessity if subtle takes amidst swirling currents are to be detected. Trout instantly spit out frauds, so quick reactions are mandatory. In strong riffles and pocket water, additional weight on the leader may be required to sink the fly into the relative calm of the hydro-dynamic cushion found along the bottom. Strike indicators should be held back during the drift as the surface currents are swifter than those along the bottom.

Tuck casts present the fly upstream by allowing the line and leader to roll out completely prior to landing on the water. The nymph lands first, plummetting to the bottom. Follow the indicator with the rod held high and as the nymph drifts past, lower the tip and follow the fly downstream. The majority of takes can be expected when the indicator swings directly in front.

The Brooks method is an alternative to traditional floating-line tactics. Famed angler Charlie Brooks used a high-density sinking line, short leader and weighted fly in the same manner as a floating line, especially in deeper runs and slots. No matter what the method, keep the casting distance at a minimum to maintain maximum control. It is better to shotgun an area systematically with short, controllable casts than to over-reach with long casts. ✺

Selected Menu

Redside Shiners

Stocking of the native rainbow trout strains known as Gerrards, Blackwaters and Tzenzaicuts has changed the way anglers perceive redside shiners in British Columbia. No longer an 'infestation' to be checked at all costs, redside shiners are the single most important food item for these aggressive, piscivorous trout. As the number of lakes stocked with such trout strains increases, growing numbers of anglers are becoming devotees of the once-vilified redside shiner.

Native to many B.C. waters, shiners are one of the most-studied forage fish due to their potential impact on other species, most notably rainbow trout. With locust-like efficiency, an unchecked shiner population out-competes other species in short order. Rooting deep into weeds and bottom structure, shiners feed where larger species seldom venture, laying waste to scuds, mayflies and other desired trout fare in the process.

The dark olive to brown backs, large yellow eyes, distinct red stripe and skittish swimming make the shiner easy to spot. Zonker-style dressings displaying a large surface area and a distinct lateral line are ideal. Amongst the shiner fraternity there is a definite pecking order, with the smaller members relegated to the security of shallow water, so a variety of fly sizes, from a large #2 down through #8, are a sensible precaution. Big streamers will require the backbone of heavy-calibre rods to turn over – and punch out against afternoon winds.

Scouring the lake in large schools, shiners spread onto the shoals as water temperatures rise, making high summer prime shiner time. Diving birds such as loons target these shiner balls, fracturing the school into smaller splinter groups. Trout working in squads haunt the edges, singling out stragglers with wolf pack precision.

Structure such as large weedbeds and fallen or sunken timber is a shiner magnet. Steep shorelines with deadfall trees can be targetted with intermediate or slow-sinking fly lines. The shiners will be congregated amongst the outstretched sunken branches. Secure in the depths, marauding trout hunt up from below, knifing through schooled shiners with startling ferocity.

The attendant savagery will leave anglers awestruck, but a quick cast followed with a fast-paced, panic-stricken retrieve will result in rod-thumping strikes. During spells of inactivity, fan cast around the boat using a lazy, random strip retrieve to imitate the meanderings of a single shiner. Large trout venture into the shallows early and late in the day, feeding under the security of low light. Latching onto one of these aggressive fish is a real thrill, both because of the violence of the strike and the shallow water battle which ensues. Ensure the reel is amply loaded with backing. ◄

Bus's Shiner

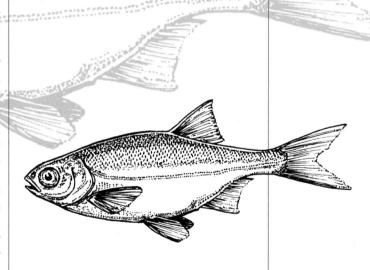

Selected Menu

Waterboatmen

Krystal Boatman

Although available year-round, waterboatmen only slip onto the menu of stillwater trout immediately after ice-off and again in the late fall. These stillwater beetles are common inhabitants of the shallows in productive lakes throughout British Columbia. Breathing through a process known as plastron respiration, waterboatmen are air-breathing insects, making them prisoners of the shallows. Trapping a bubble of air against their bodies, boatmen have a distinct silvery shine which often masks their true body color. Radiant patterns featuring mylar, Flashabou or Krystal Flash are required to mimic this sheen and are essential when trout feed selectively.

Boatmen are often mistaken for their larger cousins, the backswimmers. Characterized by dark backs and light bellies the color of masking tape, waterboatmen seldom exceed half an inch in length. Backswimmers have light backs and dark bellies and grow as long as three quarters of an inch. The prominent oar-like legs common to both insects should be a primary feature on any pattern.

Prime time to fish boatmen imitations is in the late fall after the first frosts of the season. Capable of flight, mature boatmen mate and disperse, crashing headlong into lakes all over the south-central Interior of the province. These cascading boatmen give the illusion of rainfall. Slamming onto the surface of the water, boatmen spin wildly, as though knocked senseless by the impact. After breaking through the surface film, boatmen scoot down to the bottom, depositing their eggs on weeds and other subsurface debris. Trout sometimes become fixated on the surface-spinning boatmen. Traditional patterns will not tempt these selective fish, but anglers lucky enough to have buoyant boatmen patterns in their fly boxes can reap huge rewards at this time.

The key to successful presentation is duplicating the U-shaped path boatmen follow as they travel to and from the bottom to replenish their oxygen supply. In shallow water, weighted patterns fished on floating lines are effective, provided the front portion of the hook is weighted, achieving the nose-down attitude of diving boatmen. In water deeper than 10 feet, a high-density, full-sinking line works well. The heavy belly section of traditional full-sinking lines pulls the fly down to the bottom as it sinks. A brisk, choppy strip retrieve back to the surface completes the U-shaped travel path.

No matter what presentation technique is used, strikes are invariably savage. The rapid sculling swim of the waterboatmen causes trout to strike quickly and aggressively.

Selected Menu
Three Spined Stickleback

Stickleback tend to be ignored by all but the most seasoned of coastal anglers despite their status as the food item of choice for larger cutthroat trout. Presenting a broad profile due to prominent spines which might grow as long as three inches, stickleback are particularly important in spring and early summer. Males are fearlessly aggressive in defence of their nests during the spring spawning period, making attractive targets for predatory cutthroat.

The trout do take full advantage, to the point of working in teams, herding stickleback to the surface. Predation studies show cutthroat prefer stickleback above other prey fish, including often abundant kokanee and sockeye fry populations. Shallow-water spring and summer patterns should mimic the common grey and olive stickleback coloration, but black patterns are an option in deeper water and when profile matters more than precise color.

During the cooler months, probe the deeper regions with fast-sinking lines. In coastal lakes such shoals tend to be devoid of trout until water temperatures moderate in spring, making fast-sinking lines invaluable. Goal posts for feeding zones are established using the count-down method (usually in 10-second increments). Once in the zone, be prepared for very light takes, often no more than a slight ticking sensation, as if the fly were passing through grass or light weeds. Standard response is to pause, count to three, then strike.

There are few commercial stickleback patterns available, but those included in the Selected Patterns for this book are proven veterans. Tied-down minnow variations make good imitations of the smaller stream-dwelling sticklebacks, but in lakes, a vibrant, mobile pattern with a broad silhouette is ideal. Exact replication is rarely necessary, but patterns should suggest the darting movements of the natural. Eyes are a critical focal point for attacking cutthroat, proven by the fact that blind patterns are less successful.

Contrary to popular belief, strikes to stickleback and other forage fish are often more subtle than savage. Trout will bump and nudge prey fish prior to swallowing, causing them to bleed from the gills. A dab of red on imitations can be as important a trigger as prominent eyes.

Dart the fly in and around cover using a varied strip retrieve, from fast to slow. Stickleback hover in helicopter fashion, fanning their pectoral fins like rotors, so occasional pauses should be part of the retrieve, provided the pattern 'breathes' on its own. In moving waters, swim the fly down and across as stickleback cannot manage prolonged upstream travel. Presentations parallel with the bank are ideal as stickleback congregate in the nooks and crannies along the margins of rivers and streams. Marauding cutthroat often vault up from below to take their prey, so patterns incorporating foam and other buoyant materials are a wise addition.

Lohr's Stickleback

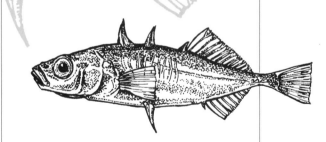

Selected Menu

Damselflies

The Undulating Damsel

Easily recognizable by their long, slender profile and distinctive swimming motion, damselflies occur in staggering numbers in many British Columbia lakes, but especially in the nutrient-rich waters of the Interior plateau. Trout prowl the stillwater jungles of these lakes, picking off large numbers of this food source. Damselflies are available to the trout through the year, but become most vulnerable during their long and potentially hazardous emergence swim from the depths to shoreside vegetation.

Favoring long-stemmed vegetation, damsels lurk in ambush, waiting for their food to pass by. The undersides of leafy vegetation such as Potamogeton are preferred hideouts. Sporting variegated color schemes, damsel nymphs in clear-water marl lakes are a pale watery green, a finicky color to duplicate. In algae or tannin-stained waters, traditional olive to olive-brown nymphs predominate. Skinny, spartan patterns are required to imitate the sleek profile of damselfly nymphs. They are fierce predators, consuming large quantities of chironomid larvae, mayfly nymphs and scuds. Under ideal conditions, mature nymphs can attain lengths as long as 1.5 inches.

In late spring, damsels migrate en masse towards emergent shoreside vegetation to complete the transformation to the adult stage. Rather than creeping shoreward through the relative safety of the weed beds, damsels expose themselves by swimming just sub-surface. Trout ravage these emerging hordes with bold, aggressive surface strikes. Often, anglers must nestle amongst shoreline vegetation so the fly can be retrieved in step with the migration, from deeper water into and over the shoals.

Horizontal presentations can also be key. Floating or intermediate fly lines are needed to keep the fly in the top band of the water column. Waddling shoreward less than a foot beneath the surface, the nymphs tire quickly, making a slow hand-twist retrieve, coupled with frequent pauses, the most effective. A slow strip retrieve while jiggling the rod tip seductively to add attractive movement can draw strikes when the trout seem finicky. Under ideal conditions, trout follow the nymphs right to shore, making for exhilarating strikes, lost flies and broken leaders as the panicking trout run in and around the tules or other shoreline obstacles.

Perhaps the most difficult aspect of fishing the damselfly hatch is duplicating the sinusoidal swimming motion of the nymphs. Patterns incorporating rabbit fur, marabou or aftershaft feathers are a must. Knotted onto the leader using a Duncan loop, these patterns wiggle and shimmy with a natural animation trout find hard to resist.

It would be a mistake to assume damsels are important only during the peak of activity associated with the emergence. Immature nymphs are available in good numbers year-round and may be regularly seen laboring from one hideout to the next. Foraging during the fall in preparation for winter, trout will stuff themselves with immature damselflies. At this time of the year simple, tiny #10 or smaller patterns can work wonders. ◄

Selected Menu

Chironomid Pupae

I f scuds can be likened to an infestation, then chironomids can be thought of as an epidemic. Available through the year, chironomid pupae are a regular feature on the menu of trout, and the number one food source in stillwaters.

Imitating the slender pupae has become a science. The silvery glow of trapped air and gases which cocoon the pupae makes fly patterns incorporating materials such as Frost Bite, Flashabou and Krystal Flash mandatory for selective fish. The hovering pupae take up to four days to ascend, so trout have ample time to gorge before there is any sign of activity at the surface. Figuring out what depth the trout are feeding at is the key.

Standard practice calls for the use of floating lines in conjunction with long leaders – 15 feet or more, depending on depth. Leaders about three or four feet longer than the depth being fished allow for the angle of the line as it is retrieved. Weight should be added in windy conditions as sub-surface currents will otherwise carry the pattern away from feeding trout. Systematically counting the pattern down before initiating a painstakingly slow retrieve is the most popular approach. Five-minute retrieves are not unheard of.

For precise depth control, attach a strike indicator to the leader. Begin by placing the fly about one foot from the bottom, then adjust the indicator on succeeding casts until feeding trout are located. The strike indicator tethers the fly to the feeding zone throughout the retrieve. A slow, one-foot strip retrieve followed by a long pause often triggers strikes when the action slows. Takes most often occur immediately following the strip.

The floating-line presentation reaches its limits in about 20 feet of water. When chironomids emerge in water more than 20 feet deep, switch to a full sinking line of at least type II density. Firmly anchored, pull off a length of sinking line equal to the depth being fished. Cast and allow the line to sink until it is hanging directly below the rod tip before beginning a slow hand-twist retrieve. Trout tend to follow the pattern to the surface, finally taking the fly in a vicious downward motion.

Fish key very specifically on size and color as the hatch builds. Chironomid pupae tend to be larger than the hatching adults, so pupal imitations one size greater than the emerged adults make sense. Using even larger pupal patterns as the hatch becomes increasingly intense helps the fly stand out in the throng of ascending pupae. Newly emerged adults tend to be brighter in color than the rising pupa, so choose patterns a shade darker than the adults.

The largest chironomid species (the 'bombers') favor mud-bottomed lakes, while chironomids found in clear marl lakes tend to be smaller. Early in the day, smaller-sized pupae predominate, with larger pupae more prevalent as the day progresses. Size also varies with the seasons. Pupae will be largest in the spring, tapering down in size as the season progresses through August and into October. A selection of patterns ranging in size from #8 through #16 will cover most situations. ◄

Ice Cream Cone

Selected Menu

Sculpins

Wool Head Sculpin

Big-ticket food items such as sculpins become increasingly important to trout as they mature and grow to the trophy sizes prized by anglers. Worthy of serious consideration by any angler, sculpins are capable of living in such diverse habitats as lakes, rivers, streams and salt water. A number of British Columbia Interior lakes boast healthy sculpin populations and most coastal lakes hold their share of these spiny-rayed bottom dwellers. Where they occur, trout, char and bass readily include sculpins in their menus.

Successful presentations require the fly to be on or near the bottom. Mottled masters of camouflage, sculpins dart or use their enlarged pectoral fins to creep amid bottom rubble and weedbeds. In rivers and streams, sunken timber, rocks and boulders make prime sculpin habitat. Undercut banks should be probed with either parallel or perpendicular presentations; even the largest stream trout will stir from its deep-cover lie for the chance to snap up a fleeing sculpin.

Primarily nocturnal feeders, sculpins scuttle along the bottom, feeding opportunistically on a wide range of food items including fish eggs, insects and the fry of most other species – trout and bass included. A sculpin worked near the bottom in the spring can be dynamite on early-season smallmouth bass. Aggressive, pre- and post-spawn smallmouth zealously guard their nests and clearly recognize sculpins for the efficient egg and offspring predators that they are. Beach fishing for coastal cutthroat is also a prime opportunity for sculpin imitations. Sea-runs prey heavily on sculpins, so much so that it is not uncommon to have them regurgitate a number of sandy, speckled salt water sculpins prior to release.

Full-sinking and sinktip lines are the best choices for lakes and streams respectively. Weighted patterns presented on or near the bottom and swum down and across to present a broad silhouette work best. Upstream casts followed by a series of mends effectively sink the fly, but split shot may be required on the leader in heavy water. Leader length should be kept relatively short to offset the natural buoyancy of monofilament.

In lakes, count the fly down to bottom and keep it there on each successive cast, which requires consistent timing. Whether in lakes or streams, use a darting strip retrieve with distinct pauses. Sculpins are bottom lurkers, often resting against the bottom on extended pectorals. Rarely will they put on a burst of speed, and never for any extended period. Takes range from smash-and-grab to surprisingly subtle, so standard practice is to strike at anything out of the ordinary.

Matuka-style patterns incorporating feather or rabbit-strip wings mixed with a broad head of mixed deerhair or wool have proven very effective. ✎

Ice Cream Cone
(Contributed by Kelly Davison)

Hook: TMC 2302, #10–18
Tying Thread: Danville's 6/0 (blk.)
Rib: Red copper wire
Body: Super Floss (color to suit)
Thorax: Built-up tying thread
Head: Blk. metal bead spray painted wht.

Floating Carey
(Contributed by Duncan Laird)

Hook: TMC 5263, #6–10
Thread: Olv. Monocord or 6/0 Uni Thread
Body: Deerhair mix (spun and clipped)
Hackle: Blu. phase pheas. rump
*Note: Deerhair is mixed & blended in
same manner as dubbing*

Butler's Bug
(Contributed by Glenn Butler)

Hook: TMC 5263, #4–10
Thread: Blk. Monocord
Tail & Under-Body: Nat. deerhair
Rib: Fine gold oval tinsel
Body: Seal fur
Wing Case: Pheas. tail
Thorax: Seal fur
Legs: Knotted pheas. tail fibres (6)
Eyes: Pheas. tail fibres
Head: Peacock herl

Hook: TMC 2457, #6–12
Thread: Tan or olv. 8/0
Rib: 2 strands yel. or grn. embroidery floss or 1
strand Super Floss
Body: Dubbing or rug yarn
Thorax: Pheas. tail Angel Hair spun in a dubbing loop
Head: Copper or gold bead

Hollywood Caddis
*(Contributed by Gord
Honey)*

Undulating Damsel
(Contributed by Ryan Pohl)

Hook: TMC 200R, #8–12
Thread: Light olv. 6/0
Tail: Marabou
Rib: Fine copper wire
Body: Twisted marabou
Hackle: Dyed yel. guinea
Eyes: Pre-made mono.
Head: Olv. ostrich herl wound arnd. eyes

Krystal Boatman
(Contributed by Phil Rowley)

Hook: TMC 3769, #10–14
Thread: Blk. 6/0 or 8/0
Tag: Silv. Flashabou
Shell Back: Blk. Krystal Flash
Body: Yel. to tan dubbing spun in a loop of pearl. and silv. Krystal Flash
Legs: Brn. or olv. Super Floss

Glenn's Leech
(Contributed by Glenn Gerbrandt)

Hook: TMC 2457, #8–12 (weighted)
Thread: Red 6/0
Tail: Rabbit fur strip
Rib: Fine gold wire
Body: Marabou wound by the tips

Hook: TMC 2457 or 3769, #10–16
Thread: Olv.
Rib: Fine copper or gold wire
Shell Back: A strip of pearl. sheet mat. or paper twist
Body: Seal fur dubbing mix or substitute

Pearl Shrimp
(Contributed by Phil Rowley)

Bus's Shiner
(Contributed by Bus Ellis)

Hook: TMC 5263, #4–8
Thread: Wht. or blk.
Body: Silv. or pearl. mylar tubing
Under-Wing: Wht. bucktail, polar bear or Antron
Mid-Wing: Gold or copper Krystal Flash
Over-Wing: 8-10 strands of peacock herl
Head: Tying thread
Eyes: Stick-on eyes or Jungle Cock

Hook: Mustad 9671, 2X, #4
Tail: Sandy brn. marabou
Under-Body Head: Flattened lead wire
Under-Body Back 1/3: Packing foam
Body: Sandy brn. dubbing w/marabou fibres tied in on top
Fins: Barred body feather from grouse or partridge
Head: Spun wool dubbing chen. trimmed to wedge shape, flat on top & bottom, wide at sides. Make dubbing chen. w/different colors of wool – tan, brn.
Eyes: None or glued-on baby doll eyes
Note: Fly fishes hook point up

Wool Head Sculpin
(Contributed by Ian Forbes)

Lohr's Rubber Leg Stone
(Contributed by Harold Lohr)

Hook: TMC 200R, #4–8
Thread: Brn. 6/0
Tail: Peccary bristles
Rib: Stripped brn. hackle stem
Body: Brn. Larva Lace
Wing Case: Mottled turkey tail folded
Legs: Brn. Span Flex
Thorax: Med.–coarse brn. dubbing
Eyes: Plastic nymph eyes (blk.)
Antennae: Peccary bristles

Hook: TMC 5263, #10–12
Body: Silv. Diamond Braid
Sides: Silv. holographic Flashabou
Back & Tail: Dyed olv. mallard flank
Eyes: Pearl or silv. prismatic eyes
Tying Note: Once fly is complete, cover body and shell back completely w/epoxy

Lohr's Stickleback
(Contributed by Harold Lohr)

Hook: TMC 3761, #12–16
Tail: Partridge
Rib: Fine copper wire
Wing Case: Shell back & pheas. tail
Body: Dirty yel.–tan dubbing
Thorax: Same as body
Legs: Partridge

Lac des Roches Nymph
(Contributed by Brian Chan)

Black Red Butt Chironomid
(Contributed by Brian Chan)

Hook: TMC 2547, #16-10
Tag: Red Flashabou
Rib: Fine silv. wire
Body: Blk. Flashabou
Thorax: Peacock herl
Shell Back: Drk. brn. pheas. tail fibres
Gills: Wht. Antron yarn

Many chironomid larvae are red or maroon in color and some red coloration is often retained in the abdomen of pupae after transition from the larval stage. This pattern takes advantage of the fact that trout often select red-butted pupae out of the many thousands that are solid colored. Best fished as close to bottom as possible on a floating line and 16- to 24-foot-long leader, the fly should be retrieved with a dead slow hand twist. Most chironomids emerge in water less than 25 feet deep; strike indicators allow the fly to be presented at precise depths.

Hook: TMC 5263, #10–12
Thread: Olv. grn. 8/0
Tail: Med. olv. marabou
Rib: Fine gold wire
Body: Med. olv. Antron dubbing
Thorax: Med. olv. Antron dubbing
Wing Case: Syn. raffia
Eye: 15-lb. mono. melted
Legs: Olv. Flashabou dubbing

Flashy Damsel
*(Contributed by
Dave Paille)*

Originally designed for damselfly migrations in lakes with dense algae blooms, the pattern stands out in such murky or cloudy water, but has a proven track record in clear water lakes as well. Best fished on a floating line and leaders at least 15 feet long, the fly is retrieved with a slow hand twist consisting of four-inch-long pulls. On windy days, retain control and achieve better strike detection by using the same retrieve but with intermediate sinking lines.

Hook: TMC 5263, #8–12
Rib: Bright grn. Super Floss
Body: Med. to drk. grn. Antron dubbing
Thorax: Peacock herl
Shell Back: Drk. brn. pheas. tail fibres
Throat: Peacock Angel Hair
Legs: Drk. brn. pheas. rump fibres

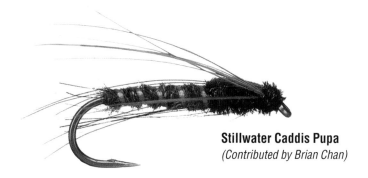

Stillwater Caddis Pupa
(Contributed by Brian Chan)

Tied in a variety of sizes, this pattern is an excellent imitation of the caddis pupae commonly found in Interior lakes. The bright green ribbing is an important element, as it is quite pronounced on the natural. Fished on either floating or intermediate lines, fast strip retrieves of between four and eight inches with one-second pauses work best. Long leaders of 14 to 18 feet are used with floating lines, allowing coverage of the shallows and deeper parts of the shoal by varying the length of time the fly takes to sink. Intermediate lines are used to probe the bottom of the shoal. Wind drifting the pattern is effective, as undulating wave action imparts a very natural movement to the fly.

Furry Foam Dragon
(Contributed by Phil Rowley)

Hook: TMC 9457BI, #6-8
Thread: Olv. or brn. 6/0 Uni Thread
Over-Body: Furry Foam strip, brn. or olv. mottled w/permanent markers
Body: Light grn. or dirty yel. deerhair spun & clipped to shape
Legs: Olv. or brn. rubber hackle or Sili legs
Head: Same combination as the body; trim the foam strip over the eye to simulate the triangular head of the sprawler nymphs

Designed to imitate Libellulidae dragonfly nymphs, the fly allows use of a slow, plodding hand-twist retrieve which mimics the pace of these largely sedentary nymphs. The blend of stiffness and flexibility in the fly's legs perfectly mirrors the wiggling legs of the natural as the nymphs amble along bottom. Effective in most lakes, it is at its best in clear marl lakes featuring large beds of Chara. Use a full sinking line and nine-foot leader to place the pattern on or near bottom. Takes are subtle, opposite of the savage takes when fishing darner nymphs.

Burnt Shrimp
(Contributed by Hermann Fischer)

Hook: TMC 2457, #10–14
Tail: Hackle fibres same color as body
Body: Fine Crystal Chenille in various shades of grn.

A unique combination of Crystal Chenille and heat forms the basis of this design. After forming the body, trim the sides and top, leaving the bottom fibres to serve as legs. Pinching the fly between thumb and index finger, pass the back of the fly through the flame of a lighter. This melts and seals the plastic fibres. At its best in early spring and late fall, the fly is retrieved with a series of short pulls followed by a five- to eight-second pause. To get an exact color match, use white Crystal Chenille and add color with permanent markers.

Crystal Caddis
*(Contributed by
Phil Rowley)*

Hook: TMC 2302, #6-8
Thread: Color to match body
Body: Crystal Chenille spun in a dubbing loop of syn. dubbing or seal fur
Wing Case: Pheas. rump
Thorax: Syn. dubbing or seal fur
Wing Pads: Lacquered mottled turkey trimmed to shape
Legs: Grouse
Antenna: Two fibres from wing case mat. tied back over the body
Head: Peacock herl or Arizona Syn. Peacock dubbing

At its best when large traveller sedges are active, a weighted version of this pattern, fished on a long leader and floating line, is often effective just prior to the hatch. Bring the pattern up from bottom using a slow, chironomid-paced retrieve – most often anglers retrieve caddis pupa imitations too quickly. As the hatch builds, switch to an active retrieve using an intermediate line to duplicate the angled trek of the ascending pupa. A slow strip retrieve mixed with pauses duplicates the swim/pause motion of the sculling pupa.

Hook: TMC 5263, #2-8
Thread: Gry. Monocord
Rib: Fine silv. wire
Lateral Line: Bright orng. chen.
Body: Pearl. or silv. Crystal Chenille
Wing: Drk. olv. rabbit strip
Gills: Red Krystal Flash
Head: Olv. or gry. lambswool spun & clipped
Eyes: Molded eyes epoxied to wool head

Rabbit Shiner
(Contributed by Phil Rowley)

Presenting the broad profile of the redside shiner, this fly is best worked in and around weedbeds, sunken debris or downed timber with Stillwater or intermediate fly lines. With trout aggressively slashing through schools of shiners, a quick erratic strip will draw attention. When searching, use a slow 12- to 14-inch strip retrieve to imitate rambling, solitary shiners. When trout are focussed on large shiners, a seven- or eight-weight rod will punch out large versions of the pattern.

Mikulak Sedge
(Contributed by Phil Rowley)

Hook: TMC 200R, #6–10
Thread: Olv. 6/0 Uni Thread or Monocord
Tail: Nat. elk hair
Body: Olv. seal fur
Wing: Nat. elk tied in 3 clumps along body
Hackle: Brn. trimmed flush along bottom

Art Mikulak's sedge is perhaps the finest stillwater caddis pattern ever designed. The mixture of natural elk and seal fur provides a realistic outline that hugs the water just like the natural sedge. A 12-foot leader and long strip retrieve achieve the surface-creasing V wake created by scampering naturals and result in aggressive takes from trout. In windy conditions, retrieve the fly up-wind, as the naturals tend to scurry into the wind. At dusk, fish the *Mikulak* into the fading light for as long as it is possible to see the take. Fishing after dark is possible by listening for the takes or using a strip retrieve to feel the strike.

Damsel Leech Thing
(Contributed by Gordon Honey)

Hook: TMC 5262, #10-14
Thread: Olv. Uni Thread
Tail: Olv. marabou and 2 strands gold Flashabou
Body: Mixture of Antron dubbing & a snippet of peacock Angel Hair twisted together in a loop of fine copper wire
Head: Small gold bead

This pattern's olive coloration breaks from traditional dark leech-type designs. Using a blend of predominantly golden green mixed with light green, medium green and brown Antron dubbing creates the perfect brown-olive mix. A fly for all seasons, the pattern is best during the crisp days of late fall when trout mass in the shallows, gorging prior to ice-up. Rolling or moving fish in 12 feet of water or less can be intercepted with a floating line and leaders of 14 feet or longer. Use a slow hand twist retrieve with lots of pauses if there is no response to the fly as it sinks.

Hook: TMC 3761, #12–16
Tail: Micro-Fleck Turkey Flats
Rib: 1 strand pearl. Krystal Flash
Counter Rib: Fine gold wire
Body: Ozark turkey quill, cinnamon or olv.
Legs: Micro-Fleck Turkey Flats
Wing Case: Mottled turkey quill tied double-back style

Turkey Quill Callibaetis
(Contributed by Phil Rowley)

Designed for trout accustomed to Callibaetis mayflies, the pattern uses Ozark turkey quill to present the mottled, fuzzy silhouette of the natural to fussy trout. Worked near or along the shoal edge with either floating or intermediate fly lines and 12-foot-long leaders, a very slow hand twist punctuated with pauses often works best. As the season progresses, downsize the pattern. In fall, ply the shallows with #14 or #16 versions of this fly.

Crystal Chenille Backswimmer
(Contributed by Brian Chan)

Hook: TMC3769, #10–12
Shell Back: Drk. turkey tail fibres (coated w/ Flexament)
Body: Peacock-colored plastic chen.
Legs: Drk. brn. Super Floss

Important early in the spring and again late in the fall, a prominent feature of diving boatmen/backswimmers is the bubble of air that engulfs the underside of the body. This allows the insects to breathe while underwater, and the peacock chenille material of this fly offers a good impression of the trapped air bubble. Using a floating line in shallow water, allow the fly to sink close to the bottom before initiating a quick, short strip retrieve of two- to four-inch pulls. In deeper water, use a type II or faster sinking line; the thicker portions of the line sink faster than the thinner tip section, creating a belly in the fly line. A fast strip retrieve will pull the fly down, then back up through the water column.

Dragonfly Nymph #1
(Contributed by Jack Shaw)

Hook: Mustad 9672, 9673 or 79580 lng., #6-10
Thread: Med. olv. grn. 6.0
Body: Seal fur or substitute
Sub-Body: 4-ply wool of any olv. or brn.-olv. color
Thorax: Half dozen strands of brnz. colored peacock herl
Wing Cover: Flue fibres from the sides of a drk. turkey tail feather (the brn. barred part)
Hackle or Legs: Fibres off the side of a hen pheas. centre tail feather.
Head: 3-4 strands of brnz. peacock herl

Designed to imitate the nymphal stage of the large blue dragonflies of the order Ondonata, species *Anax Junius*, this fly is highly effective when fished with knowledge and intelligence. With a life span of three to five years in the nymphal stage, they live where dead cattails and other detritus litter the bottom. The olive brown coloration of this pattern well imitates nymphs dwelling in such bottom areas.

Hook: Mustad 9673 lng., #6–8
Thread: Olv. grn. 6.0
Body; Med. to drk. mole grn. seal fur or substitute
Thorax: Grn. or brassy grn. peacock herl
Wing Cover: Drk. turkey tail feather
Hackle or Legs: Hen pheas. centre tail feather
Head: Grn. peacock herl

Dragonfly Nymph #2
(Contributed by Jack Shaw)

The slightly larger, older nymph this pattern was designed to imitate lives on marl beds with patches of green bottom growth. Seldom active, it lurks in wait for its prey to come by, mainly shrimp and other insects. The best fishing strategy is very tedious, but often productive. Let the fly sink close to bottom growth in a likely-looking area and move it only once in awhile. The movement will kick up a bit of marl, like smoke, attracting fish to the bottom disturbance. A sudden fast retrieve at that point will often entice a fish into getting careless.

Dragonfly Nymph #3
(Contributed by Jack Shaw)

Hook: Mustad 9673 or 79580 lng., #6-8
Thread: Light olv. grn. 6.0
Body: Seal fur or substitute
Color: Med. to light mole grn.
Thorax: Light grn. peacock herl
Wing Case Cover: Taken from the side of a light gry. goose quill dyed with a pale grn. ink pen (I use the Pantone pens)
Hackle or Legs: Flue off the side of a hen pheas. centre tail feather
Head: Bright grn. flue from the side of a peacock sword feather

This version is probably the most productive as it represents a dragonfly nymph that has just shed its skin as it grows from one instar to the next. This is a vulnerable time for these nymphs. Their color, a very pale green, and their huge, dark bulbous eyes are not conducive to hiding. They are very shy at this stage of their development, immediately moving to the far side of a plant stem or the underside of a rock if anything moves near them. This sudden movement is obvious to hunting fish and many of these insects fall prey. Fish this pattern when floating; empty nymphal cases are seen in quiet bays or over large patches of Chara weed. Watch the line carefully as fish take these nymphs quite gently.

Bloodworm
(Contributed by Jack Shaw)

Hook: Mustad 9672 or a 9673 lng. shank, #8–12
Head: Fine blk. 6.0
Tail: Blk. bear hair
Rib: Fine copper wire
Body: Originally, fine drk. maroon chen., later a single-ply or 4-wool yarn of the same drk. maroon color
Hackle: Drk. brn. feather from saddle patch of cock pheas., as drk. as possible from approx. halfway up from the tail

Designed to imitate mud-dwelling chironomid larvae, this pattern must be fished close to the bottom, preferably on nine-foot leaders with three-foot-long tippets. Let the fly sink, then start a slow hand-over-hand retrieve, recovering about 12 to 15 inches of line per second, with frequent pauses for up to 10 seconds. Often when larger bloodworms are close to pupating, they leave the larval tube before the transformation is complete. They then have the white plumosis, but the body retains the full appearance of the bloodworm. It is a good idea to have a few flies tied with this feature on them, particularly early in the season. Keep the added plumosis small, not larger than 1/8 inch round, even smaller on any but the largest patterns.

Blood Leech
(Contributed by Jack Shaw)

Hook: Mustad #6–12; best on hooks smaller than #8; use lng.-shanked 9672 & 79580 w/ #10 & 12 hooks
Thread: Fine blk. 6.0
Tail: Drk. maroon mohair wool
Body: Drk. maroon mohair

When fishing this pattern in lakes with marl bottoms, allow the fly to rest on bottom, then work it in the marl with a series of rapid pulls, followed by a few steady, slow pulls. Let it rest there for 10 or 15 seconds before again starting it with a few rapid pulls. In areas of trash bottom, use the countdown method to fish as close to bottom as possible. When fishing mid-water zones, so-called short takes are common. Resist the tendency to retrieve the line and recast or to ruin the fly by shortening the tail. Instead, let the fly sit for up to 20 seconds; usually there is a terrific smash in about five or 10 seconds. Fish suck leeches in from behind, but imitations tied to a line will not move backwards. Usually the fish circles and comes back at the fly from the side, thus getting hooked in the side of the mouth or well back on the tongue.

Selected Patterns
Chapter
2
Cariboo Chilcotin Coast

Chilcotin Mayfly
(Contributed by Doug Porter)

Hook: 3906B, #12 or equivalent
Thread: Blk. or drk. brn. 6/0 or 8/0 Monocord
Tail: 3 pheas. rump fibres
Body: Dubbed light grn. wool, kept thin
Thorax: Peacock herl
Wing Case: Pheas. tail
Legs: Pheas. tail fibres

Developed to match the mayfly hatches on clear water Chilcotin lakes, this fly is at its best when retrieved on a long leader and floating line in water up to 20 feet deep. Weight the fly using .010 lead wire for floating line presentations; unweighted versions work fine on sinktip lines. Once keyed to this insect, fish take the imitation with vigor. Over the years it has proven to be a multi-purpose fly as it also makes a suitable Gammarus shrimp imitation.

Krystal Dun
(Contributed by Phil Rowley)

Hook: TMC 100, #12–16
Tail: Micro Fibbets
Body: Arizona Micro Sheen (Adams gry. or Callibaetis)
Wing: Single post of pearl. Krystal Flash
Hackle: Blu. dun, trimmed flush along bottom

This thorax-style dry fly offers a realistic silhouette to cautious, surface-feeding trout. Winding the hackle forwards, backwards and forwards again in a palmered fashion through the thorax builds the realistic outline. During an intense hatch it is easy to become distracted by the multitude of opportunities. Choose one fish to target and allow the fly to drift naturally with the breeze.

Foam Callibaetis Emerger
(Contributed by Phil Rowley)

Hook: TMC 2487, #10–14
Tail: Micro-Fleck Turkey Flats
Rib: 1 strand pearl. Krystal Flash
Body: Arizona Micro Sheen (Callibaetis)
Wing: Gry. poly yarn
Wing Case: Gry. sheet foam
Hackle: Griz. palmered over thorax
Thorax: Tan dubbing

Dense populations of Callibaetis mayflies in many Cariboo/Chilcotin lakes make for highly selective trout. Designed to float just sub-surface, this emerger pattern is superb when fussy fish key exclusively on emerging mayflies and ignore the many duns littering the surface. Presentations should be dead drift on floating lines with 12- to 14-foot-long leaders. Grease only the poly wing and thorax, which is all that should be visible on the surface.

Lohr's Damsel
(Contributed by Harold Lohr)

Hook: TMC 3761, #10–12
Thread: Light olv.
Eyes: Blk. Ultra Chenille
Body: Light olv. marabou segmented by knotted light olv. tying thread
Rib: Fine gold wire
Wing Case: Olv. turkey quill
Legs: Light olv. pheas. tail fibres, knotted
Thorax: Light olv. marabou wrapped in front & behind legs

A realistic imitation designed for trout feeding selectively on damselfly nymphs, the pattern focusses on the three key features of the nymph: its slim body, outstretched legs and prominent eyes. The eyes are formed by tying two overhand knots in the Ultra Chenille, one beside the other. Keep retrieves simple and slow – a hand twist with intermittent pauses is enough. Work the pattern shoreward from deeper water, mimicking the migrating nymph's slow emergence swim.

Ken's Dragon
*(Contributed By
Ken Ruddick)*

Hook: TMC 300, #4–8
Thread: Blk. 6/0
Tail: Olv. goose biots trimmed shrt.
Under-Body: Fine olv. chen.
Rib: 10–15-lb. mono.
Body: Mixture of light grn. and drk. olv. chen. pulled over under-body
Wing Case: Moose body hair
Thorax: Drk. olv. chen.
Legs: Knotted pheas. tail fibres
Beard: Pheas. tail fibres

With a loyal following across B.C., this pattern is simple yet has everything needed in a great dragonfly nymph pattern. The body is unique, consisting of individual strands of chenille pulled forward over the under-body as a sheath, thus creating the dark dorsal and light ventral look of the natural. Pop-and-strip retrieves, where the fly is lifted off bottom by popping the rod tip up sharply and following with steady four-inch strips, are ideal. Periodically stop the retrieve and allow the pattern to parachute back to bottom. Fish often take on the drop.

Hook: TMC 5263, #6–10
Thread: Blk. 6/0
Tail: Brn. *Woolly Bugger* marabou & blk. pearl Accent Flash
Rib: Blk. pearl Accent Flash
Body: Spectrum Mohair Plus dubbing
Head: Blk. conehead bead

Lohr's Conehead Leech
(Contributed by Harold Lohr)

This consummate big-fish pattern combines a flowing marabou tail with a conehead bead head to give the fly an irresistible undulating motion. The buggy body provides additional movement and a large silhouette to draw trout. Type III full uniform-sink fly lines are most often used, except when fishing shoals in the evening, for which either intermediate or floating lines are suitable. Primarily creatures of the benthic regions, leeches are best presented on or near the bottom.

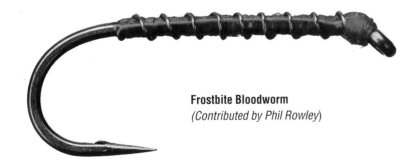

Frostbite Bloodworm
(Contributed by Phil Rowley)

Hook: TMC 5262, #8-16
Thread: Red
Rib: Fine copper wire
Body: Red Frostbite

This spartan pattern uses Frostbite to create a skinny natural profile that sinks fast. Using the rib material to build a solid under-body will increase sink rates. Wind the body over the wire under-body, then wind the rib forward, but do not counter-rib as this will unravel the under-body. A 15-foot or longer leader coupled with a floating line gets the pattern down to bottom where bloodworms lurk, but expect to wait three minutes or more in water 15 feet deep. A slow strip or hand-twist retrieve keeps the fly in the feeding zone. Takes are very soft, requiring ruler straight fly lines to detect.

Lohr's Chironomid Pupa
(Contributed by Harold Lohr)

Hook: TMC 200R, #10-16
Thread: Olv. 8/0 Uni Thread
Rib: Gry. Micro Tinsel
Body: Olv. Scud Back
Wing Case: Olv. Thin Skin
Thorax: Peacock herl
Gills: Wht. ostrich herl

Mirroring the reflective look of the natural, this pattern is best dead drifted under a dry line and strike indicator. Wave action will impart sufficient movement. Rough conditions require a sinking line be used in conjunction with the countdown method to locate the preferred feeding depth. Takes range from aggressive to a gradual disappearance of the indicator; swift hooksets are needed.

Hook: Mustad 9672, 3X, #10 or equivalent
Thread: Blk. Monocord
Head: Gold bead
Body: Dubbing mixture of blk., maroon and red wool w/maroon & brnz. Angel Hair
Note: After dubbing, tease the fibres out & up & down w/a Bodkin or Velcro strip

Spring Leech
(Contributed by Doug Porter)

Designed primarily for ice-off on Cariboo/Chilcotin lakes when the trout are still keyed to food items which sustained them over the winter, this fly is best fished in shallow water off a floating line. The body dubbing is a 60-30-10 blend of black, maroon and red wool with a pinch of maroon and bronze Angel Hair for added sparkle. Keep the wool fibres long prior to blending to provide lots of movement to the finished fly.

Draggin
(Contributed by Phil Rowley)

Hook: TMC 300, #4–8
Thread: Olv. or grn. 6/0 Uni Thread
Under-Body: Small Rainy's Float Foam
Body: Peacock Crystal Chenille spun in a dubbing loop of Arizona Syn. Peacock
Wing Case: Nat. drk. brn. raffia
Thorax: Olv. deerhair spun & clipped
Legs: Olv. or brn. rubber hackle or Sili legs
Eyes: Small Rainy's Float Foam
Head: Arizona Syn. Peacock

Influenced by British flies such as the *Booby* and the *Razzler*, this pattern's buoyant materials allow it to be fished slow and low. Ideal when imitating weed-dwelling nymphs from the Aeshnidae family, a type II or III sinking line and nine-foot leader will allow the fly to hover just over the weed tops with minimum fouling. A slow hand twist coupled with sparse four-inch strips imitates the foraging nymphs.

Chan's Chironomid
(Contributed by Brian Chan)

Hook: TMC 3761, #14–10
Tail: Wht. Antron (posterior gills)
Rib: Fine copper wire
Body: Cock ringneck pheas. tail fibres
Thorax: Peacock herl
Shell Back: Cock ringneck pheas. tail fibres
Gills: Wht. Antron fibres

Found in most Cariboo lakes, brown chironomids range in size from 1/4 inch to more than 3/4 inches in the pupal stage. All species have anterior gills and most of the larger species have posterior gills. Most pupal emergences, which occur in water between five and 25 feet deep, can be covered with floating lines and various leader lengths. The key is to keep the fly in the right depth zone, often within a foot of bottom where trout feel safe from predators. Strike indicators afford precise depth control and are a must for fussy trout.

Hook: Mustad 94831, #2–10
Thread: Blk.
Tail: Moose body hair
Body: Deerhair
Wing: Single post of deerhair
Hackle: Griz.

Spent Mayfly
(Contributed by David Cooper)

With its realistic profile, this imitative fly fools even picky trout in rivers and lakes across the Cariboo-Chilcotin. The arched tail and single wing post allow it to imitate virtually all mayfly species, from the largest through to the smallest. Under selective hatch conditions, use 12-foot-long leaders tapered to 5X, thus allowing space between fly and leader.

Stonefly Dry
(Contributed by David Cooper)

Hook: Mustad 94831, #2–10
Thread: Blk.
Body: Deerhair spun & clipped to shape
Wing: Lacquered turkey quill trimmed to shape
Legs: Striped goose quills
Thorax: Orng. or yel. dubbing
Antenna: Moose body hair or stripped hackle stems

Buoyant and realistic, this adult stonefly dressing will float like a cork, thanks to its spun and clipped deerhair body. It regularly dupes selective trout and will match most stonefly species if size and color are varied; orange and yellow have proven consistently reliable. Finer tippets and longer leaders are required as flow rates stabilize and water clarity increases in late spring and summer.

Black Peril
(Contributed by Peter Hobot)

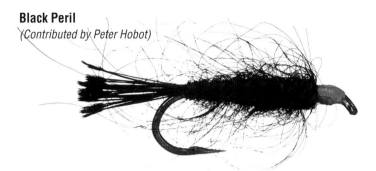

Hook: TMC 5262, #8–12 (weighted w/15 turns of lead wire substitute)
Thread: Body blk. 6/0, head Danville's Flymaster Size A, Coachman red
Tail: 12 gold. pheas. tippets dyed blk.
Body: Blk. seal fur or Crystal Seal Dubbing brushed out

I deal in spring and fall, this pattern is designed to imitate juvenile leeches less than one inch long. With the trout on the shoals through the spring, floating lines are best, but no matter what line is used the goal is to achieve a naturally paced horizontal presentation with as few hang-ups as possible. When fish are active, an eight- to 10-inch strip retrieve works best, otherwise a slow hand twist suffices.

Hook: Mustad 9671, #4–6
Tail: Barred body feathers (soft marabou style) from Plymouth rock chicken; dyed red. brn. 3/4 lngth. of hook for darner; dyed sandy brn. 1/4 lngth. of hook for Gomphus
Body: Soft marabou-style body feathers fastened in sections alng. the body so the whole hook is encased; dyed red. brn. for darner; dyed sandy brn. for Gomphus
Hackle: Dyed orng. guinea fowl body feather
Eyes: Either gold bead, copper pull chain or foam tube

Shaggy Dragon
(Contributed by Ian Forbes)

This pattern's soft body feathers become very lifelike when wet, imparting suggestive movement even when at rest. It is productive when trolled, cast or dead-drifted under a strike indicator; the brass head works best with a floating line, quickly sinking the fly and adding an effective jigging action. With foam tube eyes, the pattern almost floats and can be worked over shallow weedbeds without fouling. Effective when fished on the bottom or at midwater, it is at its best on the edges of rushes or in weedbeds.

Floating Scud
(Contributed by Ian Forbes)

Hook: Mustad 9671, #12–14
Body: Rough dubbing of olv./gry. fur or syn. mixture w/bits of olv. Flashabou mixed in
Rib: 2 strands of Krystal Flash twisted together or 4-lb. test mono.
Shell Back: Thin strip of packing foam protected w/pliable glue (thinned Goop or Soft Body) after fly is complete

D esigned to be fished very slowly over marl or weedbeds in super clear water, this pattern has the advantage of swimming right side up, unlike many scud patterns. Trout seldom waste energy chasing active scuds, but will quickly pick up stationary ones, and this floating pattern can be left inactive for long periods. A single attention-getting twitch when trout approach is normally all that is needed. The packing-foam back imitates marl-bed scuds, but dye can be added to the thinned glue to achieve a variety of colors.

McLeod's Snail
(Contributed by Bruce McLeod)

Hook: TMC 2457, #8–12
Thread: Dark olv.
Hackle: Brn., tied in at base of body
Body: Drk. olv. dubbing or peacock herl
Rib: Copper wire
Antennae: Mono. burnt to form antennae

In lakes where they exist, snails are a significant item in the diet of trout. Simple to tie, snail patterns can be fished on both floating and sinking lines. The floating line technique is similar to that used when imitating chironomids – allow the fly to sink and retrieve with a slow hand twist. Snails do not swim, but they do fall off weeds or are knocked off by cruising trout. Casting along the edges of emergent plants can be effective; strike indicators are a big help as trout will take the fly as it sinks. With full sinking lines, cast out just enough line to reach bottom with the line hanging straight down. Trout normally take as the fly sinks, but a slow hand twist back to the surface is also effective.

Hook: TMC 7999, #6-2/0
Thread: Blk. 6/0
Tail: Blk. over prpl. polar bear or bucktail, mix w/sparse blk. & pearl. Krystal Flash, top w/single yel. gold. pheas. feather
Rear Body: Prpl. haze SLF dubbing ribbed w/large pearl. myl. and palmered w/a blk. saddle feather
Mid-Body: Dyed orng. gold. pheas. tippets fanned around the rear body section; two pairs of silicone legs are tied in on each side of the body
Mid-Wing: Blk. or burgundy marabou
Front Body: Same combination as the rear body
Front Legs: 2 pairs of silicone rubber legs
Front Wing: Blk. or burgundy marabou
Antenna: 2 lng. strands of pearl. Krystal Flash
Hackle: 2 large bright red gold. pheas. rump feathers

Marabou Prawn
(Contributed by Tyson Gogel)

This suggestive pattern works wonders on steelhead across the province and especially in the Skeena drainage. Using a type IV or V sinktip line, sweep the fly through the run with a down and across approach. Mending allows the marabou and silicone legs to jiggle seductively. Be sure to work the near shore shallows where steelhead rest in calmer flows, and to systematically comb all runs. Allow the pattern to hang in the current momentarily before recasting – steelhead regularly strike the fly as it dances at the end of a taut line.

Gold Bead Hare's Ear
(Contributed by Phil Rowley)

Hook: TMC 3769 or 3761, #10–14
Thread: Olv. or brn. 8/0 Uni Thread
Tail: Partridge
Rib: Fine gold oval tinsel or wire
Body: Nat. Hare's Ear
Hackle: Partridge
Head: Gold bead

This shaggy, nondescript version of the venerable *Hare's Ear* is suggestive of a number of food items, from mayflies and stoneflies in running water to caddis and scuds in stillwaters. The gold bead provides extra weight and the touch of flash often needed to attract fickle fish. In the North it makes an excellent searching pattern and is particularly good for grayling. A natural presentation with the odd twitch should be enough to convince grayling to take a swipe. Body color can be varied to mimic available natural food items.

Red-Throated Pike Fly
(Contributed by Brian Chan)

Hook: TMC 800S, #3/0-1/0
Thread: Hot org.
Body: Silv. Diamond Braid
Under-Wing: Pearl. Polar Flash
Wing: Red over prpl. over wht. Angler's Choice Poly Bear
Over-Wing: Pearl. Polar Flash
Throat: Bright red Angler's Choice Poly Bear fibers
Eyes: Stick-on eyes, yel. w/blk. pupil, coated w/Soft Body

Extremely adaptable, this fly covers all depths and can be fished on floating, sinktip or full sinking lines as conditions dictate. No matter what the choice of line, use a six- to 10-inch strip retrieve to keep the fly fast and active right back to the boat or shoreline. Pike love to follow an offering for quite a distance before engulfing the fly.

Try moving the rod tip from side to side to add enticing movement. Cast as far as possible into any openings in vegetation. Other popular ambush spots include rockpiles and sunken timber. Remember to use a wire leader as pike, the barracudas of the North, are notorious for shredding both fly and leader with their razor-sharp teeth.

Trailer Hook: Mustad "Stinger" 37187, #2–1/0
Front Hook: Shank attached to trailer w/loop of 40-lb. test mono. or wire
Thread: Kevlar thread, gry. or brn.
Whiskers: Blk. bear hairs
Head: Spun deerhair
Ears: Spun deerhair (lacquered)
Collar: Rabbit strip, nat. or chinchilla wrapped around shank
Body: Rabbit strip, nat. or chinchilla wrapped around hook
Tail: Rabbit strip, nat. or chinchilla tied in lngth.-wise

Lemming
(Contributed by Peter Morrison)

Prepare for heart-stopping takes and be sure to have a forgiving rod and stout tippet when offering this pattern to any of the North's opportunistic feeders. Where small feeder creeks spill into a lake, cast the *Lemming* across the current, allowing it to be swept into the lake. Retrieve so the pattern swims parallel to the shoreline. On larger rivers, cast the fly to mid-stream and allow a

deep line belly to drag the *Lemming* down and across towards the bank. Smash takes can occur anywhere during the drift, so hang on. On lakes, search out ambush points such as sunken logs, weedbeds, or partially submerged brush. Probe these areas methodically. When the fly hits the water, allow it to sit until the rings of its arrival disappear, then begin a steady strip retrieve back to the boat.

Golden Stone Adult
(Contributed by Ian Forbes)

Hook: Mustad 9671, #6–8
Tail: Dyed yel. goose biots from flight feather
Under-Body: Warmed & flattened Friendly Plastic molded onto full lngth. of hook & tapered at each end
Over-Body: Closed-cell foam cut in thin strips & wrapped around hook, then colored w/Pantone pen: brn. on back, yel. on belly
Wing: Zing Wing mat. or thin piece of clear myl. string
Hackle: Gold. badger saddle hackle

Designed for wary, selective trout suspicious of anything but very realistic imitations, this pattern's foam body will keep it floating properly in the surface film, just like a natural. Golden stoneflies are common in rivers throughout the province and hatch in

the spring: June/July in northern and mountain rivers, and April/May elsewhere. The yellow belly color may vary from river to river, but the fly can be adjusted on site with the help of a waterproof marker pen (Pantone or similar art pen).

Golden Stone Nymph
(Contributed by Ian Forbes)

Hook: Mustad 9671, #6–8
Tail: Dyed yel. goose biots from flight feather
Under-Body: Warmed & flattened Friendly Plastic molded onto full lngth. of hook & tapered at each end
Over-Body: Latex rubber cut in thin strips, wrapped around hook, then colored w/Pantone pen: yel. belly, brn. back
Thorax & Legs: Dyed amb. rabbit hair spun on dubbing loop, then trimmed top & bottom
Wing Pad: Strip of latex rubber pulled over fur dubbing & marked w/brn. Pantone pen

Unlike weighted patterns, this fly will swim right side up. It must be sunk with a fast-sinking line to keep it on the bottom where the naturals are found. Stoneflies crawl and seldom swim except when knocked off their perch in high water. Trout target the large nymphs when they migrate to shore to hatch into adults. For weighted patterns, substitute flattened lead wire for the Friendly Plastic and tie the body upside down. Concentrate on fast, aerated pocket water. A heavily weighted fly can be used with a floating line, but this pattern is fished better with a short sinktip line and four-foot leader.

Hook: Mustad 9671 or similar, #14
Tail: Goose biots from flight wing
Body & Head: Deerhair dyed chartreuse grn. folded alng. & around hook shank, then held in place w/bright grn. tying thread
Wing: Zing Wing or section of thin, clear plastic string mat.
Hackle: Griz. dyed bright grn. w/lime Koolaid
Thread: Bright grn.

Lime Sally
(Contributed by Ian Forbes)

The little green stonefly, which this pattern imitates, is common throughout the province, especially in more northerly rivers such as the Chilko, Blackwater, Stellako and upper Babine. They often hatch in blizzard numbers in July, but can appear throughout the season. Trout can be very selective to returning egg-laying adults. Standard deer or elk hair caddis patterns are too bulky and will be refused. Naturals struggle a bit in the current, but float drag free. Floating lines, long, fine leaders and short casts are preferred to maintain line control. The slightest drag will affect this small fly.

Futabugger
(Contributed by Brian Niska)

Hook: TMC 5263, #4–12
Thread: Red 6/0
Tail: Blk. marabou
Shell Back: Peacock herl
Body: Silv. Diamond Braid
Hackle: Blk. saddle palmered over the body

This Chilean import combines just the right amount of flash, color and movement to fool many species including salmon, trout, steelhead and char. Its scruffy look mimics a variety of food items found in both moving and stillwater. Try a variety of retrieves, from dead drift in rivers to hand twist or strip retrieves in lakes. The best retrieves are varied to provide maximum animation and movement. Don't be afraid to experiment with various color combinations such as burgundy, olive, brown, tan or grey. Swapping the silver body for one of gold is worth a try too.

Hook: Mustad 9672 or TMC 5263, #8–10
Thread: Blk.
Tail: Peacock sword herl
Body: Dyed blk. deerhair, spun, packed & trimmed
Over-Back: Peacock sword herl
Wing: Micro-web winging mat. cut to shape
Hackle: Blk.
Head: Peacock sword herl

Deerhair Cicada
(Contributed by Rod Zavaduk)

This chunky terrestrial emerges along the Columbia River between Castlegar and Waneta in April, following the first spell of hot spring weather. While the hatch lasts only a few weeks, strong prevalent winds blow the beetle-like bugs onto the river, providing trout with an early-season treat. The cicadas get stuck in the Columbia's big back eddies, where trout easily pluck the struggling insects off the surface. The cicada emergence marks the start of the Columbia's dry fly season.

Big Purple May
(Contributed by Rod Zavaduk)

Hook: Mustad 94840 or TMC 100, #8–10
Thread: Blk.
Tail: 3 or 4 strands of blk. horse tail
Body: Maroon Phentex or Antron yarn
Rib: Bright yel. Super Floss
Wings: Griz. hen hackle shaped w/wing burner
Hackle: Furnace or drk. coachman brn.

The natural's maroon color and bright yellow striped body make this mayfly unique. Hatching sporadically during summer evenings along the Columbia River below Castlegar, the nymphs are excellent swimmers that crawl out on shore prior to hatching. Duns get caught in the Columbia's eddies and are as eagerly picked off as the fluttering spinners during their evening egg-laying flight. Seldom heavy, the hatch is nonetheless enthusiastically greeted by the trout, likely due to the large size of these insects.

Jig Minnow
(Contributed by Mike Labach)

Hook: Wright McGill DN1197, #1–2
Under-Body: Conehead, lead wire, packing foam at rear
Over-Body: Pearl. myl. tubing
Body Glue: 5-minute epoxy or Angler's Choice Soft Body
Wing: Covering hook point; polar bear, goat hair or syn. hair in colors wht., red & blu./grn.
Eyes: Plastic stick-on
Note: Fish fly hook point up

Designed to sink quickly and not hang up on bottom, this prey fish imitation is used for bull trout and larger westslope cutthroat holding in deep pools and under brush piles – places conventional streamers cannot easily reach. The fly has a unique jigging action which, along with its weight, allows it to target and entice deep-water bull trout. A slow sidearm cast is required to lob this heavy fly, which swims hook point up to prevent snagging bottom.

Mahogany Parachute Mayfly
(Contributed by Mike Labach)

Hook: Mustad 94840 or TMC 100, #14
Tail: 4 strands of moose mane
Body: Red. brn. dubbing
Thorax: Drk. brn. dubbing
Wing: Drk. gry. hen hackle shaped w/wing burner
Hackle: Furnace wrapped around wing base parachute style
Thread: Brn.

Westslope cutthroat love deer or elk hair caddis patterns, but become selective whenever mayflies hatch in numbers. This slate wing mahogany dun is common to the Elk, St. Marys, and Wigwam rivers in late summer. The spinners' reddish color actually glows in the sun. The pattern floats flush in the surface film and works equally well for the emerger, dun and spinner stages. Drag-free drifts are essential as the trout will refuse unnatural mayfly presentations.

Hook: Mustad 94840, #16
Tail: Wood duck flank feather
Body: Moose mane, nat. gry. & dyed pale olv.
Thorax: Pale olv./tan sparkle dubbing
Legs: Wood duck flank feather
Wing: Zing Wing or section of myl. string mat.

Pale Evening Dun Emerger
(Contributed by Ian Forbes)

Important on a number of streams in the Rockies, particularly the upper Elk, trout often take this small mayfly in preference to anything else. The emerger seems the tidbit of choice, especially when greased and presented just under the surface. A downstream slack-line cast or an upstream reach cast are both effective, and while dead drifts are mandatory, the slightest of pauses will often induce strikes. Tippets no heavier than 5X are needed if the fly is to drift naturally.

Deerhair Caddis
(Contributed by Ian Forbes)

Hook: Mustad 94840 or 9671, #8–14
Thread: To match body color
Tail: Deerhair, 1/2 body lngth.
Body: Spun fur dubbing; choice of colors to match nat. caddis, stonefly or grasshopper – olv., yel., brn., gry., blk., orng.
Wing: Deerhair tied low atop dubbed body
Hackle: Med. brn. or ging. var. wrapped over head
Head: Spun deerhair

The mainstay pattern for dry fly fishing streams in the Rockies, this fly will produce 90 per cent of the time, imitating caddis, stoneflies or grasshoppers equally well. Trout will accept a bit of drag and the odd twitch from this pattern. While buoyant, it should be dressed with floatant, although trout will take the fly even when soggy. A change in size and/or color will entice trout grown wary of the original.

Foam Red Ant
(Contributed by Ian Forbes)

Hook: Mustad shrt. shank 94838, #16–18
Thread: Blk. nyl.
Body: Closed-cell foam cut w/leather punch, trimmed & colored w/red Pantone pen, then lacquered
Hackle: 2 turns of furnace

Ant patterns are a 'go to' fly when trout become shy after being hooked a few times. Lying flush on the surface, this tiny fly is hard to see, except in flat water where trout are most fussy. Follow the line with the rod tip and watch the tippet carefully for the slightest movement. Concentrate on where the fly should be and strike gently at the dimple rise. The fly is of less value in fast broken water, but can be used with a short line in pocket water.

Hook: Mustad 9671, #14
Tail: Dyed brn. teal flank feather
Under-Body: Lead wire flattened w/pliers
Body: Fur dubbing mixed 50/50 med. olv. and tan
Back: Hologram silv. myl. tinsel
Thorax: None or peacock herl
Rib: Fine copper wire
Legs: Dyed brn. teal flank feather
Head: Brass bead

Bead Head Flashback Nymph
(Contributed by Ian Forbes)

This fly will take trout, grayling or whitefish anywhere in the world. Designed for rivers, trout will pick it off rocks in alpine ponds as well. It sinks like a stone and can be floated dead drift under a strike indicator or swung through a current on a tight line. More strikes will be detected with a strike indicator. It is also effective when highsticking, the term for short-line pocket fishing. The fly is small enough to be cast with a light rod, but requires at least a 4X tippet to turn over. With long, light leaders slow down the casting stroke.

Cinnamon Caddis
(Contributed by Eric Schulz)

Hook: TMC 900BL, #12-16
Thread: Brn. 8/0
Tail: None
Rib: Stripped brn. hackle stem
Body: Rust brn. rabbit dubbing
Under-Wing: Brn. CDC feathers
Wing: Mottled turkey quill dyed rust brn. w/Pantone pen
Hackle: Brn.

**Selected Patterns
Chapter
5
Vancouver Island**

Trout Patterns

Fished in the traditional dead-drift manner, this dry fly is effective on Island rivers from mid-April to early June. Floatant should be applied only to the hackle, as silicone will stick the CDC feathers together. A lightly greased tippet aids flotation and helps to keep the fly on the surface film, where it can be skittered to entice a strike.

Hook: TMC 9394, #8–10
Thread: Fine, clear mono
Tail: None
Rib: None
Body: Flat silv. or gold tinsel
Under-Wing: None
Wing: Marine grn. Polar Flash/Griz. hackle tips tied to simulate parr marks
Hackle: None
Eyes: 1.5 mm pearl or gold prismatic eyes glued w/clear 5-minute epoxy

Der Uberminnow
(Contributed by Eric Schulz)

This unique minnow pattern was designed for early-season Cowichan River brown trout, but has proved equally effective for sea-run cutthroat in estuaries. A long piece of lead core line will get the fly down in the water column during heavy spring flows; a most effective retrieve consists of fast one-inch strips with occasional pauses. In the salt, a Stillwater line with fluorocarbon tippet works best.

Crawdad
(Contributed by David Wallden)

Hook: 3XL nymph, #4–6
Thread: Brn.
Antenna: Stripped hackle stems
Eyes: 30-lb. mono., burned
Over-Body: Rust bucktail, coated in Flexament
Weight: .030 lead wire palmered to bend of hook
Pincers: Squirrel tail, coated in Flexament
Legs: Brn. saddle hackle
Body: Blended brn. & red dubbing

Deadly on large, wary brown trout in the Cowichan River, this crustacean is best fished dead drift on the bottom with a floating line and sinking leader or piece of lead core. For the deep, slow-moving pools preferred by browns, a type VI sinking line is best; twitch the Crawdad periodically during the drift and retrieve. This pattern can be tied in lighter colors to imitate the soft-shelled, reshly molted version of the natural.

Hook: Standard dry fly, #12
Thread: Brn. or camel
Tail: Moose mane fibres
Rib: 1 strand brn. floss
Body: Rusty brn. syn. dubbing
Under-Wing: None
Wing(Post): Moose mane fibres trimmed to shape
Hackle: 2 brn. hackles

Western March Brown Dun
(Contributed by David Wallden)

This fly will produce through the month of May on the Cowichan River. While most mayflies in B.C. streams hatch in June and July, the Cowichan March Brown is a true May- hatching mayfly. Use it as a searching pattern, or fish it directly to rising fish during a hatch, using the traditional dead-drift method, typically during low light.

Hook: TMC 5262, #8
Thread: Blk. Monocord
Antenna: Blk. mink guard hairs coated in Flexament or blk. goose biots
Bead: Gold
Tail: Blk. mink guard hairs coated in Flexament or blk. goose biots
Rib: None
Body: Blk. Larva Lace w/blk. Hare-Tron dubbing for thorax
Under-Wing: None
Wing Case: Tyvek building paper dyed blk. w/Sharpie marker
Hackle: None

Black Robertstone
(Contributed by Ian Roberts)

This durable stonefly pattern takes no time to tie and is eagerly accepted by trout. While there are virtually no black stoneflies on Vancouver Island, this fly is effective for brown and rainbow trout, notably when fished deep in early spring. An upstream approach with a sinking leader on a floating line works best. The fly can be tied weighted or not; using a curved hook imitates the posture of free-floating nymphs.

Ian's March Brown Nymph
(Contributed by Ian Roberts)

Hook: TMC 3769, #12–14
Thread: Brn.
Bead: Brn. glass
Tail: Pheas. tail feather fibres
Rib: Fine copper
Body: Brn. dubbing
Thorax: Peacock herl
Wing Case: Pheas. tail feather fibres coated in Flexament
Hackle: None

The March Brown is the number one hatch on the Cowichan River for several weeks in late April and May and provides the best trout fishing of the season. This pattern was evolved as a durable replacement for the ubiquitous *Pheasant Tail Nymph*, which tends to wear out after four or five fish. The glass bead head gives the pattern some translucence and the overall shape matches the short, stubby proportions of the Cowichan's version of the March Brown. Fish it upstream, dead drift, with a sinking leader.

Hook: Mustad 9671/TMC 9394, #6
Tail: Orng./brn. marabou
Thread: Wht. covering entire hook
Body: Translucent packing foam, cut to shape & glued on hook w/527 glue
Over-Body: Pearl. myl. tubing
Back: Dyed olv. barred pintail or teal flank feather glued on hook w/527 glue.
Eyes: Plastic stick-on
Body Glue: Soft Body

Floating Coho Fry
(Contributed by Ian Forbes)

Designed to fool wary fish in shallow water where standard patterns would snag bottom, this fly will take piscivorous fish the world over. In clear, shallow water, cast well in front of cruising fish and allow the fish to come to the fly. When sea-run cutthroat are feeding in the shallows along a beach, fish the fly from shore into deeper water. The fly will not foul on the rocks, nor will it be thrown onto shore by waves. This floating pattern always remains upright and works equally well with floating or sinking lines.

Thread: Mono., fine
Hook: Mustad, TMC, or Eagle Claw Shrimp Hook, #8–14
Tail: Nat. deerhair, 6, fine
Rib: Mono. thread, fine
Body Rear: Med. Crystal Chenille, 3 or 4 wraps, colors – grn., prpl. or lavender
Mid-Body: Fluor. Uni Thread, 2 or 3 wraps
Body Front: Crystal Chenille, 3 or 4 wraps; colors – grn., prpl. or lavender
Shell Back: Thin skin to match color; pull over entire body, then wind mono. thread rib over, 3 or 4 wraps to secure the shell back; whip finish

Pregnant Shrimp/Amphipod
(Contributed by John O'Brien)

A highly effective dual-purpose pattern, this fly can be used in both fresh and salt water for a variety of species. In bright chartreuse it imitates freshwater shrimp both on Vancouver Island and in Interior lakes. A slow, one-inch strip retrieve works best in weedbeds or over shallow shoals with either sinktips or full sinking lines. In salt water, purple or lavender works well for estuary sea-run cutthroat, pink, coho and chum salmon. Use a very fast one-inch strip retrieve with a floating line and weighted poly leader. Fished near bottom, it has proven its worth on Island lakes in January and February.

Saltwater Patterns

Chartreuse Sandlance
(Contributed by Shim Hogan)

Hook: TMC 911S, Mustad 34011 or equivalent, #4–1/0
Thread: Clear mono. tying thread
Under-Wing: Silv. holographic Angel Hair
Top Wing: Chartreuse Angel Hair
Body: Chartreuse Body Stuff
Eyes: Small molded epoxy eyes – red
Body Coating: Soft Body thin formula or epoxy
Note: This fly can also be tied weighted

Originally tied as a variation of an East Coast sand eel, the pattern was subsequently adapted for use in the often brown-stained waters of Clayoquot Sound. The chartreuse color shows up extremely well during algae blooms and can be fished with the characteristically slow and steady retrieve imitative of sandlance and needlefish. Interspersing this retrieve with occasional twitches and pauses allows the Angel Hair to move in a natural, lifelike fashion. An extremely durable fly, it has proven to be consistently effective, a trait it shares with all the saltwater patterns selected for this book. It is a very good 'big fish' fly.

Hook: Daiichi 2546, TMC 811S or equivalent, #4–1/0
Thread: Clear mono. tying thread
1st Under-Wing: Silv. holographic Angel Hair
2nd Under-Wing: Light olv. Angel Hair
3rd Under-Wing: Peacock Angel Hair
Top Wing: Baitfish Angel Hair
Belly: Silv. holographic Angel Hair
Throat/Gills: Red Angel Hair
Eyes: Small or extra-small molded epoxy eyes – red
Head: Soft Body thin formula or epoxy
Note: This fly can also be tied weighted

Shim's Sardina
(Contributed by Shim Hogan)

Originally tied smaller as a sea-run cutthroat fly, the pattern was adapted for saltwater coho by using a stout stainless hook and enlarging the pattern to suit. As well as coho, it has proven its worth on a variety of species found in areas of Baja, Mexico. For coho, use a fairly erratic retrieve with short twitches and jerks. The fly consistently outfishes many popular patterns and is particularly effective in and around kelp beds or in shallow bays. It does a good job as a juvenile herring pattern or can be dressed down to imitate needlefish – its shimmering undulation seems to be the key to its success.

Pink Sparkle Shrimp
(*Contributed by Peter Morrison*)

Hook: Daiichi 2546 or equivalent
Thread: Clear mono. tying thread
Antenna: 2 strands pink Krystal Flash
Body: Pearl Diamond Braid
Over-Body: Pink Krystal Flash
Legs/Beard: Pink Krystal Flash
Eyes: Small blk. bead chain eyes

Euphausid shrimp or krill comprise about 70 per cent of the coho salmon's ocean diet. Simple yet effective, this pattern was designed for use when competing food sources – prey fish such as herring or needlefish – are absent. In sandy-bottomed bays the pattern has proven effective dredged along the bottom, while in open-water situations it works best near the surface. In all instances the retrieve remains constant, a copy of the natural shrimp's steady straight-line swim interspersed with occasional bursts of speed. This is best imitated with a long-draw retrieve and an occasional 'popping' of the rod tip. Takes are most often marked by the fly stopping and the line gradually tightening. Set the hook with a quick hard pull.

Hook: Daiichi 2546, TMC 811S or similar, #2–3/0
Thread: Clear, fine mono.
Body (Optional): Fluor. grn. Diamond Braid (behind eyes)
Over-Wing: Chartreuse bucktail or substitute
Under-Wing: Wht. bucktail or polar bear, etc.
Lateral Line: 2-3 strands each side Krystal Flash or Angel Hair
Eyes: Med. plated or painted lead eyes with prismatic stick-on eyes (coated with epoxy for durability)

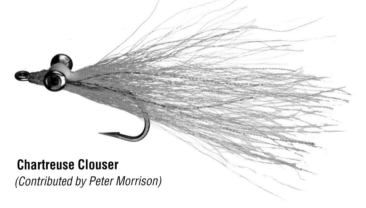

Chartreuse Clouser
(*Contributed by Peter Morrison*)

A variation of Bob Clouser's *Deep Minnow*, this fly can be used for a range of species as it readily imitates a variety of prey fish simply by changing retrieves. The materials themselves lend the fly a wonderful lifelike action and the lead eyes serve two important functions. Tied on top, they cause the fly to ride upside down, making it relatively weedless. Second, they ensure the fly is always fishing; during pauses in the retrieve, the weighted eyes pull the pattern down, perfectly imitating a prey fish diving for cover, an action predatory fish find irrestible. Finally, the chartreuse color (which may be substituted) is very effective in the brownish-tinged salt water found in such destinations as Clayoquot Sound. This fly is an absolute must for salt water.

Catface Streamer
(*Contributed by Shawn Bennett*)

Hook: Mustad 34011, #1
Thread: Uni Mono .004, clear
Body: Pearl Diamond Braid, red polar bear
Wing: Wht. & chartreuse polar bear, chartreuse Polar Flash, peacock herl, from eye
Sides: Dyed over griz. saddle hackle, grn.
Eyes: 1.5 mm chartreuse myl. stick-on

This pattern's full dressing matches the broad profile of small perch or shiners, but it slims down considerably in the water and may be taken for a juvenile anchovy. Originally designed with the waters surrounding Clayoquot Sound's Catface Mountain in mind, it will produce in similar saltwater locales anywhere off the Island's west coast. A moderate retrieve alongside patches of kelp has proven effective, while a fluttery, fleeing prey fish-style retrieve works best in shallow bays. The chartreuse color is crucial when fishing for salmon, and the red beard or gill at times makes all the difference.

Hook: Mustad #34011SS or #34007SS, #1/0–5/0,#1–6
Thread: Silv.
Body: Silv. tinsel chen.
Throat: Bright red wool, Fishair
Wing: Peacock sword
Tail: Peacock sword, silv. Krystal Flash

Silver Thorn
(Contributed by Barry M. Thornton)

Evolved through a series of experiments dating to the 1980s, the current design emerged when it became clear very sparse patterns often worked best for Pacific salmon. As originally conceived, the fly was extremely simple and, while its simple silver coloration remains a common theme, there are now more than 20 variations to suit changing ocean conditions such as algae blooms or the exceptionally clear waters found on the north and central coasts. All 20 variations have taken coho and chinook in open waters. More a pattern concept than a fly with inflexible dressing, it can be used with a variety of hook sizes and dressing variations to match water conditions or size of prey fish encountered.

Lohr's Sandlance
(Contributed by Harold Lohr)

Hook: TMC 9394, #2–6
Thread: Clear mono. or wht. 6/0
Body: Silv. Diamond Braid
Topings: Wht. Super Hair; pearl or silv. Accent Flash; baitfish Angel Hair; blk. dyed over pearl Accent Flash; drk. olv. rabbit strip
Eyes: 2 mm silv. prismatic eyes
Note: Toppings are tied down at the front and back; apply a thin coat of epoxy to the sides and bottom when finished

Designed to match the size, shape and color of Clayoquot Sound needlefish/sandlance, the fly presents a long, slender profile and swims with a distinct side-to-side, undulating movement similar to a snake slithering through grass. Retrieves should be varied and depths covered can range from near surface to just off bottom. When retrieving against tidal currents, feeding line out and allowing the fly to flutter back downstream for two or three feet can be very effective. Promising spots encountered during a retrieve can be probed by allowing the fly to hang in the current for up to a minute; feeding line out helps sink the fly and may be needed to get it in the zone.

Flashy Glow
(Contributed by Shawn Bennett)

Hook: Mustad 34011, #1/0–2
Thread: Uni-Mono .004, clear
Body: Grn. sparkle braid
Wing: Bottom–yel. glow Flashabou, top – lime glow Flashabou, lateral line – grn. Flashabou
Note: Whole fly sleeved w/pearl. myl. tubing; 2.0 myl. glow eyes head coated w/epoxy; fray tubing to just behind eyes

Having confidence in the pattern being fished is a necessity, and this pattern gives saltwater fly fishing guide Shawn Bennett lots of confidence. Consistently productive through the season, the fly works best when retrieved at a steep angle or even straight up with the fly line hanging vertically. Cast against or into the tide stream with lines such as a Teeny TS 350, and allow the fly to sink as it is pushed towards the boat, thus achieving a near-vertical retrieve. The materials used ensure the fly stands out in low light conditions, making it a good choice early and late in the day when fish are closer to the surface.

Hook: Mustad 79580, #2–4
Thread: UniThread 6/0 iron gry.
Weighted Body: Lead tape folded over hook shank, cut to form belly w/out impeding hook gap
Body: Med. myl. tubing, pearl., unravelled at tail end 1/2" and extended to form under-tail
Over-Tail & Wing: Rabbit strip, nat. drk. gry. tied *Zonker*-style leaving 3/4" tail
Side Accent: Olv.-brn. marabou (10 fibres)
Cheek: Red hackle fibres

Steely Zonker
(Contributed by Peter MacPherson)

This classic prey fish pattern has proven its worth many times on steelhead in the Vedder and Chehalis rivers, but will prove effective whenever salmonids feed on forage fish. Most often fished on a sinktip line, full sinking lines are useful when the fly must be kept down through the momentum of the swing. Line control, as always, is critical to feeling the strike. Productive in deeper runs with moderate currents, it may be necessary to feed line out immediately following the cast to allow the fly to reach optimum depths.

KCK Red/Yellow Butt
(Contributed by Kelly Davison)

Hook: Mustad 9672 or TMC 5263, #6
Thread: Uni Thread 6/0 fire orng.
Tail: Red hackle fibres
Body: Plastic chen., rear quarter fluor. yel.; front 3/4 fluor. red
Throat: Coachman brn. hackle
Wing: Teal flank feather
Over-Wing: 5 strands pearl Krystal Flash

The KCK series of patterns is highly effective for coho throughout the season in both fresh and salt water. Used extensively in the slack waters of the Harrison River and area sloughs, the fly is at its best with transparent, slow-sinking fly lines. These clear lines can be fished over the coho without spooking them, even when the water is clear or the fish fresh in from the ocean. Cast the fly over the lie, keeping the rod tip low to the water and allowing time for the fly to sink before retrieving with erratic, foot-long strips. Keep the fly moving – coho love to chase.

Hook: Mustad 36890, #2–8
Butt: Small fluor. chartreuse chen.
Body: Small fluor. pink chen./med. on #2 hooks
Rib: Large pearl flat tinsel
Wing: Pearl. myl. tubing, frayed
Collar: Fluor. pink rooster hackle
Thread: Fluor. pink Flymaster Plus 2/0

Flintoft Pink
(Contributed by Bill Flintoft)

Capitalizing on the pink salmon's preference for pink, this fly is best fished in shallow water runs with a floating line and a bit of weight on the leader (or on the fly itself). When fishing waters four to six feet deep, use a 10-foot sinktip line (type III) with a short leader. Cast slightly upstream, mend the belly out of the line and allow the fly to swing through the run close to bottom. Sockeye will take it as well, but for pinks, pay particular attention at the end of the drift when the fly hangs downstream, especially in shallower reaches. Near-shore current seams should be carefully probed.

Hook: Talon SA224, #2–4
Thread: Flymaster 6/0, fluor. salmon
Tail: Polar bear, light pink (lngth. of body) 10 strands tied on each side; 1/2" clump of shrimp pink Glo Bug yarn tied in on top of & between split tail; salmon pink rabbit fur added outside the polar bear strands
Shell Back: Swiss straw, light pink, tied in over shrimp pink Glo Bug yarn
Hackle: Soft saddle, shell pink, palmered & trimmed to 1/8", 3/4 of the way back from the hook eye
Eyes: Plastic, large blk.
Body: Med. chen., light pink
Rib: Med. brass wire, counter-wrapped

P.D.'s Shrimp
(Contributed by Peter MacPherson)

Used in rivers, shrimp patterns trigger saltwater feeding memories in anadromous salmonids. *P.D.'s Shrimp* is particularly effective for steelhead, but the fly needs to be fished in deep water, ticking along the bottom. The action can be likened to bottom-bouncing with a fly rod, with more action than when fishing an egg, but not as much as when using a low-water pattern. Distinguishing between bottom and fish strikes is difficult, so the general rule is to strike at everything. The more direct the contact between angler and fly, the easier it is to detect fish. Keeping the belly out of the line while imparting a measure of action is the key to success with this technique.

Gold Conehead Flashfire Muddler
(Contributed by Harold Lohr)

Hook: TMC 5262, #6-10
Thread: 6/0 red
Tail: Wing 'n Flash, gold
Body: Flashabou dubbing, gold
Wing: Wht. Z-lon or nat. polar bear hair
Over-Wing #1: Wing 'n Flash, gold
Over-Wing #2: Firefly, gold
Collar: Deer, nat.
Head: 3 mm conehead, gold

Incorporating all the advantages of a *Flashfire Muddler* with a heavy conehead, this pattern fishes deeper and faster water most effectively. Proven on both rivers and sloughs in the Vancouver area, it is best fished with clear, intermediate sinking lines, notably in the slower portions of the Harrison and Maria Slough. A type III full-sink or sinktip line covers most deep water situations. When coho hang suspended, as they often do two to three feet below the river surface, a floating line is adequate for this weighted pattern.

Hook: Eagle Claw L182 or similar, #1-4
Thread: Flymaster Plus 2/0, to match yarn
Body: Glo Bug yarn (salmon egg colors)
Eyes: Plated lead eyes

Among the best all-around steelhead and salmon patterns, egg flies are often difficult to fish deep due to the yarn's buoyancy. Lead eyes make the difference, allowing the fly to probe small pockets and deep holes. As with all egg patterns, a dead drift is mandatory; the fly's weight makes mending relatively easy, but frequent mends are required to maintain a direct link between angler and fly. Wait for the loop to completely straighten out when casting, and hold the rod slightly sidearm to avoid being pelted. Using different-sized eyes allows a variety of depths to be covered. Colors should range from cerise to chartreuse – combinations of pink, peach and orange have proven reliable.

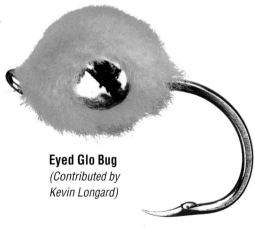

Eyed Glo Bug
(Contributed by Kevin Longard)

Harrison Fiord
(Contributed by Kevin Longard)

Hook: Eagle Claw 1197, #2-6
Body: Flymaster Plus 2/0, blu.; lightly wrapped up hook shank
Wing: Polar bear, blu.
Cheeks: Krystal Flash, prpl. 8-10 strands per side
Beard: Polar bear, wht. (use same amount as for wing)

Designed for Harrison River coho, this fly is ideal any time coho school up, as at the confluence of the Harrison and Chehalis rivers. The fly is best worked with a slow-sinking line or a five-foot mini-tip. Present the offering gently in slack or still water, allowing it to sink halfway to two-thirds down before beginning a very slow retrieve. The take will be surprisingly similar to that of trout. The pattern performs particularly well in low water conditions where its subtle coloring and wispy appearance are non-threatening.

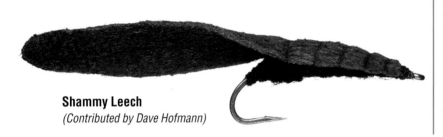

Shammy Leech
(Contributed by Dave Hofmann)

Hook: Eagle Claw LO52 or similar, #6-10
Thread: Monocord 3/0 blk.
Body: Rough blk. yarn or dubbing
Over-Body: Shammy cloth, dyed blk.
Rib: Monocord 3/0 blk.
Special Instructions: Cut shammy into a spatula-like shape & tie narrower end in at front; wind thread back to rear of hook under the shammy & return to eye, ribbing over the shammy

This pattern is at its best right on the bottom in the shoal areas of lakes. Fast-sinking lines get the fly down with minimum loss of fishing time, while long leaders prevent the fly line from spooking fish as the fly is dragged along the bottom. The retrieve is unique in that it combines short strips with a roll of the hand in between. To keep the fly on bottom, the retrieve must be executed very slowly. The hand roll, accomplished by rotating the wrist while holding the line between thumb and index finger, imparts life without causing the fly to rise. Its track record on such lakes as Buntzen, Sayers, Hoover and Weaver is outstanding.

Lohr's Alevin
(Contributed by Harold Lohr)

Hook: TMC 3761 or similar, #10-14
Thread: Uni Thread 6/0 gry.
Body: Holographic tinsel, silv.
Over-Body: Gry. Ultra Chenille, regular
Yolk Sac: Orng. egg yarn, furled
Eyes: Prismatic eyes, silv., 1.5 mm
Special Instructions: Chen. over-body tied on 'tied-down minnow' style & lightly burnt at the end for taper; eyes may be attached using epoxy, Softex or similar

This pattern is best fished when salmon first hatch out of the gravel in coastal river systems such as the Harrison and Fraser. Alevins appear as early as January and continue to emerge through March. These tiny salmon move awkwardly at first, becoming faster and more efficient as their egg sacs shrink. By varying both the speed and consistency of the strips, it is possible to mimic both types of movements when retrieving. Use a full-sink or sinktip line with a short leader to get the fly down. Strikes will be very aggressive, and care must be taken not to set the hook too hard. Broken tippets mean losing both fly and fish.

Hook: Mustad 94833 or similar, #8-14
Thread: Uni Thread 6/0 blk. or to match nat.
Body: Uni Thread 6/0, wrapped on just enough to cover hook
Wing: Deerhair, med., tied on elk hair caddis style

Bodiless Caddis
(Contributed by Kevin Longard)

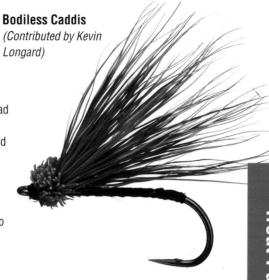

Simple, durable and versatile, this pattern is used in lakes and streams across southwestern B.C. Absorbing almost no water due to its lack of materials, it is one of the simplest dry flies to use. On lakes, it serves as a caddis when tied on #8-12 hooks or an adult chironomid on #12-14 hooks. Imparting movement to the fly as it floats will increase success. On moving water, the pattern is best dead drifted in moderate to fast currents where it imitates caddis, mayflies and stoneflies. Clear, placid waters are better left for more precise patterns. The fly can be waked and is particularly effective in tailout water. A soft, light leader is best, allowing the fly to bounce and manoeuvre in a lifelike fashion.

May Dam Nymph
(Contributed by Peter MacPherson)

Hook: Mustad 9672 or similar, #8-12
Thread: Uni Thread 8/0 olv.-dun
Tail: Blu.-phase pheas. rump, dyed olv.
Abdomen: Pheas. tail fibres, dyed olv.
Back: Same as tail
Rib: Small brass wire, counter-wrapped
Thorax: Scintilla #46
Wing Case: Same as tail
Legs: Same as tail, tied under wing case to protrude out sides.
Head: Wing case mat. is trimmed at the hook eye & left protruding from the thread head

A hybrid pattern that functions as both a damsel and mayfly imitation, the pattern is designed for south coast lakes where the two hatches often overlap. Damselflies should be fished near the surface using a hand twist retrieve to mimic the nymphs' sculling shoreward swim. For mayflies, allow the pattern to sink on a long leader with a dry line. As the fly is retrieved it matches the surface swim of the emerging naturals.

Hook: Eagle Claw LO52 or similar, #6–8
Thread: Uni Thread 6/0 olv.
Tail: Pheas. rump fibres
Under-Body: Poly yarn, olv., tied on sides of abdomen to build a wider, flatter shape
Body: Chen. #901 large, trimmed on top & bottom
Legs (2 sets): Guinea fowl dyed olv.
Head: Scintilla #17 dubbing
Eyes: Plastic, olv. or blk.

Guinea Dragon
(Contributed by Kevin Longard)

This is a mainstay searching pattern for mud-bottom coastal lakes, particularly as winter first gives way to spring. With hatches reduced to sporadic chironomid emergences, Guinea Dragons have produced reliably in the small lakes typical near Harrison Lake. Fish them down the lips of drop-offs with type III sinking lines, staying watchful for the hesitant takes common with lethargic, early-season trout. Slowly lifting the rod allows better detection and entices the fish to follow. The best retrieves often are those designed to attract notice.

Magic Carpet Leech
(Contributed by Ryan Pohl)

Hook: Daiiachi 1270 #6,8 or Daiiachi 1220 #8
Thread: Monocord 3/0 blk.
Tail: Marabou blood quill, blk. – tied shrt.
Body: Blk. seal or seal sub-base w/copper or gold fibre mixed; use dubbing loop and tease well
Head: 1/8 cyclops or tungsten bead, copper or gold

Use a Duncan Loop knot when fishing this fly to keep its body fibres breathing even with quite slow retrieves. A perky hand twist is often best with this sea-run cutthroat pattern which doubles as an effective stillwater leech. The fly is surprisingly aerodynamic, allowing tippets as fine as 4x-5x. Retrieves should always accent the undulating body fibres and be varied enough to continue enticing fish on successive passes. Sea-runs in particular quickly become inured to repeat performances.

Lohr's Little Clinger Crawler
(Contributed by Harold Lohr)

Hook: TMC 200 or Mustad 80060BR, #14
Thread: Uni Thread 8/0 camel
Tail: Peccary bristles
Body: Micro vinyl tubing
Wing Case (3 pads): Mottled turkey tail, folded
Legs: Grouse or speckled hen
Thorax: Med.-brn. dubbing
Eyes: Extra-small mono. nymph eyes
Antenna: Peccary bristles

Combining characteristics of both stoneflies and mayflies (e.g. epeorus and ephemerella), this crossover pattern is complex to tie, but extremely realistic in configuration. Staple food items on such south coast streams as the Skagit and Tamihi Creek, mayflies and stones are most vulnerable when dislodged from the stream bottom. Mimic this scenario by fishing the fly on a floating line and strike indicator, particularly after heavy rainfalls when high water flows sweep the naturals off bottom. Both insects live in fast-flowing, well-oxygenated water.

Hook: TMC 5263, #2–6
Body: Silv. or pearl chen.
Wing: 2 hackles inside to inside tied matuka style (gry., olv. or blk.)
Throat: Wht. marabou, 6 or 8 strands to bend of hook under 10 strands of red marabou 1/4" long
Over-Wing: Pearl blu. Flashabou (4–6 strands), under 8 strands of marabou the same color as the wings
Hackle: 3 wraps griz. where the over-wing and under-wing meet
Head: Epoxy head, or build head with tying thread and use pearl yel. nail polish w/blk. marker for pupil; w/the epoxy head use metallic eyes w/a clear coat of epoxy to seal the eyes

McLeod's Stickleback
(Contributed by Bruce McLeod))

In typically deep coastal lakes with little or no shoal areas, this pattern is most effectively fished on very fast sinking lines with a varied strip retrieve. Designed to imitate the cutthroat trout's favorite food item, the fly is most often taken aggressively, but cutthroat can be subtle. Slow takes feel as if the fly is being pulled through grass. The best response in these situations is to stop the retrieve immediately, count to three, then give the line a sharp tug, hopefully setting the hook on a fish that has circled back to take what it perceives as a wounded stickleback. Retrieves can be started immediately following the cast, but the countdown method should be used to locate the preferred feeding zone, which can vary from just sub-surface all the way to the bottom or anywhere in between.

BC ADVENTURE NETWORK

Discover BC's Premier Web Site!

Simply type

http://www.bcadventure.com

in your Internet browser and all of British Columbia is at your fingertips.

With over 6,000 'pages,' the BC Adventure Network is the most complete tourism resource on the World Wide Web.

Visit a city to find accommodations and services. Explore the lakes, rivers, mountains and coastline. View breathtaking scenery. Study angling, golfing, skiing, camping and resort information. Or learn about nearby hiking trails and points of interest.

Each region of British Columbia is beautifully represented with in-depth information and hundreds of maps and photos. . . the essentials for planning the vacation of a lifetime.

Discover the BC Adventure Network today and embark on an interactive journey of discovery in unforgettable British Columbia!

Interactive Broadcasting Corporation
Phone : (250) 392-2055 Fax: (250) 392-2075
Advertising Dept. toll free: 1-888-351-9826
E-mail: ibc@bcadventure.com

BCadventure
http://www.bcadventure.com

Authors &Artists

Debra Bevaart cannot recall a time in her life when she was not an artist. Her earliest memories include a childhood spent sketching and drawing British Columbia landscapes. At high school she branched into three-dimensional art by sculpting in clay and later in stone, an artform she continues to explore at her gallery in Lund, B.C., where she works primarily with hand tools on single blocks of stone. Taking her inspiration from the wildlife-rich area she calls home, she is recognized for her uncanny ability to capture the essence of her subjects, whether sea lions, wolves, bears, eagles or fish. Her many highly detailed pointilist-style drawings depicting aquatic environments grace the pages of this book.

Karl Bruhn has stood on the polar ice cap at the North Pole; dogsledded in Greenland; travelled winter ice roads with a fur buyer; lived on a trapline; was awarded two Certificates of Military Achievement without having served; danced the Tea Dance of the northern Cree as an honored guest; worked as a stevedore, as a private chauffeur, in a copper mine, for a railway, in eastern factories, as a newspaper reporter and editor; edited Canada's oldest outdoor magazine; wrote a bestselling book on lake fishing in British Columbia; and has canoed hundreds of river miles in B.C., Alberta and the Northwest Territories. He is a cum laude graduate of McGill University, an honorary lifetime member of the Powell River Salmon Enhancement Society and a lover of wilderness and the art of fly fishing. He has lived in igloos, in a teepee, under lean-tos and has restored the turn-of-the-century coastal homestead he now calls home.

Brian Chan is a professional fisheries biologist who has worked on trout management in the Kamloops region for the past 25 years, making him one of the fortunate few with a work career that focusses on his passion. An ardent fly fisher for the past 30 years, he has been active in conservation efforts and is a regular contributor of fly fishing articles to various outdoor publications. He is the author of *Flyfishing Strategies for Stillwaters* and was one of several authors who contributed to *The Gilly*. His fly tying abilities were featured in the 1994 book, *The World's Best Trout Flies*. He has also produced two volumes of an instructional video series on lake fly fishing.

Ian Forbes has cast a fly on every major trout stream in British Columbia and is diligently working his way through the minor flows. Combining his 35-year B.C. Forest Service career with as much stream prospecting as possible has provided him a unique opportunity to explore B.C. He has written and illustrated outdoor magazine articles for more than 40 years, and many of his paintings hang in private galleries. Besides extensive annual forays within B.C., never more than a year goes by without a trip to at least one of several favorite fishing haunts, including Alberta, Montana, Wyoming, Idaho, Australia and New Zealand. A fly tier for 50 years, many of his innovative original patterns are known to B.C. fly fishers. He has contributed more than 80 of his fly pattern pencil sketches to this book.

Don Holmes is a professional biologist who has made Paul Lake in the southern Interior his home. He has been an avid lake fisher since being taken in hand by the close-knit group of Kamloops 'oldtimers' as a youngster. With a Masters degree in Fishery and Environmental Science, he has been with the Ministry of Environment for 26 years, concentrating on water quality and aquatic biology. Introduced to fly fishing in the 1970s under the tutelage of master lake fishers Jack Shaw and Barney Rushton, he includes the study of lake aquatic invertebrates among his personal passions. He admits to having learned more about stillwater invertebrates from Jack Shaw than from all his university years.

Ken Kirkby is an internationally acclaimed Canadian artist, perhaps best known for *Isumataq*, the largest original oil-on-canvas portrait in the world, measuring 152 feet across and standing 12 feet high. Terming the work his "homage to the Canadian Arctic and its peoples," he spent five years in the High Arctic living with nomadic Inuit and 20 years painting to complete the project. *Isumataq* is an Inuit word for "an object in the presence of which wisdom might show itself". He was awarded the Commemorative Medal for the 125th anniversary of Canadian Confederation in recognition of his significant contribution to Canada. His paintings have been described as "wonderful works of mystical simplicity" and several are in the possession of the Royal family, including the private collections of the Queen Mother, Queen Elizabeth and Prince Philip. He has contributed paintings to assist the Inuit, the Steelhead Society of B.C., as well as a number of Canadian conservation groups. A dedicated fly fisher, some of his many angling works illustrate the Journals which close each chapter of this book.

Adam Lewis has worked as a fisheries biologist for more than a decade, studying the ecology of fish and the effects of industrial development. A Registered Professional Biologist since 1990, he acts as a consultant to government, industry and environmental organizations, monitoring environmental effects, analyzing impacts and prescribing mitigative solutions. Vice-president of operations for Triton Environmental Consultants Ltd., he is also the author of *Salmon of the Pacific, Sockeye: the Adams River Run* and *Saving Skeena Steelhead,* a publication of the Steelhead Society of B.C. He is a member of the American Fisheries Society, sits on the Advisory Board of the Sustainable Fisheries Foundation and has served as a director of the Steelhead Society for four years.

Art Lingren is a member and past president of the Totem Flyfishers, British Columbia's oldest fly fishing club; a member of the Harry Hawthorn Foundation; an honorary member of the Loons Fly Fishing club; and a long-time member, official historian and vice-chair of the B.C. Federation of Fly Fishers. In 1995 he received the Federation's Angul Award for appreciation of fly fishing heritage in art and science. He has served for many years as a director of the Steelhead Society of B.C. and is a prolific fly fishing writer with regular magazine contributions and four book titles to his credit, all on B.C. fly fishing and tying. Fittingly, he wrote the foreword to the 1997 reprint of Dr. T.W. Lambert's 1907 classic, *Fishing in British Columbia.* For the last 30 years he has balanced work and family with a passion for B.C. steelhead, trout, char and salmon waters.

Kevin Longard has been fly fishing Vancouver-area lakes and streams for 20 years, is featured in a number of videos, including two instructional tying films and the well-known *How to Fly Fish Lakes,* a guide to coastal lake strategies. A Federation of Fly Fishers certified casting instructor, he gives courses on tying and fishing, guides heli trips and is a seminar speaker at Vancouver-area outdoor shows. He is the owner of Skagit River Flies, a supplier of tying materials, flies and equipment, and is a regular contributor to a number of B.C. fishing publications.

Bob Melrose started fly fishing at age 12 and never looked back. Aside from 39 years in the sporting goods industry, with as many years fishing and hunting throughout B.C. and Alberta, he is a Fly Fishing Federation certified casting instructor, has taught the craft for 20 years, and has balanced it all with 30 years as a ski instructor. The owner of Bobsports in Prince George from 1974 to 1990, he opened a new 3,000-square-foot Bob's Sports in Prince George in 1999. He continues to teach fly fishing, dividing his non-business time between fishing, upland gamebird hunting with Sage, a German long-haired pointer, and skiing the slopes in winter.

Peter Morrison is a casting advisor to the Federation of Fly Fishers, a certified master casting instructor well known for his many fly fishing and casting seminars, a factory representative for Sage Rods and Scientific Angler Fly Lines, a former professional angling guide and a pioneering saltwater angler, most notably in the quest for Pacific salmon. A fly fisher for more than 25 years, he has angled for almost every Canadian gamefish as well as such exotic species as tarpon and bonefish. He has worked in the fly fishing tackle industry for 10 years and in 1999 was selected to join the Canadian team at the 2nd Annual New Zealand Saltfly Tournament.

Ron Nelson is a longtime, national award-winning writer whose work has appeared in *Gray's Sporting Journal, BC Outdoors, Flyfisherman, Reader's Digest* and a wide range of other magazines and newspapers. He is also a freelance book editor, contributor and author of one book (a second book, *And When You Go Fishing, Again,* is currently in the works). After a decade in British Columbia's Okanagan Valley and two decades on the Queen Charlotte Islands, he now lives with his wife and 14-year-old son in Cranbrook.

Doug Porter caught his first fish on a fly in 1958, using a fly his brother taught him to tie. He went on to become a charter member of the Kamloops Fly Fishers and, in 1980, founder of the Grizzly Anglers, the Clearwater-based group known for its trend-setting conservation work, including the prototype Dutch Lake spawning channel – the first of its kind in Canada. Having joined the Forest Service in 1975, he is currently recreation officer for the Chilcotin forest region and a member of the Chilcotin Rod and Gun Club, serving on the executive since 1991, with two years as president. A contributor to *The Gilly,* he has taught fly tying and casting since the early 1980s, always with a strong conservation message, and started teaching rod building in 1998.

Ian Roberts has a degree in still photography from Ryerson Polytechnical Institute in Toronto, spent a year of postgraduate study and work in Italy, owns a Victoria-based photography business and has been fly fishing since he was 10. He merges his love of photography with his passion for fly fishing in images which have appeared in various publications, including the color fly photography that appears in this book. He specializes in estuary fishing for sea-run cutthroat and salmon, but rarely misses an opportunity to fish B.C.'s Interior stillwaters or tropical destinations for bonefish and other warm-water species. His various written contributions to this book mark his first foray into the field of angling writing.

Phil Rowley started fly fishing as a youth at Cameron Lake on Vancouver Island and has been a self-confessed fanatic ever since. He regularly gives seminars, including presentations at outdoor shows in Canada and the U.S., teaches fly fishing and tying, is a commercial tier whose flies were among those used by Canada's 1994 world fly fishing team, and counts both Brian Chan and Gordon Honey among his clients. He is also a contract tier with Umpqua Feather Merchants and a member of the Lamiglas field staff. He writes extensively and contributes photographs to a variety of fly fishing publications, is a past president of the Osprey Fly Fishers and a former director of the B.C. Federation of Fly Fishers.

Dave Stewart has blazed so many angling trails in so many corners of B.C. it is unlikely the rest of us will ever catch him up. Born near Revelstoke in 1919 on the family homestead, now designated a historical site (Craigellachie Historic Site), he is himself a part of B.C. angling history. Aside from brief ventures to other provinces, the Arctic and U.S., he stuck to B.C., driving truck, playing jazz guitar, working as a railway telegrapher and train dispatcher, captaining his own commercial salmon troller and fly fishing for much of his angling life. He started writing in the early 1950s, selling a wide range of material, including fiction and 'fact fiction' in U.S. magazines, travel articles for major dailies and a wealth of outdoor stories. As a western stringer for Maclean-Hunter, he travelled across B.C., Alberta and the Yukon, always carrying fishing tackle and always learning. After 25 years as a freelancer to *BC Outdoors*, he became Guides Editor until his retirement in 1984. His book *The Last Casts* is a collection of 24 of his acclaimed and popular Last Cast columns, which he continues to write.

Barry Thornton is a popular and prolific British Columbia outdoor writer. He has published over 1,000 articles and an equal number of photographs, with writing awards from the Outdoor Writers of Canada and the Northwest Outdoor Writer's Association. The American Fisheries Society's northwest chapter presented him with their Roderick Haig-Brown Memorial Award. He has served as a director of the B.C. Wildlife Federation, a member of the Salmonid Enhancement Task Group, and was the founding chairman and a three-time president of the Steelhead Society of B.C. Recently retired after 35 years as a school principal, he now writes full time, contributing to regional, national and international publications.

Bibliography

Bruhn, Karl. *Best of B.C. Lake Fishing,* 2nd edition. Vancouver: Whitecap Books, 1992, 1998.

Chan, Brian. *Flyfishing Strategies for Stillwaters*. Kamloops: Brian Chan, 1991.

Davy, Alfred G., ed. *The Gilly*. Kelowna: Alf Davy, 1985.

Lingren, Art. *Fly Patterns of Roderick Haig-Brown*. Portland: Frank Amato Publications, 1993.

Lingren, Art. *River Journal: Thompson*. Portland: Frank Amato Publications, 1994.

Lingren, Art. *Fly Patterns of British Columbia*. Portland: Frank Amato Publications, 1996.

Lingren, Art. *Irresistible Waters: Fly Fishing in B.C. Throughout the Year*. Vancouver: Raincoast Books, 1998.

Lingren, Art. *Steelhead River Journal: Dean River*. Portland: Frank Amato Publications, 1999.

Nelson, Ron. *And When You Go Fishing*. Lantzville: Oolichan Books, 1984.

Shaw, Jack. *Fly Fish the Trout Lakes,* 2nd edition. Surrey: Heritage House Publishing Co. Ltd., 1998.

Shaw, Jack. *Tying Flies for Trophy Trout,* 2nd edition. Surrey, Heritage House Publishing Co. Ltd., 1999.

Stewart, Dave. *Fishing Guide to Fresh Water in British Columbia*. Vancouver: Special Interest Publications Division, Maclean-Hunter Limited, 1985.

Stewart, Dave. *Okanagan Backroads, Volume 1,* 2nd edition. Sidney: Saltaire Publishing Limited, 1977.

Stewart, Dave. *Okanagan Backroads, Volume 2*. Sidney: Saltaire Publishing Limited, 1975.

Stewart, Dave. *Exploring British Columbia Waterways: Southern Interior Lakes*. Sidney: Saltaire Publishing Limited, 1976.

Thornton, Barry. *Salgair, a Steelhead Odyssey*. Surrey: Hancock House, 1997.

Thornton, Barry. *Steelhead*. Surrey: Hancock House, 1995.

Thornton, Barry. *Saltwater Fly Fishing for Pacific Salmon*. Surrey: Hancock House, 1995.

Thornton, Barry. *Steelhead, the Supreme Trophy Trout*. Surrey: Hancock House, 1978.

Fly Pattern Index

Selected Waters Index

General Index